Pursuing a Career in Mental Health

T0323643

Pursuing a Career in Mental Health

A Comprehensive Guide for Aspiring Professionals

Ann F. Garland

OXFORD
UNIVERSITY PRESS

OXFORD
UNIVERSITY PRESS

Oxford University Press is a department of the University of Oxford. It furthers
the University's objective of excellence in research, scholarship, and education
by publishing worldwide. Oxford is a registered trade mark of Oxford University
Press in the UK and certain other countries.

Published in the United States of America by Oxford University Press
198 Madison Avenue, New York, NY 10016, United States of America.

© Oxford University Press 2022

Library of Congress Cataloging-in-Publication Data
Names: Garland, Ann F., author.
Title: Pursuing a career in mental health : a comprehensive guide for
aspiring professionals / by Ann F. Garland.
Description: First. | New York, NY : Oxford University Press, 2022. |
Includes bibliographical references and index.
Identifiers: LCCN 2021062821 (print) | LCCN 2021062822 (ebook) |
ISBN 9780197544716 (paperback) | ISBN 9780197544730 (epub)
Subjects: LCSH: Mental health services—Vocational guidance.
Classification: LCC RA790.75 .G37 2022 (print) | LCC RA790.75 (ebook) |
DDC 362.2023—dc23/eng/20220328
LC record available at https://lccn.loc.gov/2021062821
LC ebook record available at https://lccn.loc.gov/2021062822

DOI: 10.1093/med-psych/9780197544716.001.0001

3 5 7 9 8 6 4 2
Printed by LSC Communications, United States of America

Dedicated to

Saul and HannaMei for inspiring me in this and every other endeavor

Contents

Acknowledgments   ix
Key Terms   xi

   Introduction   1

 1. Why Should You Become a Mental Health Professional?   9

 2. Is This Career a Good Fit for You?   18

 3. Steps to Becoming a Mental Health Professional   31

 4. Choosing a Discipline and Degree to Pursue   46

 5. Expanding the Possibilities: Populations, Settings,
    and Types of Work   67

 6. The Business of Mental Healthcare   83

 7. Ethical and Legal Issues in Mental Healthcare   96

 8. Diversity, Equity, and Inclusion in Mental Health   108

 9. Preparing for Success in Graduate School   121

10. Occupational Hazards and How to Manage Them   138

11. Inspiring Hope and Change   150

12. Embracing the Science of Mental Healthcare   162

13. The Future of Mental Healthcare   174

14. Shared Wisdom and Suggested Inspiration   190

Notes   207
Index   223

Acknowledgments

I am so grateful to the many people who have helped me bring this book to fruition. The knowledge I've shared in these pages comes from hundreds of conversations with students and colleagues over the past few decades. Naming them all is unrealistic, but special thanks go to the following who have contributed their wisdom so generously by helping me to clarify the book's purpose, reviewing specific sections, or providing the insightful quotes that enrich this book: Mary Baker-Ericzén, Marcia Beck, Sarah Kate Bearman, Lauren Brookman-Frazee, Sandy Brown, Caroline Boxmeyer, Nick Boyd, Larry Chamow, Angela Chui, Betty Desta, Ana Estrada, Cassidy Freitas, Denise Golden, Ned Golubovic, Barry Hill, Pat Judd, Leita Koontz, Florencia Lebensohn-Chialvo, Saul Levine, Jenny Li, Carrie Morrison, Jo Ellen Patterson, Carol Randolph, Jennifer Regan, Sonja Schoenwald, Jill Stoddard, Mike Terry, Carolyn Turvey, Feion Villodas, Lily Vistica, Jill Weckerly, Katherine Nguyen Williams, and Lee Williams.

Thanks to Sarah Harrington at Oxford University Press for her encouragement and helpful advice beginning at our first meeting and to Aviva Layton for sharing her expertise by helping me translate my initial idea into an actual book proposal, as well as Gina Arnold for expert editorial advice. Thanks to Alex Ramirez, Diana Reyes, and Dorna Sepheri for their encouraging and insightful reviews from a student perspective. Tremendous thanks to Elissa Ellis-MacLeod for reading every word so carefully (likely multiple times), offering astute editorial suggestions with enthusiasm and kindness. It's been a pleasure sharing this project with you.

I am also very lucky to have so many fun and generous friends who have offered consistent encouragement as well as necessary distractions; thanks to Kathy Kim, Zac and Michael Rattner, Howard and Gail Feldman, and my wonderful book club members of almost 30 years and counting: Irena Blessent, Maria Bushong, Michelle Chen, Gayle Braun Driver, Joan Greenhood, Marla Harvey Guin, Cathy Perkins, and Dyana Woo.

I've been fortunate to have had amazing mentors. In particular, David Shaffer and Edward Zigler shaped my early career trajectory and helped me to believe in my ability to contribute to this field. Each set high standards for excellence and offered encouragement and guidance to meet those standards. I'm indebted to them and hope that I have been able to pass on some of their wisdom in these pages. Likewise, mentors, colleagues, and trainees at the Child and Adolescent Services Research Center, the University of California San Diego, and the University of San Diego have enriched my professional life in countless ways. Finally, I am so glad to have this opportunity to express my deep appreciation for my family. My parents instilled high expectations and, fortunately, provided abundant love and support to meet them. My sister Julie has always been a main source of fun, support, and inspiration. Holly, Cam, and

Drew have enriched my life in innumerable ways. Thank you also to Jaime and Karin, Mischa and Marcia, and Zachary and Catherine for welcoming me so warmly into your lives and making me a very proud Bubbie. Lastly, so much gratitude to Saul for unwavering encouragement and expert advice on this project as in everything else. You and HannaMei bring more meaning and joy to my life than I can adequately express. Thank you.

Key Terms

For clarification, it may be helpful to review the following key terms that will be used throughout the book.

	Key Terms	
Term	Definitions	Synonyms
Therapy	Talk-based intervention to address mental health issues including psychiatric illnesses; emotional, behavioral, or relationship issues; identity; wellness, etc.	Psychotherapy, counseling
Therapist	Someone who is trained to provide psychotherapy or counseling	Psychotherapist, counselor, clinician, provider Includes psychologist, social worker, psychiatrist, psychiatric nurse, marital (couples) and/or family therapist
Client(s)	Person or persons participating in psychotherapy or counseling; could be an individual, couple, family, or group	Patient, consumer, person with lived experience with mental health issues
Mental Health Discipline	The specific professional field in which a therapist is trained and licensed. The most common are psychology, counseling, social work, marital & family therapy, psychiatry, and psychiatric nursing.	Mental health profession or field
Therapeutic Relationship	The working relationship between a therapist and their client(s)	Therapeutic alliance or working alliance
Evidence-Based Practice	Mental healthcare that is supported by research evidence	Empirically supported practice

Introduction

Congratulations! The fact that you opened this book suggests you are considering becoming a mental health professional. (For simplicity, from here on I will use the term *therapist* to represent all mental health professionals including counselors, marital and family therapists, psychologists, psychiatric nurses, psychiatrists, and social workers). You are exploring a career that is extraordinarily meaningful and challenging. Where else can you find a career that will so fully engage both your heart and your mind? It is a career that offers rare opportunities to build trusting relationships with individuals from diverse backgrounds with the potential to help them profoundly transform their lives. Working as a therapist is a wonderful privilege but also a great responsibility. Therefore, it is critical that you have a good understanding of what the role entails, to determine if it is a good fit for you. This book is designed to help you make that decision and to prepare you to succeed.

Introduction to the Book's Purpose and Content

You may feel called to be a therapist to help people, building on your strengths as a "wonderful listener" or "the person all my friends come to with their relationship problems." You may be motivated by direct personal or family experience with mental health challenges, inspiring you to help others in the way you were helped. Or, alternatively, maybe you are determined to become a better therapist than the unhelpful therapist you encountered or to bring culturally sensitive mental healthcare to an underserved community. Perhaps you've been intrigued by the mind–body connection and want to delve deeper into how to optimize mental and physical wellness. Or you've grown increasingly concerned about the grip of addiction on so many and want to help ease this scourge. Maybe you've been inspired by scientific discoveries about the brain, and you want to learn how to make sure these discoveries can actually improve people's lives and reduce suffering.

There are many powerful motivations for exploring this noble career path. But how do you know if your motivations could actually translate into a rewarding lifelong career? What are the surprising realities and challenges of being a therapist? What personal characteristics and strengths may be best suited for success in this career, and what weaknesses could interfere? What do you need to know about the business or legal aspects of mental healthcare or how diversity, equity, and inclusion ideals are prioritized in mental health? These important questions and more will be addressed.

You are exploring this career at an opportune time. Workforce demand is great, with job opportunities projected to increase into the future. Demand for mental healthcare was already high prior to the COVID-19 pandemic and social unrest related to racial injustices, but it is now even greater. Experts predict that the stresses and trauma associated with these events will result in elevated rates of a variety of mental health challenges for many years to come.[1]

If you are already convinced this is the best career path for you, there are still important decisions to be made regarding which particular occupation (often referred to as *discipline*) to choose. The disciplines that will be described in this book include, counseling, psychology, marital/couples and family therapy, social work, psychiatry, and psychiatric nursing. While there are similarities across these disciplines, there are also important distinctions in graduate school pathways and costs for master's versus doctoral degrees, licensure or certification, practice specializations, and employment opportunities. The information in these pages will help you to determine which discipline and degree path might be the best fit for you.

This book will also expand your knowledge about what's possible in this career, introducing you to a diverse array of exciting job opportunities. You'll learn about the rewards and challenges of working with children, adolescents, families, or elderly adults; people who have experienced trauma or grief; those who feel hopeless, depressed, or anxious; couples who want to improve their relationships; individuals with severe mental illnesses; those with physical illnesses, eating disorders, or developmental disorders; military veterans and their families; and many others.

Learning more about possible career paths will help you find the best fit for your specific passions and strengths. Throughout this book, therapists who have pursued a variety of paths will offer advice intended to help you make important career decisions and prepare for success. They'll share hard truths about the challenges and the rewards to make sure you have realistic expectations.

These pages are full of practical "how to" guidance for pursuing a mental health career, but the book raises bigger, thought-provoking questions too. These bigger questions include exploration into the art and science of how psychotherapy works. You may be exploring this career path because you believe you have the heart and soul of a healer. That is a great start, but to be an effective therapist you'll need to fully integrate your compassionate healer identity with that of a scientist, critically reviewing research on the evidence for different practices. This book will challenge you to think about what it means to integrate the art and science of therapy—to use both your heart and mind—to offer the most effective help to those in your care.

You will also learn about future developments in mental healthcare, including how innovative technologies like mobile device apps, virtual reality, and artificial intelligence impact therapy so that you can be prepared for the future. As you read through this book, ask yourself if the dilemmas and questions that are raised are the kinds of things you want to spend your career grappling with. Do these challenges and opportunities make you more motivated to pursue the hard work of becoming a therapist? For me, and the dozens of therapists sharing their wisdom in these pages, the answer is a resounding "YES!" Where else can you find a career where you build such meaningful connections with others and utilize emerging science to help individuals and families reduce suffering and dramatically improve their lives?

Personal Introduction

Throughout this book, I will urge you to ask yourself tough questions about how your personal experiences have inspired and prepared you for this career path. Since I am encouraging this self-reflection, it seems only fair for me to start by sharing some of my experiences in this introduction. By highlighting my own career decision points and their implications, I hope to help you anticipate the decisions you'll face. I will also share lessons I've learned to give you my view of the rewards and challenges of this career. In subsequent chapters, dozens of other mental health professionals offer their advice and share lessons learned, so you'll get valuable diverse perspectives.

Looking back, I cannot imagine having pursued any other career, but I did not always have this clarity. I spent my early college years without any certainty of my desired major, let alone my career aspirations. I explored many fields. I liked the arts and humanities, studying literature, philosophy, and other cultures in anthropology. I wanted to learn multiple languages to travel the world with great fluency until it became clear that I had no aptitude for languages (resulting in a useless jumble of unidentifiable babbling when I try to communicate in a foreign language).

I was also fascinated by science courses and even liked the challenging logic of math and statistics. I know I benefited from my explorations in all these fields, but it was also clear that I was not a natural expert in any one of them. Thankfully, I discovered psychology midway through college and gravitated to it immediately because it tapped into my analytic and scientific interests as well as my humanistic and cultural interests.

When I graduated from the University of California Berkeley with my major in psychology, I had no idea how to translate my passion for this academic field into a career. (Maybe you are feeling something similar now?) I did not know anyone who worked in the mental health field and had minimal knowledge of career options. Once again, I was juggling potentially contradictory interests. I loved the stimulating intellectual challenge of psychological research, but I was also drawn to the rewarding human connections in mental health practice.

Given that I was unprepared for graduate study, having no clarity about what I wanted to pursue, I sought practice experience and was hired as a mental health worker in a group home for young men diagnosed with autism and other severe mental illnesses. Our clients had spent most of their lives in a locked state psychiatric hospital. They were part of the national "deinstitutionalization" movement, resulting in closures of many psychiatric hospitals.[2]

This initiative to move individuals out of institutions into community settings was well intentioned. However, shifting individuals who had spent most of their lives in highly structured hospital settings into suburban homes staffed by people like me with only a textbook education in psychology presented many challenges.

My job in the group home was unquestionably the hardest job I've ever had. Our staff shifts were 48 hours long, and we were responsible for everything from basic daily needs (e.g., meals, dressing, bathing) to implementing detailed educational and behavioral interventions and supervising family visits and field trips. Most of the residents had difficulty communicating, and some expressed their frustration through physical aggression. Community outings were particularly fraught. Our residents were often uncomfortable in unfamiliar surroundings, and they would occasionally run away, become very agitated, or engage in socially inappropriate behaviors.

I vividly remember a community field trip when a client became overwhelmed in a grocery store, yelling and then knocking over a large display of glass jars. He quickly ran out of the store, and I had to follow him. With all sorts of potential disasters running through my mind and my heart racing, I knew I needed to stay in control despite the possible dangers. Fortunately, I caught up to him, and we sat together to calm down. It's about 40 years later now, but I still have twinges of lingering anxiety when I hear "We're going on a field trip."

The group home job challenged me in every possible way. It was physically demanding; I sustained a few on-the-job injuries including a broken arm. And, of course, it was emotionally challenging as well. As I got to know our residents and their histories, which often included heartbreaking traumas and rejections, I was overwhelmed with sadness at times. Yet I was also profoundly inspired by our clients' resilience and their pride in achieving their goals. The job was also intellectually challenging. I wanted to figure out why our residents behaved as they did and how I could apply what I had learned in textbooks to improve their daily lives.

Despite the challenges, and maybe partly because of them, I absolutely loved that job. I think I learned more there than I ever learned in a classroom or on any job since. The topics I'd studied in college classes came to life. For example, the public stigma about mental illness that I'd studied was on blatant display any time our clients ventured into the community—with people staring, shunning, and shaming. I felt it vicariously when people expressed frustration that we staff members were clearly inept because our clients were not "better controlled."

Our clients came from diverse backgrounds and reinforced for me the powerful impact of race, ethnicity, and social class in shaping identity and others' perceptions and biases. Family visits also provided a glimpse of the family systems dynamics I had read about. I saw the real toll severe mental illness had on loving family members who often felt helpless. I was also inspired by the resilience of family members who advocated so passionately for their loved ones after many years of frustrations.

I learned a lot of essential lessons in this first mental health job that have been reinforced throughout my career and are reflected in core themes within this book. For one, I learned that empathy and compassion are essential in this work but that these must be balanced with disciplined respect for appropriate professional roles and boundaries. Compassion is a great motivator, but to help our clients most effectively, we sometimes need to keep our compassion in check and respond in more disciplined ways. For example, it would not be therapeutic to solve problems for our clients, even if our compassion motivates us to do so when clients are painfully frustrated. The role of a therapist is to help clients build insight and skills to solve problems, not to try to solve them ourselves.

My job also taught me the value of structure and the importance of communicating clearly about expectations and rules. Conversely, I also learned the need for flexibility and adaptation. I tend to be a planner, so being clear about structured plans comes naturally. This was a beneficial skill in a stressful and sometimes chaotic environment. However, planners like me often have difficulty adapting to a change in plans when things go awry. So I had to work on quickly regrouping and setting new plans when necessary (and it is often necessary). Being a good therapist relies on balancing the need for structure with the need for flexibility. The COVID pandemic reasserted the necessity of flexible adaptability for all of us.

My experiences in my first mental health job formed my initial beliefs about what makes mental healthcare work. I started out believing what many people likely assume, namely, that compassion, empathy, and authenticity are the most important ingredients of therapy. Over time, I came to realize that while these are necessary, they are not sufficient for effective practice. In other words, we cannot rely on compassion, empathy, and authenticity alone. Therapists need to build on this foundation with evidence-based strategies (practices supported by research) to help clients change. This is a theme I will return to throughout this book.

My job at the group home reinforced my commitment to a career in mental health. I still wasn't exactly sure which path to take, but I recognized that I would need a graduate degree if I wanted a job that didn't require 48-hour shifts. It took me a few more years to clarify my specific ambitions. First, I earned a master's degree in developmental psychology, which facilitated gaining a fantastic job as a research assistant at Columbia University in New York. I learned about how to conduct rigorous and relevant research from extraordinary mentors, working on studies evaluating the effectiveness of adolescent suicide prevention programs.

This research job was eye-opening because it taught me how rewarding applied clinical research could be. Prior to that I had a limited understanding of research based on my college experience, which required that I track guppies (with different colored dots painted on them) swimming in a tank. It was messy work in a lonely dank basement lab. I didn't fully understand the purpose of the study, but I knew I needed research experience, so I diligently tracked those colorful guppies night after night. I naively thought that an activity only counted as research if it were conducted in a laboratory and involved a highly controlled experimental design. It took me a few years to learn how misinformed I was, and I hope I can help you avoid the same misjudgment. Research experiences range from basic laboratory research to applied, community-based research. Gaining any kind of research experience is valuable, whether it is conducted in a basement lab or out in the community, so look for what is compelling to you.

After working with the amazing research team in New York for a few years, I finally had the clarity I'd been looking for and felt ready to take on doctoral studies in clinical psychology. I entered Yale University with a combination of pride and anxiety, wondering if I truly belonged there and thus experiencing the common "imposter syndrome" most of us feel at times.[3] I was pleased to find that I could continue to learn about both research and clinical practice, given that I didn't want to give up either. My classes were fascinating, the faculty members were leaders in their fields, and my fellow students were great. It was an amazing place to learn, full of both history and cutting-edge innovation. I still sometimes marvel at my luck in ending up there.

While my classes were often challenging (don't get me started about advanced statistics and programming), the most nerve-wracking and exciting part of grad school was the addition of clinical practice training. There is nothing quite like facing your first client who is looking to you for relief and guidance. As I try to reassure my own students now, almost everyone feels slightly terrified and unprepared as a beginner.

It's been a few decades, but I still remember very clearly when I first took the role as therapist. I say "took the role" because I didn't yet feel qualified to call myself a real therapist. Mary, my first client, was a woman in her early 40s. (Note that all client names have been changed.) She had been separated from her husband and recently diagnosed with Stage 3 colon cancer. She had three elementary school–aged sons, and she was seeking therapy to cope with all these stressors. She also wanted help figuring out how to talk to her sons about her medical issues. A faculty member gave me this information right before I met Mary, and I remember thinking something like, "WHAT!!?? This woman deserves to see an expert. I am not prepared for this at all. What do I know about facing a life-threatening illness or marital separation or parenting!?"

With trepidation, I sat down with Mary, who, in my memory, was infinitely more calm and gracious than I. I'll never forget when early in that first session she said to me, "Oh you must hear this all the time." The irony almost made me laugh out loud. I thought to myself, "No, in fact, this is the first session I've ever had as a therapist, so I've never heard anything before, everything is new to me." Fortunately, I didn't say this because I had learned about the importance of boosting a client's positive expectations for therapy. I didn't want to undermine her hopeful expectations. Authenticity is valuable but should be balanced by the best interests of the client.

Thankfully (and somewhat miraculously from my perspective), Mary returned each week for our sessions. She was very open from the start, sharing her profound fears as well as the everyday stress of her life, including details of her medical procedures and her sons' reactions. Empathizing with her was not difficult; managing the intensity of my concern for her and her family was. I found that my own anxiety and lack of confidence subsided (slightly) as I worried less about myself and focused more on how I could help her and her sons. Fortunately, for both our sakes, I had expert faculty supervision and was able to employ useful strategies to address the challenges she raised. At the conclusion of our 6 months of work together, she expressed sincere gratitude and was able to identify the ways in which therapy had helped her to cope with extremely challenging circumstances. She presented me with a small gift meaningfully selected to represent my last name, and I must admit that I still cherish it. I remain deeply grateful to her for teaching me more than she will ever know.

I completed my doctoral studies at age 32. If you are reading this at around age 20, perhaps this is discouraging, but don't despair. I took a somewhat meandering route. Those who are more certain of their career aspirations can find a shorter route. Pursuing a master's degree as opposed to a doctoral degree will also be more efficient and can offer many of the same career opportunities. However, if you are older, there is no reason for you to despair either. Many people are entering this career path in their 30s, 40s, and beyond. In fact, about 40% of those earning a doctorate in psychology are over age 35, and that number has been rising.[4]

I often speak with students who are in a hurry to finish their education. I absolutely understand the wish to finish school as soon as possible to start one's professional career and begin earning a commensurate salary. However, I've seen this impatience backfire when students find that the path they pursued quickly is not a good fit for their career aspirations.

The sidetracks I took were well worth it. The mental health worker job in the group home and the research job in New York taught me so much and were absolutely instrumental in clarifying my career choices, not to mention meeting amazing friends and mentors. One thing I've learned is that it is foolhardy to assume that our personal or professional paths will progress in a perfect linear direction. Perhaps we learn the most through the unexpected detours, roundabouts, or U-turns.

Upon graduating with my PhD, I needed to make a choice between a career of primarily clinical practice and an academic career emphasizing teaching and research. I don't believe there is any way to pursue both with equal emphasis. I chose the academic career path and have never regretted it. While research, teaching, and academic leadership have been my primary responsibilities, as a licensed psychologist I find many opportunities to remain clinically active. For example, most of my teaching is direct clinical supervision of trainees working in community settings. I also conduct applied research in partnership with other therapists.

I've been very lucky to work as a professor for almost 30 years. I get to talk with enthusiastic students and colleagues about issues that fascinate me. I am paid to read and write about topics that I like to read and write about for personal interest. I watch how students develop into expert professionals and benefit from what they teach me. There are few better feelings than knowing that you have been a positive influence on someone's personal and professional development. Some of the quotes in this book come from professionals I worked with as students. Just reading their eloquent and insightful comments fills me with pride.

My academic career has been somewhat unusual in that I've had the opportunity to teach students from multiple disciplines, including counseling, marital and family therapy, psychology, and psychiatry. It's more common for professors to work exclusively within their own discipline. Having worked across disciplines, I can tell you that there are actually more similarities than there are differences. However, the differences in emphasis are important to recognize so that you can find the best fit for your interests (as detailed in Chapter 4).

In addition to working across disciplines, I've worked in different settings, including a school of medicine in a large public research university, a nonprofit children's hospital, and a private school of education and leadership. Each of these environments had very different cultures and pursued different priorities. I believe my diverse experiences across disciplines and work settings provide valuable perspective on a wide range of potential career paths, as I'll share throughout this book.

I was motivated to write this book because of countless discussions over decades with students who are looking for clarity about how to choose a specific mental health career path and how to be successful in that career. My goals are to clarify some of the confusion about the varied graduate program and career options and to provide the best preparation for success in whichever path you choose in this amazing field.

1

Why Should You Become a Mental Health Professional?

The most rewarding aspects of this career are seeing true, meaningful, powerful growth in my fellow humans, and being able to wear different professional hats. (Jill, therapist in private practice)

Perhaps you are already certain that you want to pursue this career, or you are hoping to learn more about the realities before you commit considerable time, energy, and money to your education and training. You may already have a clear mental image of the therapist you'd like to be based on previous experience with a role model or media depictions. Maybe you picture a wise, welcoming woman asking questions about your childhood or a man in a tweed jacket stroking his graying beard and asking about your dreams. Perhaps you imagine a young woman with a soothing voice leading a meditation exercise or a creatively tattooed peer counselor supporting sobriety efforts. Maybe you even envision a bitmoji pinging your phone and asking you to rate your current mood on a 1-to-10 scale. Whatever your current image of a therapist is, or if you don't yet have one, this book will introduce you to a wide range of possibilities. Hold on to the images that inspire you.

This first chapter is intended to help you clarify why you might want to become a mental health professional and to test some of your assumptions about the realities of this career path. In the Introduction, I shared some of what I find most rewarding about this field. In this chapter and throughout the rest of the book you'll learn from many other professionals about what they find most rewarding and most challenging. They'll share insights to help you make career path decisions and set realistic expectations for each step in the journey. These insider perspectives will be valuable preparation for success.

A Meaningful Career

It is a true honor to walk with others in the ups and downs of their life. Each day is different and requires a tremendous amount of wisdom, creativity, flexibility, and realness. It is rewarding to know that your time is spent in service to others. (Caroline, professor and therapist)

Any of the diverse paths you take toward becoming a mental health professional will take you on an incredible journey. You'll find a sense of purpose and fulfillment that may be elusive in many other careers. Few other careers offer, and in fact require you to build, such deeply meaningful connections with other human beings. It is an unusual privilege to accompany someone through life's profound challenges and triumphs, partnering with them as they work to find relief from suffering. It is also a huge responsibility. You may be the first and only person with whom they have shared deep feelings, fears, traumas, and hopes. You'll experience intense emotions and witness extraordinary resilience.

> I work with children who have anxiety disorders. Being able to see a youth who was previously fearful of speaking to others, making mistakes, or even going outside, ultimately embrace those challenges makes all the difficult steps in between really worth it. What a gift to be able to facilitate that change for someone else. (Jennifer, therapist in community and private practice)

Many of us are looking for a career that is meaningful, but what does that really mean? In a survey of working Americans, 70% said that helping others made work meaningful.[1] Multiple research studies indicate that if you perceive that your work helps others and that it contributes to a greater good, your life will feel more meaningful.[2] Those who believe their work is a "calling" (i.e., it is fulfilling and socially useful) have the highest work and life satisfaction.[3] In addition, more meaningful work has been associated with lower risk for depression and anxiety; it is a buffer for managing stress.

> I learn as much from my clients as they do from me. I couldn't have predicted how much the strength of my clients would inspire me on a regular basis. (Jill, therapist in private practice)

Your clients will challenge and inspire you in different ways every day. You are likely to encounter individuals who have endured unimaginable trauma or deprivation. And you may work with those who have actually perpetrated violence or crimes against others and are working hard toward redemption. You may hear tragic accounts of child abuse, exploitation, violence, or survival of terrorism and natural disasters. You may work with combat veterans, individuals who have been homeless, or those who are facing terminal illnesses or unbearable grief. You will encounter individuals who are contemplating suicide, and you will have the enormous responsibility of figuring out how to help keep them safe.

The number of ways in which humans can suffer is infinite, but so too are the examples of resilient survival stories which will humble and inspire you. At times I've thought if I read a novel depicting the real-life experiences of some clients, I'd toss the novel aside for being too melodramatic and unrealistic. I've come to learn that real life can, in fact, be more dramatic and more surprising than fiction.

Hearing about traumatic experiences and witnessing the intense emotions they may engender can be overwhelming for therapists. Most of us who enter this field have good empathy skills. This is a strength. But the corresponding risk is that we may struggle to cope with the intensity of our clients' emotions and experiences. Chapter 10 of this book is devoted to a discussion of these types of occupational hazards. Compassion fatigue is a real phenomenon that can impact therapists and potentially lead to career burnout.[4] Likewise, therapists can experience *vicarious trauma*, the indirect effects of empathizing with a client who has been directly traumatized. Strategies to manage these occupational hazards are also presented in Chapter 10.

While you will encounter dramatic experiences and traumas in this career, you will more commonly address the drama of everyday life. Suffering and resilience are often born out of more common experiences. For example, perhaps you'll meet an individual whose loneliness weighs very heavily but who feels paralyzed by anxiety to meet people. You will be able to help them to gain coping skills that will ultimately inspire them to enter a new social group.

Or perhaps a couple will come to you, locked in years of escalating conflict over resentments about seemingly mundane daily chores. They may bring long, detailed lists of grievances about dishwashing, dirty socks on the floor, or the dreaded toilet seat position. These types of issues may not be the dramatic life events you expected to spend time discussing when you dreamed of becoming a therapist, yet you can make a big positive impact in this couple's life. You can help them develop new communication strategies to change repeated patterns and rediscover what brought them together.

Perhaps you'll work with children with severe behavioral problems and their families. Helping parents improve parenting skills is essential in this work. You may help them create a sticker chart to reward their child's good behavior. Again, working on a reward chart for teeth brushing, homework completion, and taking out the trash may not match your desire to delve into deep, dark secrets as a therapist. However, if you are successful in this work, you will have helped them reduce chaos in their home and improve the quality of their relationships. This seemingly straightforward behavioral intervention could have a dramatic lifelong therapeutic impact on the parents and the children.

The point of these common examples is to illustrate that the drama of therapy is manifested in many different ways. Yes, you will address significant trauma, and sometimes dramatic, deep, dark secrets will be revealed. But this is not what therapy is always, or even most commonly, about. More often, you will be addressing the drama of everyday life, loneliness, grief, motivational challenges, or struggles with identity issues, body image, or health challenges. You may be discussing dissatisfying jobs, relationship challenges, tensions between children and parents, conflicts about money or sex or household chores, cultural clashes, etc.; and your impact can be just as profound.

I have known a few trainees who expressed disappointment when they entered the field and realized that practicing therapy would not always be full of the dramatic intrigue they imagined (as if they were looking for a captivating Netflix series). It is important to recognize up front that the focus of therapy will be as varied as is the human experience. The everyday challenges clients face can impact their lives in very significant ways and should never be discounted.

I learned this early in my career when I was assigned a 9-year-old boy client, referred for frequent bed-wetting. I will confess that, initially, I questioned why I had spent so many years in training to address bed-wetting and the mother's frustrations about frequent loads of laundry. However, I quickly learned that this problem had a very significant impact on this family's quality of life. The boy's self-esteem was sinking, and he was withdrawing from friends. The mother was chronically exhausted. She was angry at her son but also angry at herself for blaming him. A physician ruled out any medical explanation for the bed-wetting, and she was very worried that it might signify a serious developmental delay.

Fortunately, after researching evidence-based treatments for bed-wetting, I was able to work with them effectively. Over just a few weeks, the bed-wetting problem improved significantly. It was so gratifying to see the mother and son work together to implement strategies and then to celebrate together when the strategies were successful. This example is meant to challenge assumptions you may have about the types of issues you'll be addressing as a therapist. One of the goals for this book is to help you test how your expectations measure up to the realities.

Personal Growth as a Therapist

I have been surprised by how much I have personally changed from learning more about myself and my family through my training. Being a therapist has made me look at all aspects of life differently and has helped me grow into the person I wanted to be. (Lily, therapist and instructor)

This is definitely a career that pushes you to grow and change constantly. It begins in graduate school, where you'll learn different theories of how our unique personalities develop and how a multitude of factors influence who we become. You may find yourself testing out the validity of these theories to determine how they apply (or don't apply) to you, your family, and your friends. You'll likely gain new insights into your family dynamics, your relationship patterns, and how your race, ethnicity, gender identity, and cultural background influence you. When you learn about group dynamics you'll have a better understanding of how groups often form alliances and how an individual can be ostracized. These are just some of the ways you will gain a language and explanations for all the complex behaviors and feelings you experience and observe in others.

There are also many useful "perks" you can apply to your personal life through your mental health training. For example, you'll learn specific active listening techniques to convey empathy and caring. You may believe you are already a good listener, and that may very well be true; but you will learn established techniques to improve your listening and empathy skills. You'll also learn about research-supported communication strategies to significantly improve the quality of romantic relationships[5] and effective parenting skills to use if you have children. (Of course, I've learned the hard way that sometimes all the training in the world can't help us parents avoid the inevitable embarrassing toddler meltdown in the candy aisle of the grocery store!)

If you are open and honest throughout this journey, you'll learn about your biases and your limitations. You'll confront uncomfortable challenges to your own beliefs and assumptions about how and why people behave as they do. Being an effective therapist requires that you gain self-awareness about your blind spots and biases. And yes, you definitely have some. We all do. In Chapter 10 I'll discuss ways to gain greater self-awareness and the value of participating in your own therapy.

Gaining insight into your own background, behavior, feelings, and relationships is an enriching benefit of mental health training. However, this can sometimes be taken too far. There is a risk that you'll annoy your friends and family by analyzing their personalities and relationships through your new lens of psychological theories. Also, as you study psychiatric illnesses, you may be tempted to diagnose yourself or family and friends. There is a phenomenon called the *medical student syndrome*, suggesting that when students learn about symptoms and disorders (medical and/ or psychological), they may be more prone to experience the symptoms they are learning about.[6] It's certainly possible for graduate students in mental health to experience something similar.

One study found that undergraduates who planned to major in psychology were more worried about their psychological health than those who were not majoring in psychology.[7] However, this does not mean that studying psychology causes more worries about mental health. Perhaps students who are predisposed to thinking about these issues are more likely to study psychology. In Chapter 2 I will discuss how one's own mental health issues may motivate this career choice and the extent to which this can be helpful, as well as risky.

New Challenges and Opportunities Throughout Your Career

> What makes being a therapist difficult in the beginning also makes it a rewarding career for a lifetime. If being a therapist were easily mastered, then most of us would leave the field because it no longer challenged us. Being a therapist will constantly push you to change and grow. (Lee, professor and therapist)

One of the things many of us love about this career is that it is never boring. There are new challenges around every corner as you meet new clients or take on different roles. The rapid shift to remote therapy required during the pandemic is a practical example of how therapists needed to adapt to new realities almost overnight to meet their clients' needs and to save their jobs. Even therapists who were not very tech-savvy learned to use video and telephone platforms to work with clients when in-person meetings were prohibited.

Aside from the dramatic example of adaptation for a global pandemic, there are always new scientific developments, new evidence-based assessment and treatment approaches, and new technologies for therapists to learn. Scientific advances in our understanding of the causes of mental illness and effective interventions are evolving every day. It can be challenging to keep up to date, but there is always something new to learn.

A career in mental healthcare also provides opportunities to grow in different roles. For example, in addition to practicing therapy, a therapist may teach or supervise students, conduct or collaborate in research, or consult for businesses. Chapter 5 presents a wide array of different job opportunities for someone with a graduate mental health degree. For instance, mental health professionals can take on managerial or leadership positions in nonprofit agencies, hospitals, or educational or faith-based institutions. Therapists often work for local or national government entities, global nonprofit agencies, or media operations. Some become journalists who can translate mental health research into accessible information for public mental health awareness. Mental health experts are well trained in behavior-change models, and this knowledge can be applied to a variety of health and wellness issues, such as addictions, nutrition and weight loss, and physical fitness. As technological innovations in mental health proliferate, therapists are also needed to partner with digital industry entrepreneurs. This is just a sampling of the diverse contexts in which individuals with mental health degrees may work. The exciting range of possibilities is another strong draw for this career path.

Balancing Inspiring Success With Frustrating Disappointment

> Be prepared for how high the highs are and how low the lows are. I don't think there's anything as fulfilling as seeing a client or family finally take the first steps towards improving their situation. It can be quite humbling to be present for those moments in someone's life. Unfortunately, the flip side is that you can also be in a position where you have to witness a client or family remain stuck, or further deteriorate. Those moments are particularly hard because you feel so powerless. (Florencia, professor and therapist)

This quote provides a sobering reminder of the realities of being a therapist. The majority of individuals who participate in therapy report that they benefit significantly.[8] However, not every experience will result in a good outcome. You will experience frustrations and disappointments. You will not be able to help everyone, and some people will reject your best efforts. By highlighting this, my intent is not to discourage you but to make sure you have a realistic perspective of the amazing opportunities this career path offers as well as the weighty challenges.

What Makes This Career So Fascinating: Balancing the Art and Science of Psychotherapy

Psychotherapy is extraordinarily impactful because it capitalizes on both the healing arts and innovative science. Like all healing arts, effective psychotherapy builds on clients' positive expectations. Good therapists inspire hope, and they use empathy to build healing therapeutic relationships with clients. Like all effective healthcare, mental healthcare relies on scientific advances, including identification of evidence-based practices and objective evaluation of outcomes. An effective psychotherapist is always integrating the art and the science for maximal impact.

Many of us were drawn to this field because of this complementary balance of art and science. It is what truly engages both our hearts and our minds in this work. Unfortunately, however, there is tension in the field because some people align more exclusively with either the healing art or the science of psychotherapy, dismissing the other side. As you prepare to enter this field, I hope to persuade you to appreciate the awesome healing art of a compassionate human connection, while also respecting the power of science to identify practices that are most effective. We need to marshal both art and science to help our clients most effectively.

You may encounter therapists who dismiss the importance and relevance of science in psychotherapy. They may profess that the power of psychotherapy is exclusively driven by the therapist–client relationship. These therapists also often reject any efforts to measure therapeutic outcomes using established, objective methods. As a dramatic example, a therapist told me that if she were required to use a scientifically developed measure to track her client's therapeutic progress, she would have to "throw her heart out the window." I've encountered this attitude at times from therapists who feel that practicing the healing art of therapy with compassion and empathy is incompatible with a scientific approach to delivering evidence-based practice. This false dichotomy can lead to unethical and ineffective practice.

A highly respected founding father of psychotherapy, Dr. Alfred Adler, is quoted as saying "follow your heart, but take your brain with you."[9] I love this quote because it reinforces my approach to psychotherapy. Our heart's compassion and empathy provide the motivation to help, but we need to use our brains to learn to deliver practices that are supported by science and to critically review how our clients are progressing (or not). Ignoring the science about what is most likely to help someone is as unethical as expressing indifference to our clients' suffering.

Embracing a scientific approach to therapy does not require you to reject the humanistic healing art aspect of therapy. Even though I proudly identify myself as a scientist, I love the fact that some of the power of psychotherapy feels well beyond the bounds of science, somewhat mysterious and unmeasurable by scientific methods.

This is the magic power of a human connection that is greater than the sum of its parts. It's what helps someone tap into hidden depths of resilience to gain strength and peace. Some may refer to this as a spiritual aspect of therapy, but it can just as appropriately be labeled the humanistic or healing art aspect.

Some who contemplate this career path may not think of themselves as scientifically minded. This may be due to a common but false perception of scientists as cold-hearted in their disciplined pursuit of knowledge. In fact, scientists are often poetically passionate about the mysteries they explore. Albert Einstein said that "the most beautiful thing we can experience is the mysterious. It is the source of all true art and science."[10] You may have been drawn to this career because of the humanistic aspect of therapy, but remember that when therapists use scientifically supported practices, their clients improve faster, are more likely to return, and are most satisfied with treatment.[11] Thus, incorporating a scientific approach to therapy is, in fact, the most compassionate way we can help our clients.

Embrace Science to Promote the Value of Psychotherapy

Unfortunately, there is a fair amount of skepticism about psychotherapy in our society. Some doubt that "just talking" can actually result in real behavioral or psychological change. Skeptics may question how therapy differs from a chat with a caring friend; this attitude undermines the value of professional training and expertise of therapists. We also see media reports about individuals who have been in therapy but still commit acts of violence or die by suicide. Unfortunately, these anecdotal stories reinforce public doubts about the effectiveness of mental healthcare. You and your friends may have a strong belief in psychotherapy, but it's important to recognize that these beliefs are not universal. We all have a responsibility to counter the skepticism.

When you enter this field, I urge you to become an advocate for the value of effective mental healthcare. We need to counter prevailing skepticism with hard evidence of the positive impact of therapy as well as compelling personal stories about its power to transform lives. Such evidence is readily available. Many studies document that the majority of individuals who are treated with evidence-based therapy demonstrate significant positive improvements in behavior and/or emotions, relationships, thought patterns, and/or daily functioning.[12] Exciting research demonstrates that evidence-based talk therapies can actually change brain functioning in healthy ways for children and adults.[13]

Nobel Prize–winning scientist Dr. Eric Kandel wrote that "Psychotherapy is a biological treatment, a brain therapy. It produces lasting, detectable physical changes in our brain, much as learning does."[14] This statement from such an esteemed neuroscientist is huge for our field. We need to publicize it—shout it from the rooftops! Psychotherapy, when practiced with compassion, empathy, and evidence-based approaches, changes peoples' brains in potentially life-saving ways.

In Conclusion

What an exciting time this is to be entering the mental health field. Job opportunities are projected to increase and expand, with innovative treatment methods opening up new roles for mental health professionals. Scientific and technological developments have great potential to extend and enhance the therapeutic benefits of psychotherapy. When you combine these innovations with the healing power of a therapeutic human connection, the possibilities are truly transformative.

I hope your motivation to pursue this career has been strengthened by what you've read so far. You've heard from me and other professionals about why we find this career to be exceptionally rewarding and stimulating. Subsequent chapters will provide more details to help you make decisions to chart your specific career path. Experts will share their insights to prepare you for success on that path.

2
Is This Career a Good Fit for You?

The best fit for this career? People who are empathic, curious, and who know themselves well or are willing to engage in a lot of self-reflection. (Sarah Kate, therapist and professor)

Are you truly cut out for this? Are you good at listening and NOT giving advice, taking the time to assess and to ask more questions? Do you know your own issues, "triggers"? You will need to be able to distinguish between your issues and your client's issues every session. (Mary, therapist and professor)

You've read that a career in mental health is extremely meaningful and that it can also be challenging. In this chapter, I urge you to critically examine how your own personal strengths and weaknesses may be a good fit for a successful career. I'll also push you to delve deeper into how your specific career motivations may impact your journey. The chapter concludes with some recommended activities and questions for you to further test your potential fit with this career and improve your readiness.

Shadow a therapist or "try on" a therapist role to see if it fits your personality and lifestyle hopes. It is easy to idealize being a therapist when looking from the outside. (Jo Ellen, therapist and professor)

One of the main goals of this book is to make sure you have a realistic understanding of this career. No matter how passionate someone is, this is not a realistic choice for everyone. To begin testing your fit, consider each of the following top 10 personal characteristics for effective therapists and evaluate yourself.[1]

Top 10 Personal Strengths of Effective Therapists

1. *Emotional intelligence*: The concept of emotional intelligence was popularized by Daniel Goleman in his 1995 book.[2] It refers to our ability to understand and appropriately express emotions, as well as to interpret other people's emotions correctly. It's no surprise that this type of intelligence is absolutely essential for effective therapists. In particular, *empathy*, the ability to imagine another person's experience, is crucial. A therapist needs to be good at recognizing a

client's emotions and needs and to know when to confront and push a client, when to offer support, and when to offer humor to lighten the atmosphere.

Emotional intelligence also refers to how well we manage our emotions. As a therapist, sometimes you'll hear stories that may shock you or move you very deeply, and you'll need to control your genuine automatic emotional reaction. It's not that you should be an emotionless robot but rather that you shouldn't burden your clients with the intensity of your emotions. Similarly, you will face high-risk situations, such as when a client expresses suicidal intentions; you may feel a sense of panic, but displaying your panic will not be therapeutic. You'll also need to manage very different emotions, such as boredom, frustration, or distraction, so as not to interfere with your therapeutic relationship. How effective are you in managing your emotional expressions?

2. *Open and accepting attitude*: Therapists need to embrace working with a wide range of clients who come from many different backgrounds and belief systems. You may need to build strong working relationships with people who express opinions that are offensive to you. Maintaining a curious and nonjudgmental attitude is essential. If you intend to "teach" people how to live their lives by your values, then this career is not for you.

Think about an individual who has cultural, religious, or political perspectives that are the opposite of your own or someone who tells sexist or racist jokes you find offensive. Can you imagine building a strong therapeutic relationship with such a person? Think about how well you'd be able to maintain a curious attitude when they are expressing opinions that are abhorrent to you.

I've had this experience several times, and it's tricky. For example, I had a client who made blatantly sexist "jokes" which were demeaning to women. I had been trained to be nonjudgmental, but I didn't feel comfortable ignoring these remarks. Struggling to figure out how to address this, I asked him about his intent and shared how I interpreted the comments. These discussions were uncomfortable; but I believe he gained some insight into the impact of his comments, and he made fewer such "jokes" as our work progressed.

You certainly don't need to endorse or accept offensive remarks, but are you someone who can work with people who have very different values than your own?

3. *Ability to inspire hope and optimism*: As discussed in Chapter 11, it is essential for therapists to build clients' confidence that therapy will relieve their suffering. To do so, you'll need to believe it yourself, and you'll need to explicitly "sell" the potential effectiveness of therapy to your client. This requires self-confidence, which may be particularly challenging as a beginner. No one expects you to feel totally confident at the start; you'll learn skills to build your confidence over time. For your clients' sake, you'll need to convey confidence even when it is lacking. You may have to "fake it till you make it."

To emphasize this point, imagine finally dragging yourself into a dentist's office for help with a severe toothache. You are desperately hoping the dentist will be able to offer you some relief, but when they greet you they express doubt that they can help, saying they aren't sure that they know how to do the procedures that could ease your suffering. How would you feel?

4. *Ability to be both organized and flexible*: Therapists need to balance the need for organized structure with flexibility. Sometimes plans are upended by major life events or crises, and you'll need to set aside your agenda to address unanticipated issues. If a client is not progressing, you'll also need to revise all your plans significantly. Well-developed goals and plans are absolutely necessary in therapy, but recognizing when to set them aside or revise them is also essential.

In addition to balancing planning with impromptu adaptability, good therapists need *cognitive flexibility*. This is the ability to hold on to multiple ideas and perspectives simultaneously, to be comfortable balancing ambiguous or even contradictory information. For example, imagine working with a couple and hearing opposite accounts of why they had a big argument. Your inclination may be to rush to figure out exactly which account was "correct." Alternatively, a good therapist needs to understand both perspectives and work with the couple to gain insight into the dynamics of their relationship by helping them to see the situation from the opposite perspective.

Are you someone who prefers to see the world in absolutes (e.g., absolute right and wrong), or are you comfortable with "maybes" and "it depends" explanations?

5. *Good communication skills and comfort with silence*: Therapists need to have strong verbal skills to communicate with clients fluently and accurately. Yet they also need to learn when to be quiet. Many beginning therapists are worried that they won't come up with things to say, but more often, the bigger challenge is learning to speak less. Careful listening and observing are often as important as talking.

Not surprisingly, this career path draws people who like to talk a lot (yes, I confess I'm one of them—how about you?). When I observe students doing therapy sessions, I can often see the client's eyes glaze over when the therapist keeps talking, often restating a point or overexplaining. I know the student is well intentioned and working hard to explain things to a client, but I see how therapists lose their client's attention when they talk too much. (This is analogous to professors who lecture for too long. You know what that feels like when your attention wanders and your eyes glaze over.)

Therapists need to learn to leave more space for clients to express themselves or just to contemplate. Sitting in silence can be awkward for talkative people, but it is essential for us to learn to rein in our verbosity. Even a brief 2-minute period of silence can feel like an eternity for an anxious therapy beginner, but it's an important learning experience.

While discussing verbal skills, I want to add a related note here about the value of second language skills. If you already have proficiency in or are learning a second language, this will be a great advantage in this career. Even if you are not totally fluent, clients will appreciate efforts to communicate in their primary language. Second language skills will expand your job opportunities and salary potential, so keep working on that second (or third?) language.

6. *Trustworthiness*: All mental health disciplines have established ethical codes, and there are serious consequences for therapists who engage in unethical behavior (more on this in Chapter 7). Clients need to know they can trust you. As a therapist, you are thus held to a higher standard of ethical behavior than many in other professions. Ethical codes address issues like confidentiality, informed consent for treatment, clarity in boundaries of therapeutic relationships, and responsible responses to risk and safety (e.g., how to address suicidal or homicidal risk, suspected child or elder abuse, or domestic violence).

Beyond the ethical guidelines, however, your clients need to see that you are conscientious, a person of integrity who is reliable and honest, and that you have their best interests in mind. They also need to trust you to follow up on what you've said you'll do. Basic organizational skills, like timeliness and record-keeping, may seem superficial; but they are important because clients need to know that they can count on you to be a competent professional. Conscientiousness is actually one of the best predictors of professionalism in healthcare practice.[3]

I've known students who think that their innate kindness and caring will compensate for weak organizational skills. If this rings true for you, please work on these types of organizational skills so that more people can benefit from your kindness and caring.

7. *Comfort with conflict*: Therapists will be confronted with intense emotions, conflicts, and family dramas. The therapist's job is to create a safe space for clients to be able to discuss these very weighty and poignant issues. You'll need to be comfortable with interpersonal intensity—both when it is directed at you and when you witness it expressed by clients toward others. For some trainees, this is particularly challenging. They may shy away from emotional intensity or interpersonal conflict. Unintentionally, they may communicate their discomfort to clients, sending an implicit message that these feelings aren't allowed in therapy. You'll need to learn how to use conflict therapeutically, as opposed to suppressing or avoiding it.

Sometimes therapists are overly concerned with doing something that will make their client angry. It's important to recognize in advance that you will experience anger and rejection from clients; you'll want to learn from it but not necessarily take it personally. Conflict is inherent in this work. Therapists need to provide feedback to clients that may be very difficult to hear, and clients will be angry or frustrated sometimes.

Avoiding conflict can limit the potential effectiveness of therapy. For example, let's imagine that a client hints at feeling angry at the therapist about something the therapist said last week that has been bothering them all week. Exploring this feeling more deeply would likely be valuable to the client, but if it makes them uncomfortable, the therapist may subtly convey a desire not to address this. The therapist might, for example, ignore the "hint" of the negative feeling and take the conversation in a different direction. This might not even be a conscious intention, but many kind, empathic people have a tendency to avoid or deflect potential conflict. Are you someone who tends to avoid conflict, and will you be able to work on this?

8. *Self-awareness*: You will need to develop a sophisticated awareness of how your own identity, history, family background, race, ethnicity, gender, sexual orientation, culture, spirituality, relationships, and personality contribute to how you see the world. This includes recognizing your biases and assumptions about how and why people behave as they do. Watch out if your initial response is "but I don't have biases." Being defensive about these explorations will be a problem in your training and for your subsequent career. We all have biases and blind spots.

9. *Curiosity to learn and motivation to improve*: This career is always evolving with new research and innovative technologies, as well as new problems to address. Someone who is intellectually curious and enjoys continually learning will thrive. Good therapists are inquisitive and analytical, using logic to figure out how best to understand and help their clients. Therapists also use strong critical thinking skills to evaluate how to apply research findings to benefit their work with clients. The best therapists I know are always seeking out new information for their practice, bringing in new perspectives from diverse sources including the arts (e.g., books, movies, TV, music), current events, and personal experiences. As you'll learn in Chapter 13, our field is constantly evolving, which means we need to learn how to use emerging tools, such as virtual reality, mobile apps, and therapeutic video games, to support mental healthcare. Are you someone who will embrace the opportunities to keep learning more?

10. *Being collaborative, willing to ask for help and admit when underqualified*: While self-confidence is critical for therapists, it's equally important to be aware of your limitations. You'll need to seek help and consultation frequently. And you'll need to get comfortable receiving and using critical feedback. This is crucial to maximize your learning in clinical supervision. Clinical supervision is part of all graduate programs and is offered in group and individual formats. You will show videotapes of your practice and receive feedback about your style and approach. This can be intimidating, but it is essential for learning.

Therapists need to be very collaborative and able to work well in a team. You may have a mental image of a therapist working independently in private practice, but the reality is that most mental health professionals work with multidisciplinary teams in clinics, hospitals, or schools. Working with colleagues who have different types of training and life experience is enriching.

As a therapist you will also need to recognize when a client could be better served by someone else. There may be many reasons to refer someone to another provider, including expertise with a specific clinical problem or treatment approach and difficulty in developing a therapeutic working relationship. Referring someone to a different provider may be the most caring and responsible thing you can do, but it takes some humility.

Potential Weaknesses as a Therapist

The potential weaknesses for a therapist are, in many ways, the opposites of the strengths. I will also highlight some specific weaknesses that I have encountered:

1. *Desire for clients to be dependent on you*: Our clients rely on us to support, encourage, and coach them in a variety of ways. They are usually in a vulnerable position when seeking help, and, unfortunately, I have seen a few therapists exploit this vulnerability to build their own ego. I'm not talking about egregious exploitation, such as an inappropriate romantic or sexual relationship; I am talking about a more nuanced situation when a therapist encourages their clients to become emotionally dependent on them.

   I worked with a therapist who repeatedly told her clients that she knew they would have difficulty when she went on vacation; she emphasized this so often that it became a self-fulfilling prophecy. She also found ways to subtly take credit for clients' progress, reinforcing the idea that any of their gains were all thanks to her. She often warned her clients about how difficult it would be for them to carry on after therapy ended. She would say this with a tone of empathy, but it was not at all therapeutic.

   Observing this therapist was an important lesson. I could see how this pattern was uncomfortable and detrimental to the clients. As therapists, we need to do the opposite of what she did. Our goal is to empower clients, to build their confidence in their ability to cope, to fully "own" their new hard-earned skills. We need to repeatedly stress that clients' insights and progress are due to their hard work, not to the therapist's brilliance. Make sure you are not entering this field because you want to feel needed or revered.

2. *Overconfidence in personal intuition*: A therapist once told me that he would never use any type of questionnaire to assess his clients' needs or progress because he knew better. He was particularly proud of his intuition and 100% confident of its accuracy. He told me that he always had a better understanding of his clients' feelings than they did.

   While I agree that clinical intuition is real and that some people are better endowed with it than others, it is never fail-proof. Expert therapists are well aware of the limits and biases of their intuition. We should all pay close attention to our intuition, while also critically evaluating it and looking for more objective evidence to support or refute our intuitive hunches. I teach students to embrace "disciplined intuition." I'm advocating for them to be attuned to their intuition, those valuable gut feelings and instincts, but to always critically review their intuitive hunches and impulses. Can you think of when your intuition led you to valuable insights and when it led you astray? Having some humility about our intuition and judgment is essential in this career.

3. *Sensitivity to criticism and rejection*: Therapists need to have a thick skin. Particularly during training, if you are defensive when criticized or particularly sensitive to criticism, you will not be able to learn how to help your clients. As discussed earlier (see strength 10 in the previous section), therapy training requires that you videotape (or audiotape) your therapy sessions and then play the tapes during group or individual supervision. Sometimes you will also be expected to conduct therapy while being observed behind a two-way mirror. There is no question that this is anxiety-provoking, but these are the most effective methods for learning. All your peers will be experiencing the same thing, so you can support each other through this stressful experience. I've seen students who are so afraid of criticism that they avoid showing recordings of therapy sessions where they struggled. This avoidant strategy severely limits what they will learn moving forward.

   Similarly, hypersensitivity to rejection will not serve you well as a therapist. You'll have clients who don't return for the next session and some who will actively criticize and complain about you. This will happen no matter how amazing you are. Sometimes clients just don't connect to a particular therapist, or they are not ready to address the issues you've raised. Often, clients can't continue with therapy because they are juggling so many stressful competing demands in their lives. Attending a therapy session is a low priority compared to caring for a sick family member or working to pay the rent.

   I've had many students who are overly concerned with the risk of a client rejecting them, so they never confront the client with hard truths. This could be a hard truth about a difficult diagnosis or about a recurrent pattern in dysfunctional relationships or about a behavioral change that will be challenging but essential for healing. Therapists often need to give clients difficult feedback and should not be reluctant to do so because of a fear of rejection.

4. *Unwillingness to learn new approaches*: As I get older, I have greater appreciation for the saying "you can't teach an old dog new tricks." For example, just when I am feeling comfortable with a new computer operating system, I see an unwelcome notice that a new update is required and feel slight panic. Unfortunately, our confidence and motivation to learn something new seem to wane over time.

   Many of us become set in our ways of doing things, and this goes for therapy practice too. One could argue that this isn't just fear of learning something new but also earned confidence in how we have been practicing over time. Either way, we need to embrace change throughout our careers and avoid growing complacent. Given how the science of psychotherapy evolves quickly and new evidence-based approaches are being identified all the time, it is critical for us to evolve too, to learn new effective approaches. In fact, it's unethical not to be delivering the treatments that are most likely to help the clients in our care.

A related tension is playing out as I write this book during the global COVID-19 pandemic. When in-person therapy was unadvised or prohibited, most therapists adapted quickly to remote teletherapy via phone or video, quickly learning about the ethical and clinical implications. Others refused to adapt and became essentially out of work.

5. *Difficulty compartmentalizing*: One essential skill to prevent burnout and secondary trauma as a therapist is the ability to *compartmentalize*, that is, to maintain emotional boundaries around the stressors of psychotherapy so that you are not constantly worrying about your clients during your free time. Since you are exploring this career, you are likely a caring and empathic person; thus, it is inevitable that you will occasionally be preoccupied with worries about your clients. However, you'll suffer in this career if you are unable to find ways to manage those worries. As compelling as this work is, we must be able to put our concerns for our clients aside at times so that these concerns do not totally overwhelm us. In Chapter 10 I will focus more on the risks of burnout and secondary trauma and how to prevent them.

6. *Unshakable belief in how life should be lived*: As emphasized in the description of therapists' strengths, it is essential for therapists to have an open and accepting approach to a full range of lifestyles and value systems. If you are someone who is proud that you have found "the truth" and you are hoping to lead all others to that singular truth through therapy, then you should rethink your career choice. As a therapist, it is your job not to convince clients of the "right" value system or lifestyle but to help them find what works for them. Likewise, if you feel your job is to "fix" people, you'll need to shift that mindset.

    Of course, there are some exceptions. If you are working with an individual who is harming others or whose lifestyle choices are very dangerous, you should address these risks. You'll work together to help the client identify the risks of their behavior and build alternative skills.

    Most people who want to become therapists are very open to multiple lifestyles and belief systems. However, I did work with a trainee who exemplified this weakness. She felt she had a calling to persuade everyone to embrace her specific religious belief system and hoped that psychotherapy would be the way to do this. After devoting considerable time and money to her training, she eventually learned that clients did not appreciate her subtle and unsubtle ways of advocating for her own agenda. She left the field after just a couple years.

7. *Need for clear resolution*: One thing many of us did not expect when we became therapists is how often our relationships with clients would end with limited resolution. A therapeutic relationship is so unusual because it can be very intense, and then it may end abruptly for a variety of reasons. By design, we do not stay in touch with our clients when therapy ends, and thus we rarely know about how they are doing over time. Frankly, I've always found this challenging. As I've developed a strong therapeutic relationship and become invested in my

clients' lives, their families, and professional endeavors, I'd like to know how things evolve but must accept my time-limited role.

Somewhat similarly, if you are expecting that all therapeutic relationships will reach magical "aha" moments where clients make remarkable dramatic breakthroughs and turn their lives around completely, you may be disappointed. Inspiring insight and change happen all the time in therapy, but such change is often incremental, not necessarily dramatic. Sometimes you'll never even know what impact therapy has had, and you'll need to grow comfortable with that uncertainty. Other times, you'll be blown away with the hard work that clients undertake, and they will express gratitude to you. Those moments can keep you persevering through uncertainty for a long time.

As I review the strengths and weaknesses described in this chapter, I recognize that it may seem a bit daunting, as if a therapist needs to be all things to all people. Likewise, I see how often I describe the need to balance seemingly opposite characteristics or skills. The goal of balancing contrasting aspects of therapy will be a recurring theme in this book, beginning in the first chapter with the important balance of art and science and continuing in this chapter.

Good therapists are always balancing contrasting skills, like being well organized and flexible, conveying self-confidence and humility, and trusting our intuitive hunches but also critically analyzing and testing them. I'm advocating for you to be open and compassionate and then also telling you that you must set aside or compartmentalize your compassionate caring instincts to survive as a therapist. So yes, it is all a bit daunting, and you will feel like you are on a wobbly balance board at times, just trying not to fall off. But don't be deterred because your training will help you develop the clinical judgment to keep you upright.

Understanding Your Motivation for This Career and How It May Impact Your Work

Many people choose this career path because they want to help people; wanting to help people is a truly admirable motivation. It's an excellent starting point. Now we'll delve a bit deeper into that motivation and other factors that may be driving you, helping to clarify what your motivation means to you and how it will impact your career path.

When you think about how and why you want to help people, what comes to mind? Do you want to help people who are facing challenges similar to your own or similar to the challenges a family member or friend has faced? Are there types of people you want to help and others whom you can't imagine helping? And what does *help* mean to you? These are the kinds of questions I'm asking you to explore in this section of this chapter.

Personal Experience with Mental Health Challenges as a Career Motivator

Many students explore this career path because they have struggled with mental health issues and/or their close family members or friends have struggled. Research indicates that students who have participated in psychotherapy are more likely to intend to pursue graduate school in a mental health practice field.[4] In my experience reading admissions essays for a variety of graduate programs over 25 years, the most commonly expressed motivations are personal, family, or friend mental health challenges. Some applicants describe how a wonderful therapist inspired them as a role model to emulate. Others bemoan the lack of effective, culturally sensitive therapists in their communities and are motivated to meet this need. Either way, these are powerful and worthy motivators.

Personal experience with mental healthcare can be an advantage for a trainee. Knowing what it is like to be a client can help prepare you to be on the other side of the therapeutic relationship and may give you more empathy for clients. And having some familiarity with different therapeutic approaches as practiced in real life can make the topics you will study in classes more meaningful. Knowing what it feels like to develop a working relationship with a therapist, or even what it's like not to have a good relationship, is a more impactful learning experience than reading a chapter about therapeutic relationships. These are just some of the many ways that direct experience with mental healthcare can benefit you as a trainee.

However, there are potential risks to watch out for as well. Sometimes graduate school applicants are still seriously struggling with mental health challenges and thus not yet ready to be therapists themselves. I understand that this statement may be controversial and potentially perceived as discriminatory. It is intended as a realistic assessment; those who wish to work as therapists need to have the emotional and interpersonal stability required to help others who are in a vulnerable state. Resilient individuals who have overcome challenges have the potential to be amazing therapists and role models. The point is not to discriminate against those who have struggled with mental health challenges but rather to emphasize the importance of timing and readiness. One should pursue graduate training when in the strongest position to succeed.

So how do you know if you are ready for graduate school? Discuss this with your own therapist if possible. Think about the extent to which you are feeling strong enough to be confronted frequently with potential "triggers" for your own mental health challenges. If you have experienced trauma, how will you manage hearing about a client's trauma? Or if you have experienced substance abuse personally or indirectly with a loved one, how will you feel about working with an individual who is tackling their own abuse? Even graduate course content can be potentially triggering when you are learning about different diagnoses, family dynamic patterns, relationship violence, etc.

I spoke with a student recently who requested a waiver to release her from a required course on addictions because she felt it would be too painful for her based on some family experiences. While I sympathized, I had to deny this request; and I used this opportunity to speak to her about her readiness to practice. If an academic course would be too triggering, I was concerned about how she'd manage with clients.

Do you find yourself being particularly sensitized to dramatic portrayals of mental health or substance abuse in movies or TV shows? Are you able to manage the emotions that this might trigger? Are you able to talk about mental health or substance abuse challenges you have faced without feeling overwhelmed by stressful emotions? These are preliminary ways to test your readiness.

Personal mental health experience can impact your career path in more ways. For example, sometimes our own unique experiences become the lens through which we evaluate all similar experiences. Specifically, I may view all therapeutic encounters by comparing them to my own experience. If I had a very positive experience, I may automatically assume that anything different from my experience is unhelpful or wrong. I may also assume that all clients will approach therapy the same way I did and need the same things I needed.

I have known students who struggle with this. They are so passionately driven by their own personal experience with mental health therapy that they use their personal experience as the single reference point for everything else. Unfortunately, this really limits their openness to learning about the full range of varied experiences clients may have and the wide range of effective therapy approaches.

In sum, direct experience with mental health challenges and therapy can be powerful inspiration for this career. Personal experience can contribute to empathy for clients, and firsthand knowledge of how therapy works can make graduate study more meaningful. However, if this is your motivation, be realistic about your readiness. In addition, remember that your experience is just one reference point in a vast array of experiences, and be careful not to assume that others share your unique experience or need the same thing you needed.

Other Motivators for This Career

Perhaps you've been reading the previous section and can't relate it to your own motivation. That's fine. Many people are inspired to pursue this career for other reasons, and they have no personal experience with mental health challenges or therapy. Some are motivated by their academic courses and fascinated by applied psychology and neuroscience research. Others have had volunteer or work experiences that have inspired a passion for helping people, or they've been inspired by role models in this field. Some are passionate about bridging the gaps in access to mental healthcare for underserved communities. Others have worked in a non–mental health field and have been struck by how significantly mental health challenges impact workplace culture, relationships, and productivity. I've known successful students who are driven by each of these motivators, and they are all terrific reasons to pursue this field. The important thing is to be clear about why you want to be a therapist and to be able to articulate that beyond a basic "I want to help people."

Testing Out Your Fit With This Career

> I would definitely suggest finding a job or volunteer opportunity where therapists are working, so that you can get a sense of what the career could look like. I would also promote personal therapy. There is so much value in doing your own work, and experiencing what it's like in the client's chair. (Cassidy, therapist in private practice and instructor)

So far in this chapter we've explored personal characteristics that can be strengths or weaknesses and how different factors may be driving your motivation. As you continue to examine your fit with this career, consider Cassidy's advice. Work or volunteer for a nonprofit organization, healthcare facility, or school serving a community different from your own. While you won't be able to work as a therapist per se, you can certainly gain valuable experience in a number of different roles, such as tutor, coach, organizer, advocate, marketer, behavioral aide, interviewer, crisis counselor, or case manager.

Finding a position like this may take some searching. Some job search sites like Indeed.com include volunteer opportunities, or you may find something in your area through Volunteermatch.org. Several national and international organizations, such as United Way, American Red Cross, Global Vision International, and Big Brothers Big Sisters, have multiple local opportunities. Depending on your interests, you could explore the Department of Veterans Affairs; the YMCA; the Rape, Abuse, & Incest National Network; Meals on Wheels, etc. Local libraries and municipal governments sometimes post volunteer opportunities as well.

When you find a paid or volunteer position in human services, test how it feels to work with individuals with different life experiences. Does this experience strengthen your motivation for this career or make you question it?

In Conclusion

I've pushed you to ask yourself some tough questions in this chapter. Do you have the personal strengths needed to thrive in this career, and if not, how can you work on them? What is your motivation, and how might different sources of motivation affect your career path? Are you emotionally prepared to take on the hard work of training in mental health? What are you doing to test your potential fit with this career path?

If you are currently working or volunteering in a field related to mental health and human services, do you often find yourself thinking about your clients' struggles or researching how to improve the care that is provided? Likewise, as you read anecdotes in this book about the realities of mental health practice, do you find yourself intrigued and wanting to know more? If so, you are likely hooked! Congratulations, you are fortunate to have identified a career that fits with your natural interests and strengths. As Jo Ellen's concluding quote for this chapter reflects, it is wonderful to find a career that aligns so well with our natural interests.

> My career encourages me to think about issues (i.e., suffering, redemption, healing, and forgiveness) that I would want to think about naturally. (Jo Ellen, professor and therapist in private practice)

3
Steps to Becoming a Mental Health Professional

Many people gravitate to this field because they want to help others. Learning about the many routes you can take, as well as the most cost-effective and efficient ways to get to where you want to go, can be invaluable information to have before starting a graduate program. (Angela, therapist in a hospital and instructor)

Are you beginning to believe that you've found the right career? Now you'll learn about the steps to making it a reality. This chapter outlines six essential steps for becoming a mental health professional and highlights the key decisions you'll need to make to chart your own specific path. Chapter 4 will help you make those important decisions by highlighting similarities and differences across disciplines, degrees, and specializations.

There are many possible pathways on the road to becoming a mental health professional, but all of them involve the six steps illustrated in Figure 3.1; each step will be described in this chapter.

Figure 3.1 Steps to Becoming a Mental Health Professional

Step 1: Earn an Undergraduate Degree

All professional mental health disciplines require an undergraduate degree. The most common undergraduate majors among those pursuing this field are psychology and other social science or human development fields. These majors provide a strong foundation for graduate study in any mental health discipline. However, don't worry if your major is in a different field.

Pursuing a Mental Health Career with a Non–Mental Health College Major

While a college degree in psychology or human development may be the most direct preparation for graduate study in a mental health discipline, it is not essential. People with diverse backgrounds and experiences can bring valuable perspectives that complement the more common trajectory. I've worked with terrific mental health professionals who majored in fields as diverse as chemical engineering, software development, Russian literature, Latin American history, business marketing, classical ballet, foreign languages, music, and film, to name just a few. It takes a lot of initiative to shift academic or career directions, and in my experience, individuals who have made such a shift are often among the most motivated.

Trainees who come from different fields have told me that the initial learning curve in graduate school is quite steep. Some needed to take prerequisite psychology courses to prepare for graduate study, but this was not a huge challenge. Interestingly, they've described how it is the culture of mental health that presents an unexpected challenge, as opposed to the academic content. By *culture*, I am referring to expectations about how people communicate and relate to each other. The culture of mental health encourages very open discussion of feelings and self-reflection within the academic context. People who have been immersed in other non–mental health cultures are often surprised by all the emotional sharing in mental health classes. Keep this in mind if you are coming into the field from a different professional or academic field.

Complementing Your Undergraduate Degree With Work/Volunteer Experience and/or Research Experience

Most graduate mental health programs seek students who have relevant work or volunteer experience. In the Introduction I shared some valuable experiences I had in my own educational journey. In Chapter 2 I urged you to seek work or volunteer experiences to test your fit with this career path. Many different types of work opportunities provide valuable experience. Seek out activities that offer direct interaction with diverse communities in a human service or support capacity. Don't discount relevant work, such as being a camp counselor, health aide, or tutor, just because it is not specifically mental health–focused. Gaining any experience in a human service capacity, particularly with diverse communities of people, is valuable.

Volunteer positions in nonprofit agencies are definitely worthwhile. Many students gain valuable experience as behavioral aides to children with autism or other disabilities or as volunteers on crisis hotlines. Others work as trained volunteers for organizations that support specific populations, such as those aiding homeless youth, LGBTQ+ individuals, or wounded warriors and their families. Many students work for organizations supporting racial or gender equity. Some use their passion for art, music, or sports to engage with diverse individuals or volunteer to improve literacy with immigrant or refugee families. There are an infinite number of ways to expand your experience, and those that stretch you out of your comfort zone are likely the most valuable.

Whether it be paid or volunteer work experience, both will help you to clarify the type of work you hope to do in the future (as well as possibly clarifying the work you do not want to do). You'll also build essential empathy and communication skills and learn more about how to collaborate with team members. My own early job experiences taught me important lessons about mental healthcare, which provided a strong foundation for graduate study.

Relevant work and volunteer experience will also make you a stronger candidate for competitive graduate school admissions. But please remember, it's critical that you engage fully in the activities and work on clearly articulating what you've learned. Simply listing a volunteer experience for "credit" is not going to help you progress on this career path. Sometimes students assume that an impressive job title or well-known organization is most important, but actually, what is more important is your ability to describe what you've learned from any particular job or project. Think about how your own work or volunteer experiences have influenced what you want to do next. Have these experiences inspired new interests or questions you hope to learn more about?

In addition to work or volunteer experience in a human service capacity, many graduate programs are looking for students with relevant research experience. This is essential if you are applying for a doctoral program. For master's-level programs, the expectations for research experience are more varied. Again, the important point is to be able to convey what you've learned from any research experience and to reflect on how that experience has affected your graduate study goals.

If your research experience involved direct contact with human participants (including activities such as participant recruitment, interviewing, or other direct data collection), be sure to describe this in your admissions essay and/or curriculum vitae (CV). Alternatively, if your role was more administrative or involved data analysis, writing up results, etc., be sure to identify what you learned about the rigors of the research process and/or working with a team. For example, a clerical task such as computer data entry may seem irrelevant for a future therapist, but reflect on what that job may have taught you about organizational skills, attention to detail, and complementary roles on a productive team. These skills are generalizable to all kinds of careers. Remember that every type of research experience is valuable, whether it helps you find your true passion or clarify what you are less passionate about.

Step 2: Apply to Graduate School

The common process for applying to graduate programs will be described in this section. Specific distinctions for admission to different disciplines will be highlighted in Chapter 4. Graduate school applications usually require (a) a program-specific application form; (b) letter(s) of recommendation; (c) personal essay(s); (d) undergraduate transcripts; and (e) Graduate Record Examinations (GREs) for some, but not all, programs. Many programs also require qualified candidates to interview in-person or remotely.

Advice for the Application Process:

a. Read all application instructions very carefully, and adhere to guidelines. This is critical. You would be surprised how often applicants are rated poorly because their application materials are inconsistent with the guidelines. Make sure you know the deadlines and details, such as number of letters of recommendation and word limit and desired focus of personal essay(s). Remember that the evaluators are reading dozens of applications, and if yours is too long or missing a required piece of information, it will likely annoy the evaluator, giving them a reason not to admit you.

b. Think carefully about your recommenders, and request letters well in advance (ideally, about a month). Do not request letters from friends (including friends of your family). If possible, choose one recommender who knows your academic abilities and motivations plus another who can speak to your relevant work or volunteer experience. It is wise to give your recommender a copy of your CV or résumé and a copy of your personal essay describing your goals. The strongest letters come from recommenders who know you well enough to provide a brief specific example or anecdote about you. If a person seems hesitant to write a letter, you should likely choose someone else. Sometimes applicants think they need a well-known (i.e., famous) individual to write a letter, but it is more important to have a recommender who knows you well and is motivated to advocate for you.

c. Work hard on your personal essay(s). Read the prompts and the formatting guidelines carefully, and make sure to have someone else proofread. Most commonly, graduate programs ask you to write about why you are applying to graduate school (and often why that particular program and school), what academic and other work experiences have prepared you for this field, and what strengths and weaknesses you bring to it.

   It can be challenging to strike an optimal balance of professionalism and authentic personal disclosure. For example, sharing information about personal or family mental health challenges as a motivator for this career can be powerful, but you need to frame this in a professional way. Overly dramatic disclosures that may suggest you are not yet ready for the rigors of graduate school can work against you.

Applicants also sometimes struggle with how specific their interests should be at this stage. Do you need to know exactly what clinical setting and client population you want to work with for the rest of your career? While reviewers will vary in how much specificity they are looking for, I think it's unreasonable to expect applicants to know exactly what type of work they want to do at this early stage. The goal of graduate school is to broaden your horizons to all kinds of possibilities (see Chapter 5 for lots of examples). If you are already committed to a narrow interest, you may miss other exciting opportunities.

The trick is to write about some of your interests so that you convey a depth of understanding about your chosen field, while at the same time expressing openness and enthusiasm for expanding your knowledge in different directions. I recognize this is a challenging balance to find. Your goal is to reflect some sophistication in your motivation to pursue graduate training, something that goes deeper than "I want to help people." However, the simultaneous goal is not to be too narrowly focused on just one specific career choice, suggesting that you will have blinders on to different possibilities during grad school. Maybe you do have a very specific career goal, like working with individuals with anorexia, supporting injured veteran's spouses, or conducting animal-assisted therapy with traumatized refugees. It's beneficial to express your strong interests, but make sure you also express openness to learning about a range of approaches and populations.

It is important to do research about the specific schools to which you are applying to be sure your interests align with the program. Sometimes I've read essays from applicants who are passionate about art or music therapy, but they are applying for programs that don't offer that training. Be sure that your interests are reflected in the goals and required courses of the programs to which you are applying. Try to identify particular strengths of the program that interest you, and tailor your essays to each program.

d. Don't panic if standardized tests are a weakness for you. Some graduate mental health programs do not require the GRE or any other standardized tests, and each year more programs drop this requirement. If this is a major weakness for you, look for those that don't require it. Also, keep in mind that many master's-level programs that require GREs are looking for acceptable, but not necessarily exceptional, scores. Only the most competitive doctoral programs are looking for applicants with exceptionally high GRE scores. Remember that most faculty members are aware of bias in standardized testing and will consider scores in the context of your background, for example, whether or not English is your first language.

e. Admissions decisions are based on "the whole package." Evaluators weigh factors differently for each individual. For example, if you have been out of college for years, your college grades will carry less weight. If you were a pre-med student in a highly competitive university and your GPA suffered a bit thanks to advanced math or science courses, make sure to point this out. Be sure to emphasize your strengths and resilience by describing what you've learned from any challenges you've faced. Highlight experiences with diverse communities and how you've pushed yourself outside your comfort zone. Help the essay reader get to know your authentic personality, but maintain a professional tone.

Advice for Interviews:

a. Project confidence (but not arrogance). Everyone recognizes that interviews are anxiety-provoking, so they will empathize with you if you are a bit nervous. However, if your anxiety significantly interferes with your ability to communicate clearly about your strengths and your interests, this can be a problem. Practice interviewing to manage potential anxiety. Also, remind yourself that if you have been invited to an interview, it means that you are already considered a viable candidate. Your achievements have been recognized, and the program wants a chance to get to know you a bit better.

   Also remember that everyone you interact with is likely providing input about the admissions decision, including all staff members and current students. Unfortunately, I've seen applicants interact very respectfully with faculty but not with current students or administrative staff members, and this can be a significant barrier to admission.

b. Prepare for interviews. Ask experienced peers or faculty members to share what types of questions to expect. Think about your responses, and ask a friend or mentor to do a mock interview with you. If possible, speak to previous applicants of similar programs about their interview experience and questions they were asked. I'm not recommending that you prepare scripted responses—in fact, that would be a bad idea. Rather, work on clarifying your thoughts so that you are prepared to speak about the types of issues that may come up.

   In addition, think about your strengths and the major reasons you are confident about your fit with the graduate program. Don't hesitate to advocate for yourself and emphasize these even if a specific interview question hasn't addressed them. You will usually have an opportunity to add something that you feel hasn't been well addressed by the interviewer's questions.

Common Interview Questions May Include Versions of the Following:
Questions about your interest in becoming a mental health professional:

1. Why do you want to become a mental health professional? And why did you select this particular discipline? Or this particular program?

2. How have your academic, work/volunteer, or research experiences prepared you for this career path?
3. Tell us about your experiences with diverse communities and what you've learned.
4. Give us an example of how you have worked with someone who had a very different belief system than your own.
5. What clinical populations are you most interested in working with, and which are you not interested in?
6. What are your long-term career goals?

Questions about your interpersonal style, insight, and self-awareness:

7. What strengths would you bring to this field, and what challenges might you face?
8. What is your usual role on a group project?
9. Give us an example of an interpersonal conflict and how you resolved it.
10. Tell us about a personal challenge or an ethical dilemma you've faced and how you handled it.
11. How might your family experiences influence your work as a therapist?
12. What were your favorite (or least favorite) college courses and why?
13. What do you like to do when you are not working or studying?
14. What questions do you have about the program?

Think of some potential questions in advance. For example, you could ask to hear more about the types of practicum placements in which students work or opportunities to work with faculty on research or to attend professional conferences. Or you could identify something about the program that you're interested in and would like to hear more about. Faculty members are usually very happy to answer questions about the program and the university.

However, some types of questions are better to ask students directly. For example, don't ask faculty members questions like, "Do I need to attend classes regularly?" "Is the food good on campus?" "Is there a lot of dating among the students in the program?" (Believe it or not, I've been asked all sorts of questions like this by applicants.)

A Note About Applying to Doctoral Programs

All of what's been described so far applies to master's- and doctorate-level programs, but applicants to doctoral programs need to address additional points. First of all, compared to terminal master's programs, most doctoral programs will be looking for more information about your research experience and research interests in essays and in interviews. Doctoral programs also look for indicators of scholarly productivity, such as an honors thesis project or co-authorship on academic publications or conference presentations. Remember to emphasize what you've learned from these activities, not just a list of what you accomplished.

Smaller doctoral programs also often take a personalized approach to admissions. In these programs it is very important for you to try to find a good fit with one or more specific faculty members. You'll need to take initiative by reaching out to faculty members whose research interests align with yours to some extent. You will not always hear back from faculty members, but it is still wise to express interest and request to speak with them about the program.

Potential Pitfalls (i.e., When You Are Unsuccessful in the Admissions Process)

Many graduate programs are highly competitive, and even well-qualified applicants are denied admission. (Chapter 4 will offer some guidelines about the competitiveness of programs in different disciplines.) If you are unsuccessful in the admissions process, don't despair. I was actually unsuccessful in my initial application to doctoral programs when I graduated from college. I didn't know enough about how to find a good fit with a faculty mentor and didn't realize the importance of research experience. Many people like me are successful after reapplying if they refine their approach.

You are welcome to contact the admissions department to ask for feedback to improve your application. Sometimes you'll get a response, and other times you will not; but it may be worth asking. Often, the decisions are based on the "hard data" of grade point averages (GPAs) and test scores. If GREs are your weakness, consider enrolling in a preparation class and retaking the exam. There are many in-person and online prep services, some with low cost. If your undergraduate grades are a weakness, consider taking graduate-level courses at a local university as a "non-degree student" to demonstrate your academic ability.

Often, even applicants with strong GPAs and excellent test scores are not offered admission due to some of the following issues:

Lack of relevant "real-world" experience with diverse communities. These applicants may have adequate or even exceptional academic achievement but limited work, volunteer, or life experience. Or they were not effective in communicating what they had learned from such experiences.

Underdeveloped knowledge of the field or lack of clarity about motivation. These are the applicants who may express that they have always wanted to be a therapist "to help others," but they don't or can't expand more on that desire. Programs are looking for a well-developed sense of why you are pursuing this career path and why you are interested in their particular program.

Poor fit with the program. These applicants may have well-developed and articulated motivation, but the program faculty has determined that the applicant's specific interests aren't a good fit with what the program offers. Programs don't want to admit students who may become dissatisfied with the program.

Concerns about interpersonal skills and/or self-awareness. Applicants may be denied admission based on how they related (or did not relate) to program faculty, staff, students, or fellow applicants during an interview. Likewise, they may have communicated a lack of self-awareness, curiosity, and openness to other people's perspectives. Graduate programs are looking for individuals who demonstrate interpersonal maturity, tolerance, and respect for others.

Selecting Your Graduate Program

Selecting your graduate program might be easy if your choice is based solely on practical factors, such as financial aid, class scheduling convenient for your work, or geographic preferences. However, if you do have the luxury of choosing among multiple programs, here are some factors to consider.

Factors to Consider in Selecting Your Graduate Program:

a. Check the accreditation status of the program. National accreditation (such as the American Psychological Association for psychology, the Council for Accreditation of Counseling and Related Educational Programs for counseling, the Commission on Accreditation for Marriage and Family Therapy Education for marriage and family therapy, and the Council on Social Work Education for social work) is often important for licensure and portability of your degree across different states and is required for some jobs. Accreditation also offers scholarship opportunities and can facilitate membership in professional organizations. Don't assume all programs are accredited since many are not.

b. Check the student outcomes that are usually posted online. These may include passing rates for licensure exams and alumni employment rates.

c. Review the required courses for the degree program and the practicum/field-work options to see if they fit your interests. Find out how the practicum placement process works. Specifically, do you have to find your own placement, or does the program facilitate placement? To what extent are placements vetted for quality of experience and supervision? Look for evidence of innovation in the curriculum and extracurricular opportunities that enrich traditional course-work. For example, are there active clubs or volunteer service opportunities that fit your interests? Global travel courses? Research opportunities? An emphasis on multicultural issues, diversity and inclusion?

Chapter 13 highlights future developments in mental healthcare, and you should explore the extent to which programs address innovations that will best prepare you for the future, such as an emphasis on evidence-based practices, attention to emerging technologies, and neuroscience applications.

   d. Consider all the financial factors including tuition and cost of living, as well as the feasibility of working while earning your degree. Consider what the "value added" may be for more costly programs in terms of the quality of the training, professional networking opportunities, and meeting your specific career goals.

   e. Don't discount quality-of-life considerations, such as geographic location, cultural diversity, and proximity to friends, family, or other social supports. Be sure to ask to speak to current students about what it is like to be a student in the program and (if relevant) what it's like to live there. You're not likely to thrive in a program where you are unhappy or overly stressed about finances, no matter how prestigious the program's reputation.

   f. Finally, consider the long-term career prospects and the networking opportunities that will set you up for career success in a geographic area in which you'd like to live.

Step 3: Complete Your Graduate Program and Earn Your Degree

> Be clear about your choices for education and where you want to go after (i.e., what is your ideal job), prepare for that during graduate school if you can. Also, have realistic expectations of salary after—make sure you can afford 2–3 years of school plus an additional 2 years before getting licensed. (Jenny, therapist in a hospital clinic)

In general, most master's programs will require 2–3 years of full-time coursework, including 1 year of practicum (may also be called *internship, residency, fieldwork,* or *field placement* where you are actually practicing therapy with clients). Doctoral programs will require at least 4 years of coursework and practicum, plus 1 year of internship and completion of a doctoral dissertation. If you enter a doctoral program with a master's degree, the duration may be shorter; but this is not guaranteed (more on that in Chapter 4). Many graduate degrees can also be completed part-time, extending the duration of the program.

Graduate School Is Not Just an Extension of Your Undergraduate Education

Chapter 9 is designed to boost your preparation for graduate school, addressing many ways that graduate school is different than undergraduate college. As a preview, you'll have less class time but more reading, writing, and project work outside of class. Your classes are likely to be smaller, especially if you attended a large undergraduate university. Smaller classes provide more opportunities for discussion with your peers and instructors; they also offer less anonymity, so you need to be fully engaged. Your professor will know if you are spending lots of time on social media in class—trust me.

Graduate school also requires a shift in your mindset, away from a primary focus on grades, toward a focus on professional development. Graduate school is designed for you to gain the knowledge, skills, disposition, and networking connections to practice as a mental health professional. Much of the essential personal and professional growth in graduate school has nothing to do with points on an exam or grades. It's about gaining deeper self-awareness and interpersonal skills that will be essential for your career. Remember that graduate school is your professional training ground, not just an extension of your academic education.

The social aspect of graduate school is also different than undergraduate. Obviously, students are generally older, and many have their own busy lives outside of school (e.g., families, jobs). While you will likely make several lifelong friends in graduate school, it is also very important to remember that your fellow students and faculty will be professional colleagues one day too, so you are building a professional network and establishing a professional identity from the first day forward. Remember that this professional identity is reflected in all your in-person contacts, as well as your social media presence.

Balancing Coursework and Practice Training

Chapter 9 describes the types of courses you will take in most programs and how to prepare for those courses. Often, your first year will be devoted to classes only, with actual practice (i.e., assessment, counseling, or therapy) training beginning in the second year, although this varies by program. Even within your coursework, you'll likely have a mix of classes that are more content-based to build your knowledge (e.g., learning about theories) and others that emphasize actual skill-building (e.g., learning active-listening skills or group-counseling skills). You are also encouraged to continue to expand your experience with work or volunteer opportunities while taking classes.

The beginning of your practicum training is usually the most exciting and the most stressful step in your career path. You'll still be taking classes, but you'll add many hours per week of practicum. No matter how well prepared you are, there is still nothing like stepping into the role of therapist or counselor for the first time. Many trainees struggle with a lack of confidence at this stage; so prepare yourself for that, and recognize that you will not be alone. Be sure to be as open as possible with clinical supervisors who can help you gain confidence in your knowledge and skills.

Clinical Supervision

Clinical supervision is an integral part of your training in graduate school and for at least a couple years after you graduate. Each profession has specific requirements about the ratio of direct service hours (when you meet with clients) to supervision hours (when you meet with your supervisor). High-quality supervision should include review of your actual practice with clients using video or audio recordings or live supervision (i.e., when your supervisor actually watches your practice in real time). Sometimes students also partner with experienced therapists to do co-therapy. All these supervision experiences can be intimidating at first, but they are essential learning experiences.

Step 4: Find a Postgraduate Job or Internship

> Talk to people in different mental health fields and ask what decisions they consider key to getting to their current position. Mentors are critical throughout your career, not just at the beginning. Seek out peers and more senior people whom you trust and are invested in helping you develop. (Lauren, professor)

Earning your master's or doctoral degree is arguably the most important step in your career journey, and that achievement should be celebrated. However, it's not the final step in becoming a fully independent mental health professional.

Learn Exactly What Type of Practice and Supervision Is Required for Licensure

All of the disciplines require that you complete supervised hours of practice after graduation and pass licensing exams to get your professional license. Most states have a process for registering as an associate or intern right after you earn your degree. Your graduate program should provide guidance on the process.

Each discipline and each state within the United States has slightly different specific requirements for licensure, but virtually all require at least 1000–3000 hours of postgraduate practice that is supervised by a licensed mental health professional within a specified time period (often about 5 years). It is absolutely critical that you clarify licensure requirements from a reliable source instead of just "hoping for the best." When you reach this stage you will have devoted considerable time, money, and energy to your career development; and you want to make sure you are accurately informed and prepared to get your license. Consult the licensure requirements in your discipline and in the state in which you want to be licensed. As a warning, this is a bureaucratic process, and the online information can be somewhat dense and confusing. Professional organizations in your state may provide more user-friendly resources for information on licensing processes. Also, be aware that requirements change fairly frequently, so don't rely on a friend's advice from their experience of 5 years ago.

A license is critical for independent practice and for most jobs in hospitals, clinics, and nonprofit agencies. Obtaining your license also increases your earning potential significantly. It's important to know your state's licensure requirements when you are looking for a job after graduation so that you will meet the specific practice and supervision requirements.

Tips on Finding a Job After Graduation

Networking

If you are going to stay in the geographic area of your graduate training and practicum work, you'll be wise to be working on professional networking throughout your graduate training. In fact, even if you aren't intentionally thinking about it this way, be aware that others are. Remember that a colleague or supervisor you meet in one context (academic or social) may be connected to a colleague or potential hiring supervisor for a job you want later. The mental health communities are often well connected, even in large cities. This can be beneficial if you make a good impression but can be problematic if you behave unprofessionally. And, again, let me remind you that this includes impressions you leave on social media as well.

I have known students who, unfortunately, seemed to assume that because they were "just a student" (i.e., not yet a professional seeking a job), they didn't have to worry about their reputation. Cultivating a strong professional reputation is important from the beginning. You may think of networking as a formal process of reaching out to a professional contact, but remember that you are informally networking all the time through peers, instructors, and even social acquaintances.

Word of mouth is one of the most common ways people find their first job out of graduate school. You'll want to let all your supervisors and colleagues know that you are looking and highlight your strengths and interests. Often, the organizations that place students in practicum will also have postgraduate employment opportunities.

Of course, you should also explore professional networking sites online, including LinkedIn and Indeed.com. Local professional organizations for your discipline may also be useful resources. You'll be able to find these online, and they often host social events and/or continuing education opportunities. Attending a training for a specific interest can also provide good networking opportunities.

Prepare Your Materials

Make sure you have polished your résumé and cover letters. Utilize career counselors at your university who are trained to help you put your best foot forward. Seek advice about the level of detail to include in your résumé and how to highlight your strengths. Sometimes students make a mistake by including too many details about unimportant elements of their accomplishments and/or too little detail about important elements. Highlight any leadership roles, experience with diverse communities, and specialized training (including clinical, ethical, second-language, or administrative training). Don't discount your skills that may seem less relevant to therapy, such as organizational and writing skills, technology expertise, research and program evaluation experience, advocacy and marketing. Employers are looking for candidates who bring complementary skills beyond "just" clinical care. Highlight unique experiences or talents that reflect maturity, creativity, compassion, and dedication.

Cast a Wide Net

When looking for a job, try to be as open as possible to varied job descriptions. Counseling and therapy jobs can be called many different things, including *case manager, social service worker, mental health worker, intake coordinator, community counselor,* and *behavioral specialist.* Even if the posting includes specific language regarding the desired disciplines, such as *social work, counseling,* or *psychology,* and your degree is in a different discipline, feel free to contact the employer to express interest. You may be surprised to find they are interested in your discipline too but just didn't list it. Likewise, if there is an organization you are particularly interested in working for, don't hesitate to contact them even if you don't see a specific job posting.

Step 5: Pass Licensure Exams

All disciplines have licensure exams in each state. The requirements vary by state, but there are often two exams, one covering clinical practice and the other covering mental health laws and ethics. There are usually free or low-cost test preparation materials offered through the licensing board, including sample exam questions. Many companies also sell test prep materials and workshops. The pass rates for these exams vary by discipline, state, and year but are often around 75%. You are allowed to retake the exams if you are unsuccessful at first.

Step 6: Practice and Maintain License with Continuing Education

Obtaining your professional license represents the culmination of many years of hard work and definitely deserves a celebration. At this point you will have completed all the necessary steps to becoming a fully independent mental health professional. Now you just need to be sure to maintain that license and keep your knowledge and skills up to date. That's right, the learning never stops, but the good news is that there are no more exams!

Every state and discipline has specific requirements about how to maintain your license. The requirements usually include completing a number of approved continuing education courses to make sure your knowledge is up to date. This may range from 20 to 40 hours every year or two. You'll need to pay fees to renew your license and follow all state guidelines regarding the specifics of the continuing education experiences (e.g., online vs. in person). Note that professionals can also lose their license (temporarily or permanently) if they engage in unethical or illegal behavior.

In Conclusion

This chapter has described the six steps to becoming a mental health professional, including key decision points and advice for success at each step. Maybe you are still working on finishing Step 1 (completing your undergraduate degree) or you are contemplating Step 2 (applying to graduate school). No matter where you are in the process, having accurate knowledge of what's coming next is critical to your preparation for each step. While it can be a daunting process, remember why you are passionate about this field, and you'll actually enjoy the work along the way. You are exploring a particularly meaningful career, and it doesn't come easy.

Review of the Six Steps to Becoming a Mental Health Professional:

1. Earning an undergraduate degree.
2. Applying for admission to a graduate program in the discipline of your choice.
3. Completing a graduate program, including all coursework and supervised practicum experience.
4. Earning a job as a prelicensed trainee (often called an *intern*) to gain supervised hours of postgraduate clinical practice to qualify for licensure. Most disciplines require 1 year or more of full-time supervised practice after earning your graduate degree to qualify for license eligibility.
5. Passing a clinical licensure exam in your discipline and (often) an ethics exam in your state.
6. Maintaining a license with required continuing education throughout your career.

4
Choosing a Discipline and Degree to Pursue

> It would have been helpful to have a broader understanding of the multiple paths that one can take within the field of mental health. There are many decisions along the way that influence where one might go—Which of the multiple mental health disciplines is the best fit? What type of degree should I pursue? (Lauren, professor)

One of the main motivations for writing this book was to address the confusion that many students have about choosing a discipline and degree path. It is difficult to find accurate and comprehensive information about the range of available options. You may be in this position right now. Perhaps a mentor or family member is suggesting you pursue a particular discipline (usually the one they pursued). You are aware of other options; but the implications of choosing one versus another are not clear, and you may even be getting contradictory advice. There are many misconceptions about these disciplines and career opportunities. This chapter is designed to help you choose the discipline and degree that best fit your career interests, strengths, timeline, and budget.

The very good news is that expert analyses project increasing workforce growth across all disciplines—simply put, the number of mental healthcare jobs is projected to increase significantly. The US Bureau of Labor Statistics predicts that healthcare jobs will increase at double the rate of the overall job market from 2018 to 2028 (a 14% increase in healthcare compared to 7% overall). And for mental healthcare jobs specifically the forecast is even better, with projected workforce increases of over 20% across some disciplines.[1] These projections were estimated prior to the global pandemic, which is expected to accelerate the need for mental healthcare even more.[2] Thus, all signs indicate increasing need for well-trained mental health professionals of all kinds in the United States and globally.

Table 4.1 summarizes information on the disciplines covered in this chapter. Note that some disciplines (e.g., counseling, social work, and psychology) have many sub-specialties. Also, the number of providers, projected workforce growth, and salary ranges are all rough estimates compiled and averaged from multiple data sources[3]; they should not be interpreted as precise estimates. In terms of salary, for example, there are major differences by geography, type of workplace, unique skills (such as bilingual skills), etc. The factors that impact salary will be detailed in Chapter 6, which is devoted to the business aspects of this career.

Table 4.1 Summary Table on Major Mental Health Disciplines in the United States

Discipline	Degree Options	Licensure/ Credential	Estimated Number in the United States	Projected 10-Year Workforce Growth	Estimated 2019 Mid-salary Range across the United States
Counseling Addiction, clinical mental health, college or career, school, rehabilitation	MA & PhD	LPC/LPCC with master's PPS credential for school counseling	250,000	23%	$38–70K MA
Marital/Couples and Family Therapy (MFT)	MA & PhD	LMFT with master's	43,000	22%	$40–70K MA
Social Work Administrative, clinical, policy/ public welfare	MSW & PhD	LCSW with master's	117,000 (LCSW)	17%	$39–70K for MSW
Psychology Clinical, counseling, school/ educational	PhD & PsyD	Psychologist license with PhD or PsyD	174,000	14%	$75–125K PhD/ PsyD
Psychiatry	MD	Medical license	40,000	16%	$158–230K
Psychiatric Nursing	RN or APRN	APRN for independent practice	14,000 (APRN)	15%–20%	$45–70K RN $80–107K APRN

APRN = advanced practice resident nurse; LCSW = Licensed Clinical Social Worker; LMFT = Licensed Marital/Couples and Family Therapist; LPC = Licensed Professional Counselor; LPCC = Licensed Professional Clinical Counselor; PPS = Pupil Personnel Services.

Each of the major mental health disciplines will be described using the same format so that you can compare and contrast. At the end of each discipline section, you'll find recommended sources for obtaining more information. I'll start with descriptions of the three disciplines that offer professional mental health licensure at the master's degree level: counseling, marital/couples and family therapy (MFT), and social work. These can all lead to similar career paths, but I will describe how the training emphasis differs. As noted in the summary table, they each offer both master's and doctoral degrees; but the vast majority of students earn terminal master's degrees in these disciplines. The minority of students who go on to seek doctoral degrees usually do so to pursue careers as professors, researchers, or leaders of organizations.

Following these three discipline descriptions, psychology and psychiatry will be described. Both require a doctoral degree for licensure; there is no universal licensure at the master's degree level for either of these disciplines. Psychiatric nursing is described last as it is the smallest in terms of number of providers in the United States and has a very specific training path.

Counseling

Overview

Professional counselors work in a variety of settings to promote mental health wellness as well as academic and career fulfillment. Counseling is a very popular discipline that includes a variety of subspecialties. For the purposes of this book, I'll focus on the subspecialties that prepare you for a career as a mental health provider, as opposed to subspecialties that are more peripheral to mental health, such as college or career counseling.

As noted in this section, each subspecialty within counseling has different licensure, credentialing, or certification processes. If you are interested in becoming a psychotherapist, clinical mental health counseling is the subspecialty to pursue. Licensed professional clinical counselors (also called *mental health counselors* in some states) work with individuals, families, or groups in a wide range of clinical settings, including community-based clinics, schools, hospitals, and private practice.

Subspecialties

The major subspecialties in counseling programs include addiction counseling; career counseling; clinical mental health counseling; marriage, couple, and family counseling; school counseling; student affairs and college counseling; geriatric counseling; pastoral (or faith-based) counseling; rehabilitation counseling; and counselor education and supervision. In addition, some programs offer tracks, concentrations, or certificate programs in areas such as Latinx counseling or international counseling.

Graduate School Admissions

Admissions criteria for counseling programs vary across specializations and programs. The accrediting agency for counseling is the Council for Accreditation of Counseling and Related Educational Programs (CACREP). In general, programs with CACREP accreditation are likely to be somewhat more competitive for admission. Earning a degree from a CACREP-accredited program offers several benefits, often including a more efficient path to licensure, ease of transferring licensure across states, and priority for employment in some organizations. Some states are moving toward requiring CACREP accreditation for licensure. CACREP accreditation also confers a high standard of training quality, as well as access to some scholarship programs.

Most counseling master's programs prefer an undergraduate grade point average (GPA) of at least 3.0, but there is sometimes flexibility if an applicant's personal and work experience compensates for a lower GPA. Graduate Record Examination (GRE) scores are often optional or not required for master's degree admission. Relevant work or volunteer experience in a human services or social services capacity is highly valued.

In terms of doctoral program admissions, there are approximately 80 CACREP-accredited doctoral programs in counseling (often called *doctorates* in counselor education and supervision) in the United States (as of 2021). Completion of a CACREP-accredited master's degree in counseling facilitates transition to a doctoral program for students interested in careers as professors, researchers, and clinical supervisors. Admission to doctoral programs requires strong grades in a master's program; evidence of scholarly productivity, such as research presentations or publications; and excellent letters of recommendation. Doctoral programs are also more likely than master's programs to require the GRE.

Students are often understandably confused about the distinction between a doctorate in counseling, compared to a doctorate in counseling psychology (described below in the "Psychology" section). These are distinct degrees with different accrediting agencies (CACREP vs. American Psychological Association [APA]).

Licensing/Credentialing

Most people in the counseling profession have master's degrees (as opposed to doctoral degrees), and all licensure, credentialing, and certification for counselors require only a master's degree. As noted, the licensure and credentialing processes differ by subspecialty.

School counselors earn a credential to work in schools when they complete an accredited master's degree program in school counseling; they do not need to complete postgraduate hours of practice. States differ in the specific requirements for credentialing as a school counselor, so students should consult the American School Counselor Association website (www.schoolcounselor.org) for requirements in their desired state. In California and some other states, this credential is called a Pupil Personnel Services (PPS) credential.

Mental health counselors (sometimes referred to as *community mental health counselors* or *clinical counselors*) pursue licensure as Licensed Professional Clinical Counselors (LPCCs) (also referred to as *Licensed Professional Counselors* [LPCs] in some states). They need to complete postgraduate hours of supervised practice and pass clinical and ethics exams to be licensed to practice independently, as described in Chapter 3.

Credentials to work as a school, career, or college counselor are different than licensure to practice as a licensed professional mental health counselor. These are not interchangeable, which is why it's important for you to figure out which path you want to pursue prior to entering graduate school. One notable exception is that some universities are now offering combined programs which allow you to pursue both a school counseling credential and a clinical mental health license. This is a great option for someone who wants to work with kids and families in schools for children with special needs while also having the flexibility to pursue independent clinical practice.

Pastoral, or faith-based, counseling is another very specific subspecialty with its own credentialing path. Pastoral counselors are connected to a particular faith-based organization and work with individuals from a faith-based perspective. Sometimes clergy members themselves seek training in pastoral counseling to supplement their religious education. Faith-based counselors who work exclusively within a religious organization are not necessarily required to become state-licensed counselors. If you are interested in becoming a pastoral counselor, it would be wise to investigate your particular faith's requirements and training opportunities. Keep in mind that many counseling programs across specializations will include some training in the spiritual implications of counseling even if you are not in a faith-based counseling program.

Additional specializations in counseling include rehabilitation counseling and geriatric counseling. Rehabilitation counselors work with a wide variety of individuals with disabilities and therefore address many cognitive, physical, and developmental issues in addition to mental health. Geriatric counseling is a growing field, to meet the needs of our aging population.

I have saved addiction counseling for last because it is particularly complicated, with credentialing options that vary dramatically across states. There is no single national accrediting agency for addiction counseling, and there are many different types of addiction counseling certifications. In fact, in some states, you can enroll in a certification program with only a high school diploma, while other states require an associate's, bachelor's, or graduate degree. Consequently, the scope of practice (i.e., the responsibilities and job opportunities) varies broadly, based on the level of education. For example, an individual with a high school diploma only and an addiction counseling certificate will have significantly more limited job responsibilities and earning potential than an individual who has earned a master's degree in counseling with an addictions specialization and a professional license.

To complicate this further, it's important to note that counseling is not the only discipline that offers a training in addictions. Several social work programs offer a specific track in addictions, as well as some psychology, MFT, and psychiatry programs. At the end of this section, you will find links to organizations that provide more detail about addictions training and certification requirements. Just be forewarned that it is somewhat confusing to sort through. However, if you are motivated to pursue this critically important area, please don't be deterred. The field needs you.

Good Fit for Interests?

Given all the different specialization options, counseling offers something to fit almost anyone's interests. Overall, the counseling discipline is a good fit if you resonate with the goal of promoting wellness, as contrasted with treating illness. Counseling emphasizes empowering clients to work through life challenges to fulfill their potential. Professional mental health counselors are trained to diagnose and treat psychiatric illnesses, just like other mental health providers; but the counseling discipline emphasizes approaching this work with the goal of promoting health and wellness, as contrasted to a traditional medical model of diagnosing and treating illnesses. Likewise, counselors are trained to build on a client's strengths as opposed to focusing on symptoms and pathology. Having said this, however, it is important for me to remind you that these are fairly subtle differences in emphasis as opposed to clearly demarcated boundaries. This is true for each of the disciplines described in this chapter—the differences across disciplines can often be somewhat nuanced.

When many people think about a counselor, they may envision a school counselor. School counselors have a very broad range of responsibilities and roles, from approving class schedule changes and writing letters of recommendation to leading wellness or anti-bullying programs to assessing an individual student for suicide risk. School counseling offers a wonderful career opportunity for people who like to work with youth in an educational setting but who want to focus more on psychosocial challenges than on academic achievement. School counselors usually have a collaborative work team and are called on to pitch in on a wide variety of school activities, ranging from predictable routines to unforeseen crises. As a school counselor, you won't have as many opportunities for intensive, long-term, one-on-one work with students; but you'll have the opportunity to impact more students. I've met many students who were inspired to become a school counselor because of an influential school counselor in their own life, and they have been very pleased with this career path.

Addiction counseling offers an opportunity to make a big impact on individuals and families facing major challenges. As we all see in media reports, rates of addiction are alarmingly high and the health, economic, and emotional toll can be catastrophic. Even if you do not choose to specialize in addictions counseling, you will encounter individuals with addiction-related challenges in whatever work you pursue. For this reason, courses in addictions are required in most graduate programs across disciplines.

Counseling training is known for its breadth of coverage. Accredited counseling graduate programs will include a wide range of courses in human development, assessment, counseling skills, multicultural issues, career counseling, professional ethics, risk and trauma, family counseling, and group counseling. Thus, it may be a good fit for you if you want broad exposure to many different types of work and mental health problems. In contrast, if you have a very specific career goal to work with a particular clinical population or clinical problem, you'll need to look for a program that offers more intensive specialized training in that area.

For More Information

Books:

A Guide to Graduate Programs in Counseling (2016). Edited by Tyler M. Kimbel and Dana Heller Levitt. Oxford University Press.

Websites:

American Counseling Association: www.counseling.org

Council for Accreditation of Counseling and Related Educational Programs: www.cacrep.org

American Mental Health Counselors Association: www.amhca.org

American School Counselor Association: www.schoolcounselor.org

Commission on Rehabilitation Counselor Certification: www.crccertification.com/state-licensure-boards

Other useful resources:

US Bureau of Labor Statistics: Occupational Outlook Handbook: www.bls.gov/ooh/

Addiction counseling resources:

Association for Addiction Professionals: www.naadac.org

State-by-state requirements for addiction counselors: www.addiction-counselors.com

Addiction Counselor Certification Board of California/Simple Steps to Becoming a Certified Addiction Treatment Counselor (example of one state's addiction certification board): https://www.accbc.org/catc

American Academy of Health Care Providers in the Addictive Disorders: www.americanacademy.org

Marital (or Couples) and Family Therapy

Overview

Marital and family therapists (also known as couples and family therapists but abbreviated here to the more common acronym, MFT) emphasize the essential role of relationships in our lives. They work with clients who have relationship challenges and those with mental health challenges. Just like all mental health professionals, MFTs learn how to diagnose and treat the full range of psychiatric disorders, but their training emphasizes the crucial role of family and partner relationships in the development or exacerbation of mental health problems. MFTs learn a variety of therapeutic approaches, with an emphasis on treatments that focus on the family and couple system. While the training emphasis is on how relationships and family systems can be improved to relieve suffering, MFTs work with individuals, couples, families, and groups to address a full range of mental health and life challenges. MFTs are licensed to work in a variety of settings including clinics, hospitals, schools, and private practice.

Graduate School Admissions

The accrediting agency for MFT programs is the Commission on Accreditation for Marriage and Family Therapy Education (COAMFTE). Note that only a minority of programs in the country are accredited by COAMFTE. Similar to other disciplines, there are advantages of earning your degree from an accredited program, but you can still get licensed graduating from a non-COAMFTE-accredited program. Advantages include easier portability across states for licensure and higher priority with certain employers, access to some scholarship programs, and adherence to a high-quality standard for your educational experience.

MFT admissions into COAMFTE-accredited programs are often competitive, with top programs admitting fewer than half of all applicants. Many programs require an undergraduate GPA of at least 3.0. However, if your GPA is lower and there are extenuating circumstances, you still have a chance of admission. Some programs require GREs, while many are optional. Programs usually seek applicants with relevant work or volunteer experience in social or human services. Many programs are looking for candidates who can clearly express why they are interested in the MFT discipline specifically—that is, why this choice over counseling, social work, or psychology?

Admission into MFT doctoral programs is more selective, with programs looking for evidence of research experience and interest since the goal is to train academics. In many programs, applicants apply to work with specific faculty advisors, so a match on research interests is important.

Licensing/Credentialing

The MFT license is granted with a master's degree plus the required approved supervised postgraduate practice hours and passing of the licensure exams. Each state has specific requirements for the number and type of hours and license exam(s). There is a lot of variability across states in representation of MFTs. California has significantly more licensed MFTs (often referred to as LMFTs) than any other state, but all 50 states plus the District of Columbia have licensure paths for MFTs.

Good Fit for Interests?

MFT is a great fit for you if you are passionately interested in working with couples or with families to address relationships and life challenges, as well as psychiatric disorders. This discipline will prepare you very well to help couples and families with significant transitions such as marital and premarital counseling, or divorce and child-custody issues. MFT is also a good choice if you are interested in foster care or adoption, as well as parent–child conflicts. Licensed MFTs are trained to work with individuals alone (children, adolescents, and adults) when necessary, but they often attempt to work with families all together if possible. They are trained to emphasize how family relationships impact mental health challenges, including all types of psychiatric disorders, so if this emphasis resonates for you, this is a wonderful discipline.

If you are interested in working in hospitals or medical care settings, there are some MFT programs that offer specialization in integrated behavioral healthcare or medical family therapy where you are trained to work collaboratively with healthcare professionals. Other MFT programs offer specific tracks or concentrations focused on multicultural issues or specific cultural groups (e.g., Latinx communities), sexual and gender issues related to mental health, addictions, or school-based mental health. It takes some time, but exploring these types of subspecialty opportunities within programs will definitely be worth it if you find the best fit for your interests.

For More Information

Websites:
American Association for Marriage and Family Therapy: www.aamft.org
Commission on Accreditation for Marriage and Family Therapy Education: www.
coamfte.org

Social Work

Overview

Social work professionals strive to enhance well-being in a variety of ways including efforts to help people meet their basic needs as well as their complex psychological, social, and emotional needs. As a discipline, social work emphasizes support for vulnerable communities, working with clients to identify and utilize essential resources, build coping skills, and improve the environments in which they live. Licensed clinical social workers are trained to diagnose and treat the full range of psychiatric illnesses like other mental health professionals, but their training emphasizes an ecological approach to understanding and addressing factors in a person's environment that are causing distress and working collaboratively to change those factors. A person's environment can include their close relationships, family, neighborhood, school, and workplace.

Subspecialties

The field of social work is very broad, and there are many formal and informal sub-specialties. Some programs have formal subspecialty tracks, while others encourage students to select courses to meet their specific career goals. Subspecialties are wide-ranging, including administration and management, advocacy and community organizing, aging/gerontology, child welfare, developmental disabilities, healthcare, international social work, justice and corrections, mental health/psychiatric, occu-pational, policy and planning, public welfare, research, school social work, and sub-stance abuse.

Graduate School Admissions

The accrediting agency for social work education is the Council on Social Work Education (CSWE). CSWE-accredited programs are likely to be somewhat more competitive for admissions compared to non-accredited programs. The advantages of accreditation are similar to those described for the previous disciplines. The aca-demic and work-related requirements for admission are also relatively similar across these three master's-level disciplines (counseling, MFT, and social work).

Most master's programs prefer an undergraduate GPA of at least 3.0, and GREs are often optional (or sometimes required if the GPA is lower than a specified level). Letters of recommendation and personal statements of interest are important, as well as volunteer or work experience in a human or social service capacity.

Doctoral programs in social work (PhD or doctor of social work [DSW]) are de-signed for individuals who want to become professors, researchers, or leaders of so-cial service organizations. Admission to doctoral programs is more competitive and requires excellent grades, evidence of research interest and productivity, strong letters of recommendation, and, often, strong GRE scores.

Licensing/Credentialing

There is a lot of variation in licensure paths for social workers across the United States. Some states even license individuals with a bachelor's degree in social work, but this does not allow for independent practice as a therapist. For that, states have specific requirements to become a Licensed Clinical Social Worker (LCSW); this re-quires a master's degree, postgraduate supervised practice hours, and passing licen-sure exams.

Good Fit for Interests?

Social work is a discipline with a long and admirable history. It is a good fit if you are passionate about issues of social welfare, social change, human rights, economic and social justice, and advocacy. Other disciplines embrace these values too, but social work is founded on these values. Traditionally, social workers are trained to look at the larger community and social factors impacting individuals, but clinical social workers also learn about individual approaches to psychotherapy. Social workers are also well trained in case management approaches, where they advocate for clients and work to connect clients with the resources and supports they need. Again, other disciplines do this too, but it is a strong emphasis for social work.

Social work is a good fit if you want to work in the child welfare system or other public social service agencies such as the corrections system. Social work programs also often include a variety of tracks where you can concentrate on the career direction of most interest to you. If you are interested in practicing as a psychotherapist, you'll want to pursue the mental health track to be eligible for licensure as a clinical social worker. (Sometimes this may be referred to as a *Licensed Independent Clinical Social Worker* or a *Licensed Independent Social Worker*, depending on your state.) Social work offers a comprehensive education that can lead to many meaningful job opportunities.

For More Information

Websites:
National Association of Social Workers: www.socialworkers.org
Council on Social Work Education: www.cswe.org

Psychology

Overview

Psychology is defined as the scientific study of human behavior and mental health processes. It is one of the oldest of the mental health disciplines, along with psychiatry. Psychologists study how our brains influence our behavior and vice versa. They also study how our environments (e.g., the natural world, our social communities, and our families) influence us and how we influence these environments. Psychologists are taught to apply scientific principles to assessing and treating psychological problems. While this discipline emphasizes the application of scientific principles, there is also encouragement for creativity and flexibility. Psychologists are taught to tailor evidence-based treatments to the unique needs of their clients by fully considering factors such as age, gender, culture, sexual orientation, race, belief systems, and ethnicity.

Like providers in other disciplines, psychologists are trained to diagnose and treat individuals, couples, families, and groups. While some psychology programs include education on prevention programs, positive psychology, and wellness promotion, most emphasize a more traditional medical model of diagnosing disorders and providing treatment. Many programs also require students to learn about neuroscience and biological bases of behavior. In addition, most psychology graduate programs include greater emphasis on research training compared to other disciplines. This usually includes requirements to conduct an independent research study.

Also compared to the other disciplines, psychology training includes more emphasis on assessment. Psychologists learn about how to validly measure psychological and cognitive functioning and behavior. They learn how to use and interpret psychological testing (such as IQ testing), academic achievement, personality testing, and assessment of psychiatric symptoms.

A doctoral degree is the only path to independent licensure and therapy practice as a psychologist. This is a major distinction from the three disciplines previously described. However, some states allow people with a master's degree to become psychological associates, who practice under the supervision of a licensed psychologist.

Another important point is that while there are multiple subspecialties within psychology, only a few train you for direct practice with clients. Specifically, degrees in clinical, counseling, educational, and school psychology offer eligibility to become licensed to practice. Degrees in other subspecialties, such as developmental, experimental, cognitive, social, industrial/organizational, or personality psychology do not. Neuropsychology/neuroscience and community psychology programs vary in terms of eligibility for licensure, with some programs offering a licensure path and others not.

Subspecialties

For the purposes of this book, I'll focus on the subspecialties that offer paths toward licensed practice. Among these, the best known is clinical psychology. A clinical psychologist is exactly what it sounds like, a psychologist who is trained for clinical practice. I'm biased because my degree is in clinical psychology, but I believe this is a terrific option if you are prepared for a competitive and lengthy academic journey. It is a comprehensive degree offering career options in clinical practice, research, teaching, and clinical supervision.

A doctorate in counseling psychology is similar to clinical psychology and offers the same licensure path and general range of career opportunities. The difference between clinical and counseling psychology is somewhat nuanced and based on the origins of these subspecialties. Clinical psychology emphasizes diagnosis and treatment of individuals with psychiatric disorders, whereas counseling psychology emphasizes work with individuals facing more common life challenges. However, like so many of the distinctions I'm describing here, these boundaries are flexible, and you will find exceptions, such as clinical psychologists who specialize in wellness promotion for healthy clients and counseling psychologists who specialize in treating individuals with severe mental illnesses. This is why it is important to do your research and explore the scholarly interests of the faculty members in departments to which you are applying, as well as reviewing the required coursework for the degree. This will help you determine the focus of the degree program and how well it fits your interests.

Within clinical and counseling psychology there are often opportunities to specialize in different areas, such as child/family psychology, health psychology, or neuropsychology. Some programs offer specific formal tracks, whereas others allow students to tailor their coursework and practicum sites to match their interests.

Another important distinction is between the PhD and the doctor of psychology (PsyD) degrees in clinical or counseling psychology. The PhD is the original, more traditional doctoral degree, which is consistent with the PhD across other academic fields and requires an original research project (usually called a *dissertation*). The PsyD is another option specific to psychology. This degree was developed for those who want to become practicing psychologists but do not want to pursue the rigorous research training requirements of a traditional PhD. Therefore, the PsyD includes fewer research requirements and emphasizes clinical practice training; it also meets the requirements for licensure as a psychologist. PsyD programs are often found in independent professional schools, but some traditional universities are also now offering the PsyD degree path. Note that there may be fewer scholarship and graduate assistantships offered in PsyD programs compared to PhD programs.

Additional subspecializations in psychology include school and educational psychology. As you'd expect, these programs prepare you to work in school settings, with a focus on student assessment, as well as program (or curriculum) development and evaluation. Some states offer certification for school psychologists with only a master's degree; but the requirements vary across states, and certification as a school psychologist is not the same as a psychologist's license to practice psychotherapy. Likewise, requirements and responsibilities vary for licensure as a doctorate-level educational psychologist.

There are additional subspecializations within psychology that may lead to eligibility for licensure to practice. These include programs in forensic psychology, community psychology, sport psychology, feminist psychology, or multicultural psychology. Of these, forensic psychology (also referred to as *criminal psychology* or *legal psychology*) is a relatively popular option, but there are only a few accredited programs. Forensic work includes legal consultation, investigative work, or work in the corrections system. Forensic work will be discussed in Chapter 7, which addresses the legal and ethical aspects of mental health careers.

Community psychology emphasizes the social system as opposed to the more traditional psychology focus on the individual. Community psychology includes training in delivery and evaluation of preventive interventions and, often, policy-level interventions. Some community psychology programs are combined with clinical psychology and offer the courses and practicum experiences required for licensure, but others do not.

You will also find specific subspecializations in areas such as sport or exercise psychology, multicultural psychology, or feminist psychology. Many of these are master's degree programs, and it is important to remember that a master's degree will not qualify you for independent practice as a psychologist. These can be valuable degrees for other types of career paths, but be clear on what your options will be. I've known students who entered master's programs in psychology assuming that they would be able to practice psychotherapy upon graduation, and they've been frustrated to learn later that they were mistaken.

A final word on this issue of master's versus doctoral degrees in psychology: Some students assume that they need to complete a master's degree program prior to entering a doctoral program, and this is incorrect. Most psychology doctoral programs admit students with either a bachelor's degree or a master's degree. Sometimes students pursue a master's degree to build up more research experience or demonstrate strong grades in graduate work, and this can be beneficial for doctoral program admissions. However, it's important to know that you do not need a master's degree for application to a doctoral program in psychology.

In fact, doctoral psychology programs vary significantly in the extent to which they will apply transfer credit from a master's degree program toward a doctoral degree. In many cases, students with a master's degree will be starting over in a doctoral program and will have the same course requirements as a student who enters with just a bachelor's degree. This also varies across programs, and some do accept transfer course credit; but do not assume that a master's degree will automatically give you a big head start in a doctoral program.

Graduate School Admissions

The accrediting agency for psychology is the APA, and all the points made previously about the benefits of accredited programs apply to psychology as well.

Admission into many APA-accredited doctoral psychology programs is highly competitive. Successful applicants have high undergraduate GPAs, high GRE scores, and strong research experience. The most selective programs are those that offer scholarships covering tuition and graduate assistantships. These programs emphasize research training for academic careers, but students earning a degree in clinical or counseling psychology also get clinical training. Students in these programs are often admitted to work with a specific faculty mentor on their research team (or lab group), almost like an apprenticeship. Because of this, it is important for applicants to contact faculty members with shared interests during the admissions process. Reach out to faculty members whose research area is a good fit for your interests, and ask them if they'll be taking any new graduate students for the upcoming year. If possible, offer to meet or speak by phone or video chat to discuss your interests. Don't despair if many faculty members do not respond; it can still be valuable to reach out in advance of your application submission to express interest.

PhD or PsyD programs in independent professional schools are usually slightly less competitive for admission. However, they also tend to be more expensive, with fewer opportunities for graduate assistantships. These programs tend to place less emphasis on applicants' research experience.

Licensing/Credentialing

As noted, all states require a doctoral degree in psychology for licensure as a psychologist. Many years ago there was some variability about this, and you may still meet individuals who have a psychology license with just a master's degree; but this is no longer possible.

The process for gaining licensure is the same as described in the previous chapter; after graduating, psychologists need to earn supervised postgraduate practice hours (varying from 1000 to 3000 hours across states). They also need to pass clinical and ethical licensure exams. The path to full licensure as a psychologist is long, at least 6 or 7 years, and often a bit more. However, in my biased opinion, all the hard work is worth it.

Most states have a separate licensure path for school or educational psychologists. In many states one can be credentialed as a school psychologist with just a master's degree. However, this credential does not allow for independent practice as a psychotherapist.

Good Fit for Interests?

Psychology is a good fit for those who are interested in the scientific aspects of this career and for those who enjoy learning about and conducting research. While all the disciplines include a balance of training in both the science and art of psychotherapy, the emphasis on science is strongest for psychology compared to other disciplines. However, don't assume that the humanistic art of psychotherapy will be ignored by psychology. It's all about nuances in balancing these different emphases.

Psychology is also a good choice for those who are particularly intrigued by psychological assessment and neuropsychology. In fact, some psychologists devote their entire career exclusively to assessment and testing, as opposed to therapy. This includes people with strong interests in applied neuroscience and problems such as traumatic brain injury, learning and memory challenges, or Alzheimer's disease/dementia. If this sounds like you, be sure to look for programs with a neuropsychology emphasis.

Compared to the first three disciplines described in this chapter, psychology places more emphasis on the medical model of diagnosing and treating individuals with the full range of psychiatric disorders. As a symbolic example, many (but not all) psychologists refer to their clients as *patients*, whereas counselors, MFTs, and social workers usually use the term *clients*. Likewise, psychologists have historically been more likely to treat individuals with severe mental illnesses than other mental healthcare providers (except psychiatrists), but these distinctions have blurred over time.

There are several other subspecialties that may attract you to psychology, including the growing field of industrial/organizational psychology which focuses on workplaces and the workforce. This field intersects with business management and leadership studies, as well as career and vocational assessment, so taking some courses in these areas would be good preparation. In addition, some psychology programs also offer specific subspecializations in child and family psychology or health psychology (which includes an emphasis on health and wellness, working with healthcare professionals, etc.).

I imagine that many of you readers are psychology undergraduate majors. Of course, that will be strong preparation for a graduate degree in psychology, but it will also be strong preparation for any of the other disciplines. Be sure to look carefully at all options to see what emphasis you are looking for and whether or not you want to invest the time and money required for a doctoral degree. Sarah Kate's quote reinforces this point.

> I was surprised to learn how much of the front-line work force is actually made up of masters' level therapists—in the end I am glad I got my PhD because it allowed me to pursue an academic career but it is definitely not needed for direct service work! (Sarah Kate, professor and therapist in private practice)

For More Information

Book (and associated online database):
Graduate Study in Psychology (2019). American Psychological Association. (This resource describes 1500 graduate programs in over 500 schools across the United States and Canada.)

Websites:
American Psychological Association: www.apa.org
APA Commission on Accreditation: www.accreditation.apa.org
National Association of School Psychologists: www.nasponline.org/about-school-psychology

Psychiatry

Overview

Psychiatrists are medical doctors (MDs) who complete medical school (4 years after obtaining a bachelor's degree) and then additional specialization training in psychiatry (4 or more years after graduating from medical school). They are licensed to practice general medicine, including diagnosis and treatment of medical and psychiatric illnesses. Psychiatrists can prescribe and monitor medications and conduct psychotherapy. They often work in hospital or clinic settings or in private practice. Frequently, they are leaders of psychiatric units; and in that capacity, they will often supervise and collaborate with staff members from other disciplines.

Psychiatrists are trained in all medical and psychological treatments for psychiatric disorders. Some pursue psychotherapy, but many end up specializing in medication management. This balance of emphasis on psychotherapy versus medication management differs across specializations, geographic locations, healthcare systems, and reimbursement systems (i.e., insurance coverage). Some insurance companies are more likely to cover psychotherapy provided by non-medical doctors (e.g., psychologists, counselors, social workers, MFTs, etc.) because the rates are often lower than a physician's rates. This trend over recent decades has resulted in fewer psychiatrists specializing in psychotherapy practice in the United States.[4] However, many do still practice psychotherapy.

Subspecialties

Psychiatrists can pursue subspecialization training in addiction, child and adolescent psychiatry, forensic psychiatry, consultation/liaison psychiatry, emergency psychiatry, or geriatric psychiatry. However, be aware that these specializations add more years to the already demanding educational path for psychiatric training.

Graduate School Admissions

To become a psychiatrist, you must first graduate from medical school (or earn a doctorate in an osteopathic medicine program, or doctor of osteopathy [DO]). Admission to medical school is very competitive. Applicants need to have had exceptionally strong grades in college, having majored (ideally) in a biological or physical science, math, or psychology. However, students may also enter medical school with a humanities or other major as long as they have completed specific prerequisite courses. Successful applicants need very strong Medical College Admissions Test scores, excellent letters of recommendation, and preferably some relevant work or research experience.

Medical school graduates apply for residencies in their selected specialization. Students compete for spaces at the most desirable training hospitals. Residency admission is based on medical school grades, letters of recommendation, and interviews.

Licensing/Credentialing

Medical school graduates take a variety of exams to earn their medical license (MD). Most who pursue psychiatry as their specialty will also take exams to be board-certified. Board certification is not absolutely required but is strongly recommended and can be required by many employers and funders.

Good Fit for Interests?

Psychiatry is a good fit if you are interested in medical training. If you hope to be on the cutting edge of translating neuroscientific and pharmacological discoveries into actual therapies for mental illness, comprehensive medical training is an advantage. It is a very long and demanding educational path, beginning with the rigors of advanced undergraduate science and math courses. You'll need perseverance and patience for this journey since you will not be able to practice psychiatry independently until about 8 years after you enter medical school. However, the job opportunities are strong and well compensated once you are a licensed and board-certified psychiatrist.

For More Information

American Psychiatric Association: www.psychiatry.org
Accreditation Council for Graduate Medical Education: www.acgme.org

Psychiatric Nursing

Overview

Psychiatric nursing is the specialization within nursing that prepares you to work with patients who have psychiatric illnesses. Advanced practice resident nurses (APRNs) with specialized training in psychiatric nursing can diagnose and treat individuals and, unlike some of the disciplines earlier described, can prescribe and monitor medications. Psychiatric nurses often work in hospitals or health clinics in partnership with other healthcare providers, but they can also work in community-based clinics, schools or universities, home-visiting programs, and private practice.

There are a few levels of psychiatric nursing, but for licensed independent practice you will need at least a master's degree; and many APRNs complete a doctor of nursing practice (DNP) degree.

Subspecialties

Some nursing programs provide opportunities to specialize in different areas, such as child and adolescent mental health, military mental health, gerontology, addictions, or consultation-liaison nursing (which refers to working with individuals with medical challenges).

Graduate School Admissions

There are two accrediting agencies for nursing education, the Accreditation Commission for Education in Nursing and the Commission on Collegiate Nursing Education; and the websites are listed at the end of this section. As with other disciplines, there are advantages to attending an accredited program; and, on average, such programs may be somewhat more competitive for admission.

The general academic requirements are similar to what was described for counseling, social work, and MFT, such as a GPA of at least 3.0. However, nursing programs are more likely to have specific prerequisite undergraduate course requirements in the sciences. GREs are not commonly required for master's-level programs but may be for doctoral programs. One important thing to have in mind about nursing school admissions is that each step usually requires a nursing degree at the previous level. For example, admission to a master's program in nursing often requires a bachelor's degree in nursing and an active registered nurse (RN) license. However, there are exceptions. So, if you do not have an RN license or a bachelor's degree in nursing, just be sure to look for a program that is designed for individuals without these qualifications.

Licensing/Credentialing

Licensure requires completion of the requirements for an RN license plus an undergraduate degree and at least a master's degree in nursing. Licensure and certification requirements vary by state but include the steps described for other disciplines, including approved supervised postgraduate practice hours and licensure exams (these may also be called *board certification exams*).

Good Fit for Interests?

The nursing discipline is a great fit if you are interested in working in medical settings and in medication therapies. You will receive a strong foundation in general nursing practice and then greater specialization in psychiatric diagnoses and treatment as you pursue postgraduate education. Nursing is a highly respected and well-established discipline with its own culture and history. A nursing degree and licensure can be relatively portable across states and even across countries, opening up a wide range of employment opportunities. Nursing education includes a lot of "hands-on," medically oriented practice training, so think about whether that appeals to you. As noted in Table 4.1, this is a relatively small discipline compared to many others, but it is growing.

For More Information

American Psychiatric Nurses Association: www.apna.org

Psychiatric-Mental Health Nursing Programs/Psychiatric-Mental Health Nursing Graduate Programs by State: https://www.apna.org/about-psychiatric-nursing/graduate-programs/graduate-programs-in-the-united-states

International Society of Psychiatric Mental Health Nurses: https://www.ispn-psych.org/

American Nurses Association: www.nursingworld.org

Accreditation Commission for Education in Nursing (for all levels): www.acenursing.org

Commission on Collegiate Nursing Education (bachelor's and master's levels only): https://www.aacnnursing.org/CCNE

Combined Degree Programs

There are combined degree programs within and across disciplines. These are not very common but can be particularly strong training options for those with multiple interests. For example, some mental health programs offer a combined degree with a master's in public health (MPH). The addition of the MPH program offers complementary training in program evaluation, community health interventions, and/or health disparities. For the particularly ambitious student, there are combined MD/PhD programs offering intensive practice and research training.

A Note about Websites

The websites for each of the national discipline organizations provide valuable re-sources for your graduate school explorations. In addition, each discipline's ac-crediting entity offers useful information about graduate study and the implications of accreditation. Many of these websites offer in-depth information for prospective students and searchable lists of accredited graduate programs, with links to the pro-gram websites, etc.

Please be selective when you search for information about graduate programs on-line because some sites are essentially advertisements for particular graduate schools, and they will not provide a comprehensive list of available programs. Similarly, you may often see links to lists of top 10 programs in (*fill in the blank*). Be aware that these are not necessarily valid lists of quality programs; sometimes they are just advertise-ments. If you stick to the professional organization sites, you should get more objec-tive and valid information.

In Conclusion

> I wish I'd known more about the different varieties of psychological helping, such as psychologist, counselor, MFT, social worker, etc.—what the jobs actually did on a particular day, what the advancement and research opportunities were, and how to make it happen. (Nick, therapist in hospital and instructor)

I've met many students who express similar sentiments to those expressed by Nick. I hope this chapter has helped you to learn more about all your options. There is a lot of detailed information here, and much more is available through the recommended resources. It's possible that this chapter has presented you with new possibilities that you had not previously considered. Even though that might add some confusion to your decision-making, I think it's a good problem to have at this stage. It is so impor-tant to understand all your options so that you can make a well-informed choice. The time that you'll spend clarifying your desired path now will definitely pay off in the future. Too many students have not been aware of all their options or of the implica-tions of different degree path decisions, and they've wasted time and money in having to change course later on. This book is designed to help you figure out which path fits your interests, goals, and strengths best.

5

Expanding the Possibilities: Populations, Settings, and Types of Work

I didn't realize how many opportunities there could be! I thought that I would have to keep my creative side and my clinical side separate, but over time I have seen how I can integrate these parts of my identity together. (Cassidy, therapist in private practice and instructor)

Looking back, it would have been helpful to talk with other people who had made this a career and to explore different paths and opportunities that one could take within the field. I found the work so demanding and enticing that I really didn't have a long term perspective. This came much later in my career. I ended up doing consulting, teaching, training, and supervision in addition to my clinical work. In the beginning, I had no idea that these opportunities existed. (Larry, therapist in private practice, instructor, and business consultant)

My goal in this chapter is to expand your notion of what's possible as a mental health professional. Many people have only a limited knowledge of the potential career options. For example, you may assume that most therapists work in private practice. While this is a popular career option, the fact is that only a minority of mental health professionals end up working full-time in private practice, and it may not be the most realistic or desirable career path for you. In this chapter you'll learn about many other creative and enriching career opportunities for whichever discipline and degree options you choose to pursue.

To help you imagine the extensive possibilities, Figure 5.1 presents an array of populations, work settings, types of work, and potential specialty areas you could pursue. There is a lot of information conveyed in this one figure. You can think of it as a type of menu where you can mix and match selections from different categories to create job prospects to fit your interests. For example, let's say you want to work with geriatric adults in a hospital setting doing psychological assessment to address memory issues. Or you want to work with adolescents in high schools developing and evaluating programs for the LGBTQ+ community or with couples in a faith-based context offering therapy to address divorce and child custody. Maybe you want

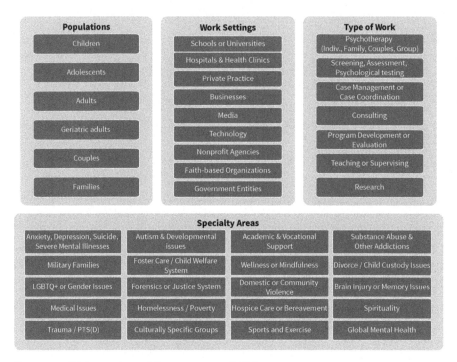

Figure 5.1 Mixing and matching career possibilities

to consult with media organizations to support military families or provide family therapy in a nonprofit agency devoted to addiction recovery.

The possibilities are vast and growing all the time. At this stage in your career explorations, the goal is to imagine all kinds of possibilities that may inspire and motivate you to do the hard work of becoming a mental health professional. There will be time to narrow your focus later.

Figure 5.1 provides the structure for this chapter. I begin with brief descriptions of the elements in the *Work Settings* and *Type of Work* categories since these will be referenced in the section that follows. Then, the next section is organized by the *Populations* category on the far left of the table. When people consider the clients with whom they'd like to work, they often describe them by age group—namely, children, adolescents, adults, or geriatric populations—while others may be passionate about working with couples or families. I'll offer a brief summary of the rewards and challenges of working with each of these populations, followed by examples of specific job opportunities for each population group.

Descriptions of Work Settings

Consider the work settings as potential work contexts. Most of these are what you would expect for mental health professionals, such as schools or universities, hospitals or health centers, and private practice. Others, such as businesses, media, or technology, may not have occurred to you. However, as the specific examples listed later in the chapter illustrate, these are all potential work contexts for mental health professionals. For example, in the business sector, corporations often have employee assistance programs that offer mental healthcare or wellness promotion for employees. Businesses may also consult with mental health professionals about how to improve the culture and climate of the organization or how to respond to crises or prepare employees for major shifts in responsibilities.

Given the general public's interest in mental health–related topics, there are also many opportunities for mental health professionals to work in all types of media contexts. We need more trained mental health professionals to cover popular topics such as stress management, substance use, relationships, parenting, depression, etc. Frankly, one of my pet peeves is when people who do not have any specialized training represent themselves in media or social media platforms as experts in these topics. It is incumbent upon us to advocate for our expertise and to work with the media to translate science-based information for public benefit.

Likewise, mental health experts are needed in the technology sector. Technological innovations for mental health are booming (as described in Chapter 13). Examples include remote access platforms for online assessment and therapy, mobile mental health apps, virtual reality, and mental health video game production. It is critical for tech companies to partner with mental health professionals to ensure that tech applications are effective, ethical, and supported by current science. I urge those of you with tech skills to consider contributing to this exciting new field.

Nonprofit agencies at the local, state, national, and international levels are also important work contexts for mental health professionals. These can be small grassroots groups serving a specific community or cultural group as well as large international organizations such as the Red Cross or UNICEF and everything in between. Faith-based organizations affiliated with religious groups also offer local, national, and international opportunities for mental health experts. Finally, US government services, such as the Departments of Education, Health and Human Services, and Corrections and the Centers for Disease Control, employ many mental health professionals. They may be hired to provide direct mental healthcare, conduct research, consult on program development or evaluation, or advise on policies and legislation. The government's Department of Veterans Affairs (VA) system is another major employer for mental healthcare providers; estimates suggest that approximately 16,000 providers were employed by the VA in 2017, and there were many vacancies left to fill.[1] The prison and child welfare systems also employ thousands of providers.

Descriptions of Types of Work

I think it is important to combine being a psychotherapist with another possible role. Being a therapist for 40 hours a week is too taxing. Other possible roles could be training other therapists, teaching, research, or consulting in a wide range of areas. (Carolyn, professor and hospital therapist)

Throughout this book, psychotherapy is the most common type of work addressed, but this chapter introduces you to a full range of complementary types of work. Even for psychotherapy, there are different modalities, including working with individuals, couples, families, and groups. Each modality has evidence-based approaches, and many providers practice in multiple modalities. You don't have to choose just one, but you do need training in whichever you choose to pursue.

All therapists are trained to do screening and assessment with their clients. In fact, research shows that therapy is more effective when providers measure their clients' progress over time using established assessment tools.[2] However, some mental health careers focus primarily on assessment as opposed to therapy. For example, providers trained in neuropsychology may devote their careers to neuropsychological assessment for brain injuries, memory challenges, or other potential deficits. Others may work in crisis assessment and de-escalation in mobile response units. Some counselors may specialize in career or vocational assessment, and school psychologists often do more psychological testing than therapy.

Case management (or case coordination) is a type of work most closely aligned with the social work discipline, but providers from across disciplines also do this type of work. It refers to determining what resources, services, or supports a client (an individual, couple, or family) needs and helping them to access those resources. A good case manager is the essential "quarterback" who coordinates other team members and services. Comprehensive, intensive case management is an evidence-based approach to helping people who have faced significant challenges get back on a more positive track. Individuals transitioning out of psychiatric hospitals or prison often benefit greatly from case management, which may be combined with psychotherapy. The rationale for case management is compelling: If clients face issues such as homelessness, unemployment, or lack of child care, traditional psychotherapy is not going to be effective without addressing these basic human needs.

Consulting is another popular type of work, as reflected in many of the job examples listed in this chapter. There are so many important ways that mental healthcare providers can share their expertise in a consulting role with the media, government organizations, schools and universities, businesses, international organizations, etc.

Program development and evaluation is yet another type of work for mental health professionals. This can include developing or evaluating public health programming at the local, national, and even international levels to promote mental health and prevent problems (e.g., substance abuse, suicide, sexual violence, harassment). Mental health professionals also develop and evaluate educational curricula for schools or universities addressing academic, psychological, or sociocultural issues (e.g., bullying, stress management, racial inclusion, LGBTQ+ advocacy, goal-setting, study skills). Program evaluation tests whether a program actually works, that is, whether it achieves the outcomes it was intended to achieve. Evaluation is absolutely essential because even the most well-intended programs can be ineffective, such as programs intended to curb substance abuse or suicidal behavior.[3] Working on program development and evaluation is very rewarding because you have the potential to impact many more people than with direct therapy.

Many mental health professionals enjoy sharing their expertise through teaching and clinical supervision. One of the main reasons some people earn a doctoral degree is to become a professor. If you pursue this route, you'll find multiple options, such as academic jobs that emphasize classroom teaching at community colleges or liberal arts colleges or research productivity at "Research 1" institutions (i.e., universities that have earned a lot of research funding) or clinical supervision in a hospital or clinic. Many therapists, either at the master's or doctorate level, find part-time teaching or supervision jobs (often called *adjunct* or *clinical faculty*), to supplement their therapy practice jobs.

One thing you may not know is that some teaching and clinical supervision opportunities are cross-disciplinary. By that I mean that a person with a degree in social work might supervise students in another discipline, like counseling; or a psychologist might teach or supervise students in marital and family therapy. I particularly like being in a work context that is multidisciplinary, with colleagues who bring different types of perspectives. Although you need to choose a discipline for graduate study, keep in mind that you will likely work with professionals from across multiple disciplines after you graduate.

Some people may assume that you need to be a university professor to conduct research. While this is the most common path to a research career, there are other creative ways to collaborate on research, including working for government entities, medical centers, or nonprofit agencies. If you are interested in research, over time you'll need to decide whether you want to lead research studies or participate as a colleague. If you want to lead research, you'll need very strong research training and mentorship, gaining experience in grant writing and management of a research team. It's an amazingly stimulating and rewarding career path, but it is rigorous.

Alternatively, if you like collaborating on research but do not want it to dominate your entire career, you can find opportunities to partner with lead researchers. Maybe you'll be the clinical partner who conducts diagnostic interviews screening potential participants for entrance into a study. Or maybe you'll be one of the therapists trained to deliver an innovative treatment protocol in a randomized study of two different types of therapy. My point is that there are many different ways to satisfy your intellectual curiosity about research.

The next section of this chapter is organized by the *Populations* category on the far left of Figure 5.1. I'll provide a summary of the rewards and challenges of working with each population, followed by a list of job options within each category.

Populations

Children

Many people may feel called to work with children who are suffering. Helping children rekindle joy in their lives and get back on a more positive developmental track is extraordinarily rewarding. Research confirms that many mental health problems begin in childhood; early identification and treatment of emerging problems can prevent more serious problems later.[4] Some of us enjoy working with children because the opportunity for change and growth is so much more apparent compared to working with adults, who are often more set in their ways. Also, working with children can be especially fun and creative.

Of course, others have no interest in working with children. Empathizing with children who are suffering may be just too painful for some people, perhaps due to their own family experiences. I know other therapists who prefer working with adults because they view children as messy, silly, inarticulate, alien beings. Many therapists crave deep, intellectual discussions about emotions, relationships, and philosophy. They may assume that children can't participate in "real" psychotherapy due to their immature verbal and cognitive skills.

Certainly, one of the challenges of working with children is that everything needs to be adapted to a child's developmental level, but their insights can surprise you at any age. I appreciate how honest kids can be. Because many haven't developed some of the social filters that adults have, they often express themselves with raw intensity. They'll let you know if your question or comment is "stupid" and tell you when they find you "boring" or "incredibly annoying." (And, yes, these descriptions are in quotation marks because they are direct quotes.) In my experience, children and teens have been more open with their frustrations about me as a therapist compared to most adults, but they've also been effusive with their gratitude when things go well.

One of the other major challenges in working with children is that they rarely seek therapy by their own initiative. They are often referred by their teachers, physicians, or parents. Therefore, they may not be motivated to participate, which presents a big challenge to a therapist. It's our job to help a child identify something they'd like to get out of therapy—maybe it is more independence from their parent(s) or, alternatively, more time with a parent. Maybe it's a tangible reward, like a cell phone or video game. I've worked with kids who reveal a specific career ambition, such as becoming an animated film director, veterinarian, or elevator technician; and setting therapy goals as steps toward these aspirations has sparked their motivation. Another challenge is that kids' goals often differ from their parents', and you'll need to navigate this; but it's critical to find a child's motivation to engage in the hard work of therapy.

When working with kids, you essentially have multiple clients. The child may be the identified client, but you'll need to also work with the caregivers (who may be the biological parents, grandparents, or foster or adoptive parents but whom I'll refer to from here on as *parents*). Research demonstrates that therapy for children will usually be more effective if parents are involved.[5] Likewise, it is often important to collaborate with teachers (with the family's permission), to reinforce work toward the goals of therapy.

This is important to think about because some students assume that if they choose to work with kids, they won't have to work with grown-ups. Many young therapists find working with parents to be particularly challenging, worrying "if I haven't been a parent, how can I relate to parents or help them with parenting strategies?" I remember having these thoughts and feeling very insecure when the parent of a child client would ask me, "Do you have kids?" I scrambled to think of a response and resorted to vague reassurance about all my child psychology education. In retrospect (as a parent now), I realize I should have empathized more with the incredible responsibility of parenting and asked the parent to help me better understand their own specific challenges. This is a good example of how we often need to tackle all sorts of issues with which we have no personal experience. The best approach to this challenge is to (a) build confidence in the skills and knowledge you gain through graduate study and beyond and (b) maintain a curious approach to learning from your clients about their unique experiences.

I've devoted much of my career to learning more about how we can improve mental healthcare for children and adolescents, so I'm biased about this client population. There is so much more I could say about the joys and heartbreaks of working with youth, but the purpose here was just to preview the major rewards and challenges to help you decide if this may be a direction for you. Some of the following specific career opportunity examples might pique your interest.

Examples of Diverse Career Opportunities With Children

- Provide therapy to children who have been placed in foster care due to maltreatment.
- Consult with technology companies to develop video games based on the principles of evidence-based treatment for anxiety.
- Work for a nonprofit agency teaching child care workers in a low-income country how to screen for developmental delays and mental health problems and how to offer basic therapeutic support services.
- Develop, implement, and evaluate a middle school curriculum addressing healthy use of social media for children and parents.
- Work in the elementary school system to provide psychological testing to identify children who may have autism, attention deficit hyperactivity disorder, or learning differences.
- Consult with media organizations about how to cover school violence incidents to reduce secondary trauma among children, drawing from trauma research.
- Provide comprehensive case coordination for children who have been discharged from psychiatric hospitals, facilitating follow-up care and necessary family services. (This is sometimes called *wrap-around care*.)

- Partner with physicians and nurses in the oncology unit of a hospital to support children undergoing cancer treatment and their families.
- Develop training materials for sports coaches, scout leaders, music instructors, etc., regarding strategies to support successful inclusion of children with non-neurotypical processing abilities.
- Offer educational support and advocacy services to children in immigrant and refugee families, including connecting them to community services and extra-curricular activities.

Adolescents

I've known many students who are passionately committed to working with adolescents and others who are equally passionate about avoiding this notoriously challenging age group. Adolescence is the briefest age range I will address, broadly defined as approximately age 12–19. It is such an intense period of psychological, social, and biological upheaval that it is, in my opinion, one of the most fascinating. Adolescents grapple with many major life challenges, such as balancing the natural drive to be more independent from family with a need to be securely connected, navigating how to be in a romantic and/or sexual relationship, figuring out academic or work goals and how to achieve them, and clarifying their sense of identity across all sorts of dimensions (gender, racial, spiritual, cultural, social, etc.). They need to tackle all this while undergoing significant physical changes and decoding confusing societal expectations. It is no wonder that the developmental stage of adolescents attracts so many of us mental health professionals.

Working with adolescents can be intense because there is often so much going on in their lives. Like younger children, they are still resilient and open to change and discovery. They are also often brutally honest! These characteristics drew me to working with teenagers. I find this age group to be most rewarding because they have better-developed verbal and cognitive abilities than younger children and often an innate desire to delve into therapeutic content like identity explorations and the meaning of peer and family relationships, for example.

However, some of the same challenges noted with children are also true. Adolescents are usually referred to therapy by others and often have very different motivations than their parents or teachers who are urging them into therapy. In addition, their natural, healthy developmental drive toward independence can translate to resisting the influence of parents and other adults, including therapists. Additional societal pressures regarding gender and cultural, racial, and ethnic expectations and biases complicate this further. For example, requiring a 16-year-old young man to sit and discuss their feelings or provide details about relationships with a psychotherapist goes against traditional societal expectations as well as the adolescent's own developmental instincts. It's critical to remember these potential challenges when working with adolescents, to discuss them openly and look for creative ways to address them.

While therapists need to be flexible with all clients, this may be especially true with adolescents. Therapy sessions might include a walk around the block, listening to the teen's current favorite song, or watching a brief TikTok video. Learning more about what inspires or entertains an adolescent and delving into what it means to them is really valuable. I'm also a strong believer in the value of humor, even at the expense of making fun of the therapist's cluelessness about current cultural references. (Yes, another firsthand experience, I'll confess.)

I've always been interested in how adolescents view psychotherapy. Several years ago I led a research study where we interviewed teenagers who were in outpatient therapy, to learn more about how they judged therapy's effectiveness.[6] The results surprised some people who had assumed that adolescents are always resistant to adult authority and never think they need therapy. In fact, most of the teenagers were incredibly insightful about what they needed and what they didn't need from a therapist. Interestingly, several said that their therapist tried too hard to be a friend. While they enjoyed the consistent support and empathy offered by therapists, they recognized they needed more. They wanted a therapist who could push them and help them build skills to solve whatever problems brought them into therapy; they said they needed help with effective strategies to change destructive or risky behaviors such as substance use. These adolescents taught me an essential lesson: While all clients want therapists who are compassionate, supportive, and trustworthy, they also want therapists who employ strategies that can directly address problem-solving and skill-building. In other words, compassion and empathy are necessary but not sufficient.

Another challenge when working with this age group is navigating potentially contradictory goals for parents and teenagers. It is an adolescent's job to become more independent from their parent(s), but this can be very hard for parents to accept. Different cultural experiences can complicate this sensitive dynamic even more. For example, when parents who were raised with more conservative cultural norms are raising teenagers in a more permissive cultural context, this adds potential conflict to an already challenging situation. Perhaps you have experienced this firsthand growing up. Culturally sensitive mental health professionals are well trained to help families deal with these challenges.

If you are motivated to work with teens and their families, I assure you that you will find this to be stimulating and rewarding work. When they trust you, they will be open and honest about their feelings; but you may need to develop a thick skin because they can be very open about their criticisms as well. Imagine some of the following job possibilities.

Examples of Diverse Career Opportunities With Adolescents:

- Consult with high schools regarding effective interventions to reduce the prevalence of stress and anxiety associated with college admissions pressures, and research the impact of these interventions.
- Conduct support groups for youth who identify as LGBTQ+ in a community-based nonprofit agency.

- Provide psychoeducation to adolescent parents about early childhood development needs, and conduct screenings to identify any maladaptive parenting practices to change.
- Partner with tribal nations to develop academic and vocational screening programs for adolescent tribal members to identify career goals and steps toward achieving those goals. Include technology partners to make these screening programs accessible remotely.
- Provide substance abuse treatment to older adolescents and young adults on a college campus.
- Consult with media organizations regarding public service announcements designed to reduce rates of dating violence and educate victims about their rights.
- Supervise adolescents in a faith-based leadership mentoring program where the teens mentor younger children in single-parent homes.
- Conduct neuropsychological testing in a hospital setting for adolescents who have sustained brain injuries (in accidents, sports, etc.) to identify specific deficits and provide treatment recommendations.
- Deliver an evidence-based intervention to identify and treat youth with suicidal ideation in a runaway or homeless shelter.
- Collaborate with a nutritionist to deliver evidence-based treatment for eating disorders and wellness education in a health center.

Adults

The majority of mental health professionals will work with adults since they represent the largest age group. Many therapists prefer working with adults because they usually seek help on their own initiative, suggesting they are motivated. Some therapists prefer to work with adults because they assume, as adults themselves, they can relate better to them. This raises the important caveat that we should never assume we can understand someone's experiences better simply because we share some demographic characteristics. For example, as a woman, I should be careful about assuming I can understand any other woman's experiences better than a man's experiences. The same is true for clients of my same race, sexual orientation, socioeconomic status, age group, etc. I need to maintain a curious stance and try to learn more from all clients about their unique experiences without assuming they may relate to mine (more on this in Chapter 8).

Another potential advantage of working with adults is that they are usually more familiar with what therapy entails. However, people can have diverse expectations about therapy that may not match common practice. Perhaps someone saw a documentary about dream analysis, and that's what they are expecting—or hypnosis or even shock therapy. In a less extreme example, perhaps a client expects that a therapist is going to give advice and make decisions for them, whereas the therapist has been trained never to give specific advice about a life decision but rather to help the client build their own decision-making skills. So, while it can seem like an advantage that adults are more likely to be familiar with therapy, it can be a disadvantage if the therapist assumes that the client's expectations about therapy are consistent with their own. Research suggests that therapy will be more effective if client and therapist expectations are explicitly discussed to reach more consensus (more on this topic in Chapter 11).[7]

While one of the advantages of working with adults can be their presumed motivation for therapy, given that they usually seek it on their own initiative, a related disadvantage can be that the problems that motivate them to seek help are often deeply ingrained and potentially more difficult to change. Imagine someone who has struggled with social anxiety for many years. They may have coped by avoiding all social situations. This coping skill may have felt helpful in the short term, but it has reinforced and deepened their anxiety over time. Once this person is finally able to enter therapy, it will be challenging (but not impossible) to change this avoidance pattern.

Often, people struggle with a variety of psychological, relationship, or identity issues for years before finally overcoming barriers and seeking help. We know that close to half of the people who need mental healthcare don't receive it.[8] Barriers include practical factors, like financial or health insurance restrictions, as well as attitudinal factors, such as the stigma of mental health problems. These factors are often complicated by cultural beliefs and bias in our health system.[9] Limited access to mental healthcare in the United States and around the globe is a major public health concern, and the practical implication is that you will meet clients who have suffered for years without help.

Even if you specialize in a different age group, virtually everyone will work with adults during their career. For example, if you specialize in child treatment, you will frequently work with parents. Working with adults to shift long learned patterns to enjoy healthier relationships and overall life satisfaction can be extremely rewarding. Some of the following specific career options may be of interest to you.

Examples of Diverse Career Opportunities With Adults:

- Work as a journalist for online and print publications responding to readers' mental health questions and translating scientific discoveries into usable information for the public.
- Provide supervision to peer advocates who run support groups for women in treatment for breast cancer in a hospital setting.
- Develop and implement a substance abuse treatment program for healthcare workers addicted to opioids.
- Coordinate comprehensive services for military veterans transitioning back into civilian life, including services for family members.
- Work with an international relief organization to develop, implement, and evaluate culturally specific trauma-focused services for people in refugee camps.

- Consult with leaders of the justice system to develop valid and feasible screening methods to identify detainees who are experiencing mental health problems, and develop referral pathways to evidence-based treatment.
- Partner with healthcare providers in a primary care community-based health clinic within an integrated behavioral healthcare service model.
- Work with the human resources department of a large financial business to provide confidential mental health support to employees.
- Supervise a peer support group for survivors of domestic violence within a faith-based organization.
- Consult with state lawmakers to develop legislation to increase funding for mental healthcare in underserved communities, synthesizing research on the cost-effectiveness of evidence-based care.

Geriatric Adults

There is no official age criterion for the designation of *geriatric adult*, and I must confess that as I age, my definition seems to shift upward. (When a student recently wrote an essay describing a 57-year-old woman as *elderly*, I had to first stifle my defensive outrage before calmly suggesting that he wouldn't endear himself to his clients by calling them elderly unless they were at least age 70—or, even better, 80.) But no matter if we use a cutoff of age 60, 70, or 80, the fact is that older adults represent the largest growing segment of our population.[10] Unfortunately, mental healthcare for this age group has been relatively neglected.[11] So one of the major advantages of working with older people is the opportunity to address this glaring need and to make a big difference in the quality of their lives during a potentially vulnerable time.

Physical health problems receive much more attention than mental health problems for older adults, but physical and mental health problems are often connected. For example, individuals with depression may report physical symptoms such as headaches, fatigue, or insomnia to their doctor without discussing the psychological aspects of depression. Older individuals may be reluctant to disclose mental health problems due to the powerful stigma they learned decades ago, perceiving these types of feelings to be shameful. Unfortunately, some may believe that depression or anxiety is simply to be expected in later life. Too often this belief is reinforced by our society. Increasingly, mental health advocates are working to refute these attitudes by highlighting the benefits of mental healthcare across all ages.

One specific issue receiving more attention in recent years is the problem of loneliness. Loneliness is not synonymous with living alone; it is the discrepancy between our preferred social contacts and our actual social contacts. Loneliness impacts people at every age, but it is most prevalent among the elderly, with estimates indicating that significant loneliness is experienced by at least a quarter of older adults. Research has shown that loneliness is a devastating public health problem. It is associated with higher risk for many mental and physical health problems including depression, heart disease, obesity, and even Alzheimer's disease.[12] Mental health professionals can play an essential role in combating these consequences.

The topic of loneliness is particularly timely as I am writing this book during the COVID-19 pandemic crisis. Most states have "shelter-in-place" rules, with restrictions on public gatherings. Even visiting family members and close friends is strongly discouraged, especially for older adults who are at greater risk for disastrous effects of the virus. Residential facilities for elderly adults have been particularly hard hit, and visiting is prohibited. I know of many older people who feel increasingly bereft, and although remote socializing is common, many find it frustrating and unsatisfying. The consequences of this isolation will be better known by the time you are reading this book.

During any era, working with older adults can be extremely rewarding, but this age group too presents its challenges. I know of therapists who specialize in this age group; they speak poignantly about feeling inspired by the wisdom and resilience of their older clients. I admire these therapists because this is an age group I know I would have difficulty with. While I can work effectively with children and adolescents who have experienced terrible maltreatment and trauma, I have difficulty compartmentalizing my emotions around issues of loss when working with older adults who are struggling. We all need to gain self-awareness about groups we are drawn to as well as those we find most challenging.

Older adults experience all the same mental health challenges as others including relationship and intimacy issues, psychiatric and substance abuse disorders, and identity concerns. Coping with declining physical health and abilities as well as loss and bereavement are also common themes for older adults. If you are someone who can manage your own emotions around loss, bereavement work can be extraordinarily meaningful. While bereavement impacts people of all ages, older adults may struggle with a variety of additional losses including identity issues (e.g., who am I if I am not working or partnered?) and physical limitations. Changes in cognitive ability and memory concerns among older adults also require assessment and intervention from mental health professionals, including support for family members. If these issues are of interest to you, I encourage you to consider pursuing work with this underserved population. Examples of career opportunities are listed below.

Examples of Diverse Career Opportunities With Older Adults:

- Supervise college students who provide home-visiting and meal delivery services through a community nonprofit agency to older adults who live alone.
- Conduct neuropsychological testing with clients who show signs of memory loss to determine diagnosis and provide psychoeducation regarding findings.
- Consult with media organizations on public service messages to address the risks of loneliness and depression among older adults and highlight supportive resources.
- Provide therapy to individuals in hospice care addressing end-of-life issues.

- Work for a large multinational Fortune 500 corporation to develop, implement, and evaluate a program for retirees that supports a smooth transition out of their professional roles.
- Supervise a peer support group for grandparents who are the primary caregivers for their grandchildren, providing evidence-based parenting guidelines.
- Partner with technology experts to develop a social media platform specifically designed for older adults to facilitate social connections.
- Work in a pain control program in a hospital setting to help patients develop mindfulness and other coping skills to manage pain with the goal of reducing prescription medication use.
- Partner with genealogical and/or genetic testing services to provide assistance and support to individuals wishing to reconnect to relatives with whom they have lost contact.
- Partner with legal experts to counsel victims and/or perpetrators of elder abuse (financial, physical, or emotional abuse).

Couples

Given how important romantic relationships are, working with couples can be very rewarding. Sometimes this work can be preventative, such as premarital counseling to help couples clarify their relationship and build skills for the long term. More often, couples seek therapy when there are significant problems in the relationship. Fortunately, there are established, evidence-based approaches with positive results. Therapists can help couples learn improved communication and conflict-resolution skills, build empathy for each other, and develop acceptance to improve the quality of their relationship. If necessary, couples therapy can also help people constructively transition out of a relationship.

Challenges in couples work include the fact that you will have two clients who may not have the same goals or the same engagement in therapy. Issues of confidentiality and secrets about issues such as infidelity or finances can also be challenging to navigate with a couple. When there is a history or risk of domestic violence, safety concerns must take precedence, and this can significantly impact therapy. Another challenge I've encountered is when one or both partners look to the therapist to make a decision about whether they should stay together. It can be frustrating to the couple, but it is not appropriate for the therapist to make that decision for them. This is a good basic example of something to think about as you imagine being a therapist; you may disappoint clients at times. You'll learn more about how to manage these kinds of tensions in your training.

The most common work settings for couples therapists are private or group practice, hospitals or health centers, nonprofit or faith-based organizations. Consider the following range of potential job opportunities.

Examples of Diverse Career Opportunities With Couples:

- Provide couples counseling for same-sex couples through a community-based nonprofit agency devoted to the LGBTQ+ community.
- Partner with a lawyer, and offer combined legal and relationship support for couples who are divorcing and negotiating shared parenting responsibilities.
- Consult with tech companies on dating apps or software to incorporate research on characteristics of happily partnered couples.
- Conduct premarital couples counseling within a faith-based organization.
- Work with healthcare professionals to provide sex therapy for couples with medical issues impacting sexual functioning.
- Serve as the mental health expert consultant to an online forum sponsored by a nonprofit agency for couples who are struggling with infertility.
- Partner with law enforcement to respond to crisis calls about domestic violence.

Families

Family therapy is another rewarding career option. There are many evidence-based approaches to family therapy which focus on intervening with the family system as a whole, as opposed to just treating an individual. These approaches can be very effective for an array of issues ranging from child or adolescent behavioral problems to substance abuse and delinquency to eating disorders and other medical problems. Family therapists work effectively on all types of family conflicts or transitions such as divorce or blended families, adoption, parent–child conflicts, or complicated bereavement. They also work effectively with families that include an individual diagnosed with a severe mental illness.

Some of the rewards of family therapy work include the potential to have a positive impact beyond the immediate referral problem. If a family is successful in improving their communication skills and relationship patterns, building empathy and acceptance for one another, the positive impact can extend well beyond resolving the specific issue(s) that brought them into therapy. Helping families shift dysfunctional patterns to build improved relationships where each member feels supported and understands their role in the family is extremely rewarding.

Challenges of family therapy are related to the same challenges with couples; namely, you will likely have variability across different family members' motivation and engagement. Good family therapists learn how to encourage engagement with multiple family members effectively and identify shared goals, but this takes time.

In my experience, family therapy can be very efficient because when you have the family in the room with you, you experience very directly how they relate to each other. You don't have to rely on secondhand descriptions about family members' personalities or communication styles. (Of course, people likely behave differently in the therapy context than at home, but at least you do have some firsthand experience.) When you have family members together in therapy, there is more "real-time" sharing of feelings and insights. This adds immediacy to the work, which can be great;

but it can also be quite challenging when raw feelings are shared. Family therapists learn important skills to help clients express potentially difficult feelings and cope with conflict. One really needs to be "on their toes" all the time as a family therapist!

If couples or family work intrigues you, it is essential that you seek out a graduate program offering intensive training in these modalities. A degree program in couples/marital family therapy may be the best choice, but some other disciplines offer specialized tracks in couples and family systems as well. Just remember that one can't simply adapt what they've learned about individuals to working with couples or families. There is a rich history of theoretical and practical knowledge about family systems and couples systems to learn, and specific skills to develop. Even if you do not end up specializing in couples or family work, you will learn more about family systems theory in graduate school given how significant our families are in shaping us. Some of the interesting ways to apply family training in a job are as follows.

Examples of Diverse Career Opportunities With Families:

- Work with international cross-border nonprofits to support reunifying families who have been separated.
- Conduct family therapy and case management with older teenagers diagnosed with autism and their families to prepare for a transition to independent living.
- Deliver evidence-based intensive family therapy with adolescents diverted from detention facilities in the juvenile justice system to reduce recidivism rates.
- Work with an adoption agency to develop screening tools and educational materials for families to determine if adoption is right for them, and provide therapeutic support after adoption.
- Partner with media and social media organizations on family programming to improve positive representations of families of color.
- Deliver evidence-based parent–child therapy programs for families in a homeless shelter.
- Work in a special education school providing family therapy for children with special needs.

In Conclusion

I hope this chapter has inspired you to expand your notion of what's possible and that you have been intrigued by some career opportunities you didn't know existed before. No matter which discipline or degree path you pursue, there are so many exciting possibilities. While I've attempted to be very comprehensive, there are certainly many specific job options that I haven't included and future jobs that we can't even imagine right now. Without doubt, a graduate mental health degree opens many doors to enriching and rewarding work.

6

The Business of Mental Healthcare

I wish that I had been able to take more classes related to budgeting in graduate school. If you decide to develop your own practice, you really need to have a mind for business and come up with a business plan that will work for you. Graduate programs do not often have this as part of required classes and it's a very practical skill that comes into play in so many different roles. Even in my administrative role, thinking about how to allot dollars for training within a service organization, it would have been very helpful to have basic training in budgeting and business planning. I would have audited a few courses in the business school if I could start over again. (Jennifer, therapist in community and private practice)

Don't be afraid of being an entrepreneur and business person even if you don't learn how in school. (Jill, therapist in private practice)

When I surveyed practicing mental health professionals to ask what advice they had for people contemplating this career, I received many comments similar to Jennifer's and Jill's. While everyone remarked on the meaningful personal rewards of this career, a large number said they were unprepared for the financial and administrative challenges. So the purpose of this chapter is to provide background on these issues for you to consider as you make career decisions moving forward.

Many mental health professionals have a complicated relationship with the economics of this career. They often feel underpaid, but at the same time, they may feel somewhat ambivalent, or even guilty, about advocating for higher pay.[1] The social justice and humanitarian values that motivate many of us can complicate our feelings about seeking payment from individuals who are already struggling. Yet it is important for professionals to advocate for their own worth and for the value of mental healthcare.

Mental health professionals shouldn't feel guilty about attending to their own financial needs. These needs include the often high costs of a graduate education to become a mental health professional. How do you know if your investment in graduate school will pay off in the long term? This chapter will address some of the financial tensions that many mental health professionals feel.

As an introduction to the business of mental healthcare, I'll begin by addressing providers' ambivalence about this topic. Then I'll provide a basic overview of how mental healthcare is funded before addressing the more personal financial implications of the costs of graduate school and factors that impact salaries. Lastly, I will review some of the pros and cons of self-employment in private practice, versus other types of employment, and share therapists' input on how some of the administrative aspects of this career can be frustrating, while also offering suggestions for coping with these pressures.

Mental Health Providers' Ambivalence About Finances

> I wish I had felt more comfortable with setting my fee with business expenses and taxes in mind. Someone recently told me, "know your worth, then add tax!" It's true! (Cassidy, therapist in private practice and instructor)

Many mental health professionals are uncomfortable talking about the financial aspects of this work. In fact, finances have been called the last taboo subject in the mental health field.[2] I think this is a fair description. We encourage direct and open discussion of topics that might be considered taboo in other careers, such as sex, drugs, interpersonal violence, and racial and cultural biases. But finances, not so much.

People who pursue mental health professions are not often motivated by financial incentives. While most therapists are able to make a very decent living, it is not necessarily a great career path for those who are primarily motivated by financial rewards. In his book *On Being a Therapist*, Jeffrey Kottler insightfully observed, "we cannot decide whether therapy is essentially a profession, or a business, or a calling."[3] If we consider therapy a calling, then the financial aspects are somewhat incidental. However, if we perceive it as a business, we need to pay greater attention to the financial aspects. Many therapists grapple with this tension, and some later regret that they did not pay more attention to the business implications of their career choices.

Societal biases can also contribute to complicated feelings about funding for mental healthcare. Unfortunately, our culture tends to undervalue the types of work associated with caregiving, where women and people of color are historically over-represented. Mental healthcare falls into this category even as a highly regarded profession, requiring rigorous postgraduate education and licensure. This undervaluing bias means we need to advocate for the value of mental healthcare (e.g., human and social value, as well as financial cost-effectiveness value). Paying more attention to the business of mental healthcare is essential for supporting your own individual worth and the worth of mental healthcare overall.

This is one of the issues where I need to work on practicing what I preach. I confess that I am uncomfortable assertively asking for payment or imposing business-driven consequences on clients. I find it difficult to push clients to pay more for needed services when they are facing other financial and social pressures. Likewise, I have often struggled with canceling services for clients when they do not meet agency expectations, for example, if they miss too many appointments without advance notice (i.e., too many no-shows).

I remember one family I worked with in which the father was recently detained by immigration officers. He was the only breadwinner and the family's only driver. The 10-year-old child very much needed mental health services for severe anxiety, and he had been benefiting from therapy. But the family missed many scheduled appointments due to all the financial and logistical challenges they faced. I advocated for them, but ultimately, after several warnings, I had to tell them that they could not be seen in our clinic anymore due to the frequent no-shows. Frankly, I still feel badly about this. It's painful to turn clients away from needed care, although, intellectually, I understand the need to impose these consequences from a business perspective.

> What I hope for the future: Funding that makes effective therapy accessible and sustainable to all who need it. (Marcia, therapist in schools and private practice)

I agree wholeheartedly with Marcia's wish for the future. In my ideal world, everyone would have access to culturally competent, flexible, and effective mental healthcare through a nationalized program. However, while I may enjoy dreaming about this ideal system, the realities are quite different. The next section introduces you to the current funding structures for mental healthcare. Gaining some familiarity with these realities is important preparation for your career path.

Funding for Mental Healthcare

> The most challenging aspect of this career is not challenging clients—I like that— but the challenging systems we work in. Many of the organizations, funding systems, and bureaucracies do not lend themselves to truly focusing on doing what the client needs but rather what the program demands. Although we are trained to be professionals we are not given the latitude to perform what we may know to be professionally needed. (Denise, therapist in community nonprofits and retired instructor)

As noted in the last chapter, many people who need mental healthcare do not receive it. This unmet need is a huge public health problem. Almost half of the people who need mental healthcare in the United States do not receive care.[4] Untreated mental health problems can become more severe and can impact every aspect of a person's life: their family, their ability to work, and their physical health, let alone their happiness.

Why do so many people not get the mental health services that they need? In a 2018 survey of 5000 representative Americans, the biggest reported barriers to mental healthcare were high costs, insufficient insurance coverage, limited knowledge about services, long waits, and social stigma.[5] Believe it or not, as bad as the situation is now, there have actually been some efforts to improve mental healthcare access in the last decade or so. Mental health parity laws have been passed which require health insurers to cover mental health services in addition to physical health services. In addition, incentives to integrate mental healthcare into primary medical care are designed to improve access and reduce stigma. Despite these advances, the mental healthcare system is still fragmented, difficult to navigate, and unable to meet the public health needs. If you are frustrated by these limitations, I urge you to become a strong advocate for expanded funding for effective mental healthcare. Getting involved with your discipline's professional organization can be one avenue for advocacy, as well as national organizations such as Mental Health America or the National Alliance on Mental Illness.

At this stage in your career explorations you do not need to know about all the complexities of the business of mental healthcare, but a preview of some basics will provide a helpful orientation. To start, do you know how mental healthcare is funded? Following is a list of the major funders.

Public insurance or public services: This may also be called *government insurance* and includes Medicare and Medicaid (MediCal in California) as well as Veterans Administration (VA) benefits. Individuals need to apply for these benefits and may qualify based on income level, disabilities, or other circumstances (such as military service for the VA). A limited number of providers accept public insurance, and there are usually restrictions on the amount of care (e.g., number of outpatient sessions, days of residential care). In many geographic areas, the waitlist for publicly funded services can be very long.

Private health insurance: Many people have health insurance through their employer, or they purchase it themselves. The Mental Health Parity and Addiction Equity Act,[6] passed in 2008, requires health insurance companies to cover mental health and addiction services on par with physical healthcare services. This represents a big advance in this field. However, there are often many constraints on this coverage, including the requirement to use an approved provider (as opposed to a provider that the client finds on their own), a limit on the number of sessions, and often, limitations on the types of problems or services covered.

Out-of-pocket: Often, individuals will pay for their mental healthcare without using insurance. They may do this because they do not have any insurance, or they may have inadequate mental health coverage. Some prefer not to use the services or providers allowed under their insurance plan. Others choose not to use insurance due to stigma; they want to avoid a formal record of mental healthcare. It is not uncommon for providers to use a sliding scale to determine out-of-pocket costs based on someone's financial resources.

Other affiliated organizations: Sometimes mental healthcare will be covered by other service sectors, such as the school or university systems, corrections, child and family services, disability services, hospital or hospice systems.

Grants or philanthropy: Some nonprofit organizations at the local, national, and international levels are able to provide mental health services funded through grants and philanthropy. This may support free or sliding scale services in specific communities or for specific issues corresponding to the nonprofit's mission.

Costs of Graduate School and Return on Your Investment

Truthfully, look at how much debt you will accrue in graduate school and as best you can, make sure this is the only career choice for you. (Lily, therapist and instructor)

This section addresses financial considerations for your educational and career decision-making. What should you expect to pay for your graduate education, and will that investment pay off in the long term? Answers to those questions will depend on lots of different factors reviewed in this section. To start, there is great variability in the cost of a graduate education. Total tuition costs range dramatically from zero to more than $200,000, depending on degree program and type of school. Of course, you also need to add in the costs of living during graduate school, which vary depending on your circumstances and geographic location but are likely to be at least $15,000 annually. Next, I list major factors that will affect your graduate education costs.

Type of Degree Program

Most master's-degree programs can be completed in 2 years with approximately 60 semester units. Doctoral programs require at least 4 years total but often 5 or 6 with approximately 120–150 semester units. Unlike most undergraduate colleges that charge tuition by the year (regardless of number of units), most graduate programs charge by the unit or credit. Overall, master's programs will generally be significantly less expensive than doctoral programs (with some exceptions as noted later in this section).

Tuition costs also depend on the type of university (e.g., public vs. private, online vs. in-person). Often, programs which are nationally accredited will have slightly higher tuition costs, but this will likely be worth the investment in terms of the quality of your education, licensure eligibility, and the potentially expanded job opportunities. Also look at issues such as class size and practicum placement support, which may be associated with tuition costs. For example, some programs may require you to find your own practicum placement, whereas others will facilitate that placement process for you, and this will be worth some extra cost.

Note that there are some highly selective doctoral programs across disciplines that cover your tuition and often even provide a small stipend for living expenses. These are programs that train people for research and academic careers. Admission is highly competitive, but if you have strong grades and test scores as well as significant research experience, it can be a wonderful and cost-effective way to earn your degree. If you are seeking this route, it is very important to gain strong research experience and to convey your interests in a research career when you apply. As noted in Chapter 3, you should consider contacting faculty members when you apply as these types of programs often admit students to work with specific faculty mentors.

Financial Aid

There are many different types of financial aid, ranging from grants to student loans to work–study opportunities. Many graduate programs also have paid graduate teaching or research assistantships on campus. Most universities have financial aid counselors who can help you determine your eligibility for different types of aid. Don't assume that your eligibility will be the same as it was for undergraduate college given that factors such as your status as a dependent of your parents may have changed.

Once you know what graduate program you will be entering, be sure to explore a range of scholarship opportunities through your university and professional organizations. Even after you graduate, some federal programs offer student loan forgiveness if you work in certain high-need areas.

Employment During Graduate Study

One of the most common questions prospective students ask is whether they will be able to work while in graduate school. The answer is that it depends on several factors such as flexible class schedules and competing personal responsibilities.

First, most graduate courses meet only once or sometimes twice per week, so you will likely be spending less time in class compared to your undergraduate schedule. Some graduate programs try to accommodate working adults by holding classes only in the late afternoon or evening. In addition, many offer online or hybrid classes to increase flexibility. The coronavirus pandemic has clearly expanded the use of remote learning exponentially, and we will see how this affects graduate programs post-pandemic. I imagine that hybrid models will be much more common even after the pandemic restrictions are lifted.

Sometimes students will opt to pursue classes part-time, thus taking fewer classes per semester to balance other responsibilities. Given that most graduate programs charge by the unit (as opposed to the year), attending part-time doesn't significantly increase the total degree cost significantly. This decision also depends on what other competing responsibilities the student may have (e.g., family).

In general, in my experience, many students can manage a part-time job in the early part of their graduate education. However, in the later part, when they are completing the practicum (or fieldwork/residency) requirements, which often include at least 20 hours per week of practice at a community site, it is much more difficult to manage an additional job. The last year of any graduate program is usually the most challenging, when you are working in the role of a mental health provider for the first time and continuing to take academic courses as well. Adding an outside job to that is tricky (but I've certainly known—and admired—students who do it).

Be sure to pay attention to Lily's advice at the beginning of this section. Think carefully about how much you will be paying for your education, and make sure that you are confident this is the best choice for you. I have known students who chose very expensive doctoral programs and went into significant debt. Perhaps they would have been better off entering a master's program, leading more quickly to licensure. When you consider the relative costs of different programs, you should also anticipate the salary implications for your future.

Factors That Impact Salary for Mental Health Professionals

It would have been helpful if I had known the financial aspect of being a pre-licensed therapist (the pay is much lower than I had researched or thought). (Jenny, therapist in a hospital)

The table at the beginning of Chapter 4 presented average salaries across the United States by mental health discipline. In general, licensed master's-level professionals could expect to earn approximately $40–$70K and doctoral professionals closer to $80K or more in 2020 in the United States. As noted, however, these are very rough estimates based on varied data sources, and there will be outliers. Given high workforce demand, these salary ranges are likely increasing annually. To put this in context compared to other careers, the salary range for master's-level providers is somewhat comparable to high school teachers' salaries or those of civil servants such as firefighters. Doctoral salaries are similar in range to those of veterinarians, physical therapists, or biomedical engineers.[7] There are many factors that will impact salary, as listed in this section.

Licensure

The annual salary figures cited in the previous paragraph are for fully licensed mental health professionals. Individuals who have just graduated but are not yet licensed can be employed as associates and must be supervised by a licensed provider. Unfortunately, your salary is not likely to be very high before you are licensed (as

Jenny states). There is an implicit trade-off whereby an agency is providing you with more training experience and the appropriate supervision to become licensed, but since you are not yet licensed, your salary will be lower. Remember this because it can be frustrating if you aren't prepared for it. You will have your degree, but you won't earn the professional-level salary until a couple years after graduation. Once you complete all requirements for licensure, including hours of postgraduate practice and passing exams (as described in Chapter 3), you can expect a significantly higher salary with greater job opportunities.

Geographic Location

Salaries tend to be higher in areas with higher costs of living, such as parts of California and the New York metropolitan area. Salaries may also be higher in rural areas where the demand for services is likely to be greater than the supply of available mental health professionals.

Type of Workplace

In general, hospital settings tend to have slightly higher salaries than nonprofit agencies or residential treatment facilities. Higher salaries may also be offered in settings that may be less popular such as prisons. Some workplace settings, such as schools or universities, may have slightly lower salaries but will provide benefits such as preferred hours or more vacation time.

Specialized Skills

I've known many mental health professionals who have earned higher salaries in their first job and throughout their careers because they are bilingual or because they have specific training or certification in a well-respected evidence-based treatment model. Particular life experiences may also be highly valued by some employers, such as military service, experience in the foster care system, or previous work in the school system.

Experience and Reputation

This is likely obvious, but your previous work experience and letters of recommendation are very important for any job prospects and salary negotiations You can often advocate for a higher salary based on your salary history or a competing offer. Likewise, your own personal reputation, as well as your academic program's reputation, can also influence your salary.

Pros and Cons of Private Practice

> In a lot of ways a therapist in private practice is a small business owner—with all the good and bad that entails. For example, if you miss work for vacation, you lose money. Young therapists should know more about financial, operational and lifestyle issues associated with their career choice—not just how to be a good therapist. (Jo Ellen, professor and therapist in private practice)

As noted previously, private practice is a popular career choice. In fact, when I meet incoming graduate students, the majority say their ultimate career goal is to open a private practice. I understand the appeal. Working for yourself allows you the flexibility to set your own schedule, personalize your office space, tailor your practice to your specific strengths and interests, select the clients you work with, etc. All this sounds really great. However, it's important to consider the trade-offs. In my experience, many trainees who planned for a private practice career end up pursuing other options they discover during graduate school.

Private practice is appealing, and given the growing demand for mental healthcare, most people in practice are very busy. Another advantage is that you can set your own rates, and those who are successful in private practice can often earn more than therapists working in community-based nonprofits. However, in private practice, your income is fully dependent on your ability to find clients who are able to pay. You must also cover all associated business expenses, such as office space rental and utilities, malpractice insurance, technology support, advertising, billing, and accounting support. Unless you have health insurance benefits from another family member, you'll need to pay for your own health insurance (and your family's health insurance, if applicable). You won't have vacation or sick time as you would if employed by an agency, hospital, or school; and any hours or days missed are lost revenue. You'll need to feel comfortable with some economic uncertainty and variations in income, as opposed to a predictable salary.

> I wish I knew a lot more about how insurance works, how to bill, how to manage payment and how to set up policies and procedures for a clinical office. (Mary, professor and therapist in private practice)

> I felt prepared clinically, but I had no idea how to start and grow a business. I had to learn through trial and error, and I wish there was more support for therapists who want to start a private practice. (Cassidy, therapist in private practice and instructor)

By describing the challenges of private practice, my goal is not to dampen your enthusiasm for this path; rather, it is to make sure you can anticipate the pros and cons and prepare for them. Many people love the autonomy that a private practice career offers. However, they'll also tell you that it takes patience and an entrepreneurial spirit to succeed. Building up a sustainable caseload in private practice takes lots of time and effort. Marketing a particular specialty may help, as well as completing advanced training in specific evidence-based practices. For example, you could pursue advanced training in evidence-based treatments for anxiety disorders and market yourself with this specific skill or market your second (or third?) language abilities and cultural competencies to serve specific underserved communities in your geographic area. You'll want to think about how you define and market your "brand." Completing rigorous bureaucratic requirements to become an approved (also called *impaneled*) provider for private insurance companies can also boost referrals significantly. If you are someone who enjoys networking and marketing yourself and you aren't daunted by the business demands of private practice, this may be a great fit. If you do pursue this path, you will benefit from resources offering education in running a small business. There are some books and webinars available on building a private practice.

> Private practice can be isolating, and finding a community can be difficult. Over time it has become easier, but it takes constant intention. (Cassidy, therapist in private practice and instructor)

A decision about private practice versus a salaried position in an agency, clinic, school, or hospital raises additional pros and cons beyond just the finances. Private practice can feel isolating. Independence is nice except when you want to consult with a colleague about a challenging clinical dilemma or even just to share a cup of coffee or a funny anecdote about your pets. For me and many I know, our collegial relationships in our work settings are essential and often what keep us going during stressful times. I know people in private practice who have to work hard to create peer consulting opportunities to counter the isolation they experience at times. As you think about career options, consider when you are most fulfilled in your work. Do you thrive on partnership or group work and collaboration? Or do you crave the autonomy of independent work?

The other important thing to remember is that a mental health career offers great flexibility, so it's not an all-or-none decision. Many mental health professionals enjoy being able to do different types of work by combining part-time jobs. For example, they may have a part-time private practice combined with teaching a course at a community college, supervising trainees at a nonprofit agency, or conducting sexual harassment prevention trainings for a corporation. Combining different work activities is a good way to diversify salary sources and to help prevent burnout (more on that in Chapter 10).

> In retrospect, I probably would have worked part-time in a job that provided benefits, retirement, etc. while working part-time in a private practice for the freedom and the autonomy to choose the type of clientele I like to work with. (Carrie, supervisor in hospital and therapist in private practice)

Some people sequence their job options over time. For example, it can be difficult for brand new therapists to be able to succeed right away in a full-time private practice. Most will seek jobs in hospitals, schools, or community agencies, which offer a steady salary and benefits. These jobs also provide invaluable networking opportunities. Networking is critical for building your reputation, getting to know other professionals who may refer clients to you, and simply expanding your professional and personal contacts. After working in an organization for a while, some therapists may start to reduce their time in the organization and build a part-time private practice. I've known many people who successfully navigated this transition, but they've told me it is tricky to figure out when to make the move. It can feel risky to take the leap away from a steady job toward the uncertainties of private practice.

A side note here regarding the concept of networking: As I confessed near the beginning of this chapter, I am definitely one of the stereotypical mental health professionals who has ambivalence about focusing on the financial and business aspects of the profession. I even have ambivalence about using the term *networking* because it sounds (to me) somewhat calculating, implying that the main reason I should try to meet new people in my field is just to benefit my own career. I recognize that this is a skewed perception of the word *networking* and that I need to "get over it."

My ambivalence about the *networking* term may sound silly to those of you who have been immersed in virtual and in-person social networks for most of your lives, with all the good and bad experiences that may have brought. However, despite my skewed perspective about the term, I am absolutely unambivalent about the benefits of meeting as many people as you can to expand your personal and professional networks. We are all enriched by meeting people from diverse backgrounds whether or not the specific tangible benefits to our career are evident. Of course, some people are more naturally gregarious, and networking comes naturally. For others, it can feel like more effort. But trust me, it will be worth it.

As clichéd as it may sound, the absolute best part of my career has been the wide array of people I've met. Always remember that people you meet in all capacities, as fellow students, teachers, social friends, and community members, may become colleagues later in your career. Again, keep that in mind in terms of how you present yourself in all forums and platforms.

Administrative Demands of This Career and How to Manage Them

Working in an agency there's always a level of bureaucracy that's unavoidable. However, it has been surprising how, at times, the administrative demands seem to outweigh the benefits to a patient. (Nick, therapist in hospital and instructor)

The purpose of this chapter is to introduce you to the financial and administrative realities of this career so that you know what to expect. Many mental health professionals share the sentiments that Nick expressed. We feel discouraged at times by how these administrative challenges take away from the meaningful human interactions we prefer. Who wants to fill out lengthy, detailed forms when you could be speaking with a suffering client and offering help? Often, there is a tremendous amount of paperwork required to get approval for mental healthcare—and then, once approved, to document the care that's been delivered. Many mental health trainees tell me that the biggest surprise in their first clinical placement is the amount of paperwork. I've known people who actually changed career plans because of this. Just remember that trainees usually find that it gets easier to manage over time.

Most providers have transitioned to using electronic record systems which can be more efficient than hard copy, but they can present different kinds of frustrations. (True for all technological innovations, right?) Public and private insurers often impose detailed specifications about how records should be kept for billing, administrative, and ethical purposes. They also audit providers (both individuals in private practice and those working in agencies and hospitals), which means that they meticulously review all the records to assess compliance. These audits are stressful because if record-keeping errors are found, there are often negative financial implications. As annoying and stressful as these processes are, they are necessary for accountability. Just be forewarned that bureaucratic paperwork demands are one of the major frustrations mental health professionals face.

So how do people cope with these administrative challenges? I'm impressed by colleagues who can keep these demands in perspective and just accept that this is part of the job. They don't necessarily enjoy it, but they just get it done so that they can spend more of their time doing the real work that drew them to this profession. Those who struggle the most are those who spend lots of time bemoaning the administrative demands instead of just getting the work done.

One thing that helps me is to remember the big picture. Entering this profession is a privilege and a responsibility. While we all find some of the financial and administrative demands annoying and even oppressive at times, there is a valid reason for these accountability mechanisms. We are often serving vulnerable individuals and are privileged to earn their trust. Accountability mechanisms ensure that we don't abuse that privilege for our own selfish benefit. But the truth is that sometimes I lose perspective of this big picture and wish these mechanisms didn't have to be so burdensome. On the positive side, I can tell you that complaining about administrative demands is a popular bonding conversational topic for therapists.

In Conclusion

You may not have expected to read a chapter about business issues in a book about becoming a mental health professional, but that's exactly why it's here. As you make decisions about your specific career path, let your passions drive you, but don't ignore the financial implications. Think seriously about how much you are willing and able to invest in graduate school and what the realistic return on that investment will be in terms of projected salaries. There are lots of online resources to help you estimate salary ranges for specific jobs in different geographic areas. Think seriously about the pros and cons of self-employment as you map out your desired career path and pay attention to the advice about getting some business training if private practice is your goal. You may not be thinking of yourself as a business person, but you'll likely make better decisions if you pay close attention to financial and administrative implications at you chart your path in this career.

7

Ethical and Legal Issues in Mental Healthcare

> When I first thought about becoming a therapist, I didn't realize all the legal liabilities and forensic issues that I might confront. I didn't know that therapists can be sued or called to testify in court. I'm glad my graduate program covered legal and ethical issues up front, but it definitely made me nervous. (Anonymous, therapist in community nonprofits)

Mental healthcare providers are held accountable to high ethical and legal standards. There are many detailed ethical and legal codes to learn and significant consequences for violating these codes. While this can be daunting, ethical accountability is critical for earning our clients' trust, let alone society's respect for our profession. This chapter will introduce you to some of the most significant ethical, legal, and forensic (relating to the legal system) issues in mental health practice so that you are not surprised when you hear about them in graduate school.

As reflected in the opening quote, when students are initially unaware of these weighty issues they can be intimidating when they are first introduced. I've even known a few students who left graduate programs after their first law and ethics course when they learned that therapists can be sued for malpractice or that therapists have a duty to warn about homicide risk. My goal is to make sure you have realistic expectations about these serious issues and that you are aware of strategies to manage them.

The bulk of this chapter is devoted to introducing major legal and ethical issues in mental healthcare, research, and teaching. I'll also describe an approach to ethical decision-making and review consequences for violating ethics. In addition, at the conclusion of this chapter I will urge you to think about how ethical practice goes beyond just following the specific laws and ethical codes. I'll challenge you to aspire to ethical practice in the broadest moral sense, advocating for social justice and inclusion, combating injustice and discrimination.

A Primer on Ethical and Legal Issues in Mental Healthcare

All mental health disciplines stress the importance of learning the laws and ethics of practice. An initial question might be, what is the difference between laws and ethics? *Laws* are legally enforceable rules for society. *Ethics* (or *ethics codes* as they are often referred to professionally in mental health) are standards of right and wrong professional behavior defined by each mental health discipline. Professional organizations, such as the American Psychological Association (APA), the American Association of Marital and Family Therapy (AAMFT), and the American Counseling Association (ACA), publish their ethics codes online; and I urge you to check them out as a good introduction.[1] Licensed providers are held accountable to ethics codes and can lose their license for serious violations.

Every graduate program I know of requires students to take a course in law and ethics, and you'll need to pass a law and ethics exam to earn your license. That should get your attention as to the importance of these issues. But don't worry, at this stage in your career, you do not need to know the specifics of the law and ethics codes. This initial introduction to these issues will make it easier to learn the details when it's time for you to do so. In the next section I'll preview six major issues and pose examples of ethical dilemmas for you to contemplate.

Maintaining Professional Boundaries

You'll hear a lot about the importance of maintaining appropriate boundaries when you enter this field. In this context, the term *boundaries* refers to the limits on the types of relationships you should and shouldn't have with clients. Therapists are taught that they cannot have dual relationships with clients. That means that they cannot have any type of additional relationship beyond the therapist–client working relationship. Prohibited relationships include a casual friendship, a business relationship, or a family connection. The most egregious examples of prohibited relationships are those of a sexual or romantic nature. Violations of appropriate boundaries are the most frequent type of ethics complaint against therapists.[2]

Why is this such a big deal? Wouldn't it be an advantage if a client and therapist know each other already? It is critically important to maintain the boundaries and roles of the therapeutic relationship. If the therapist and client know each other in some other context, regardless of whether the relationship is a positive or negative one, it can interfere with the necessary objectivity in therapy. If therapists and clients have a dual (as in an additional type) relationship, whether it is a business, family, or romantic relationship, it will complicate the therapeutic relationship. Even a virtual "friendship" through social media is unadvised. These other relationships can create a conflict of interest. Blurred boundaries for the therapeutic relationship also significantly increase the possibility for exploitation of the client or the therapist.

Think about this example. Ms. Jones is a licensed therapist working in a college town. Her cousin's 20-year-old son, Jake, is attending the college in this town, which is far from his hometown. Jake's mother calls her cousin (Ms. Jones), expressing serious concerns about Jake. She's not sure what's going on with him, but he barely speaks to his family anymore and seems to be struggling. Jake refuses to seek help, but he may agree to see Ms. Jones because he knows her. Ms. Jones explains to her cousin that it's not appropriate for her to meet with a family member in a professional capacity and offers to recommend a colleague, but Jake's mother pleads with her, telling her that she just doesn't trust anyone else. Ms. Jones sympathizes and agrees to meet with Jake, rationalizing that she is not all that close to his family.

Jake comes to Ms. Jones' office and shares that he is dealing with a few issues. He's thinking of dropping out of college. He says he's unmotivated in school, and he is also questioning his sexual orientation. He shares that he is using a lot of marijuana as a stress reliever and is getting into debt. Ms. Jones encourages Jake to speak with his parents, but Jake says he absolutely will not. He also tells Ms. Jones that he knows she is legally bound to confidentiality, and he forbids her from telling his parents anything they've discussed. Jake's mom calls Ms. Jones asking for an update; but Ms. Jones can't tell her anything, and the mother gets angry at her cousin. Jake does not return to meet with Ms. Jones because he feels her only agenda is to get him to talk to his parents, and he's not going to do that. Jake becomes even more alienated from his family, and he does not return Ms. Jones' calls either.

This is a good example of how dual relationships, even if relatively nuanced and driven by good intentions, can backfire and interfere with effective therapy. On the surface, it may not seem like a big problem for Ms. Jones to have met with Jake. While she knew it was against the ethics codes, she wanted to be of help to Jake and his family. However, her family relationship with Jake's mother complicated the therapy relationship from both the client's and the therapist's perspective; it reduced both Ms. Jones' and Jake's objectivity. Although everyone acted with good intentions, they all felt worse in the end. As a result, Jake may be even less likely to seek therapy in the future.

Confidentiality and Legal Privilege

The concept of boundaries also applies to strict limits around sharing information. Confidentiality is a crucial expectation in mental healthcare and is protected by legal and ethical codes. Clients need to feel safe to share all kinds of personal information, experiences, emotions, thoughts, and even fantasies without the risk of disclosure to others. Therapists encourage clients to share thoughts and feelings that may be embarrassing, shameful, or even potentially hurtful. How wrong it would be to share any of that outside the confines of the therapeutic relationship.

In your graduate training you will learn more about the details of maintaining confidentiality as well as the few exceptions when a therapist is either allowed, expected, or even required to break it. As a preview, therapists are expected to break confidentiality when they are significantly worried about a client's safety, as in the case of serious suicidal intent. In addition, therapists are required to break confidentiality if a client makes a credible homicidal threat toward another person. Likewise, they are required to break confidentiality to report reasonable suspicion of child abuse or elder abuse to county authorities (as discussed in the following section).

Confidentiality is complicated when working with children and adolescents. The parents or legal guardians of minors hold the legal privilege of confidentiality for their children, so therapists do not maintain the same limits of confidentiality with children and adolescents as they do with adult clients. Therapists usually explain this to parents and minor clients by reassuring them that they will maintain confidentiality regarding what's discussed in therapy unless they are worried about the youth's safety.

The rationale for confidentiality is likely clear to you now. However, as clear as it may seem, you'll encounter ambiguous situations that can be tricky. For example, what if you are working with a 16-year-old who is sexually active and asking you for guidance about how to get birth control without her parents' knowledge. She says her parents would punish her severely if they knew she was sexually active. Given what you know about the parents' culture and belief system, you suspect she is correct about how her parents would respond. Independently, the parents contact you expressing concern about their daughter's relationship with her boyfriend, and they ask if you know if she is sexually active. What would you do?

For a very different example, imagine working with a combat veteran who has been diagnosed with post-traumatic stress disorder. You have been working with him for 3 months, and his symptoms are improving; his mood has stabilized, and he is sleeping better. He and his wife both report that their relationship is getting better after a very rocky year, and he is enjoying time with his young sons. In therapy sessions, he is opening up more about his combat experiences; and during one session, he shares a very painful story about a cruel officer who brutally abused and exploited fellow soldiers. He blames this officer for his close friend's suicide, and he says very explicitly, "If given the chance, I would kill him as retribution for all the lives he ruined." Knowing that you are supposed to report credible homicidal threats to potential victims and law enforcement, what would you do?

I offer these two brief examples here to give you a preview of how challenging these decisions can be. The legal and ethical codes may require you to act in opposition to your initial instincts. In graduate school you will learn more about how to make ethical decisions in situations like these and how to deal with the potential consequences in therapy. Gaining some awareness now can protect you from the intimidation that some trainees experience when they are naive about these complicated issues.

Mandatory Reporting of Child or Elder Abuse

Therapists are considered mandated reporters of suspected child abuse in most US states; they are in good company along with teachers, law enforcement officers, and other healthcare professionals. The details of reporting requirements vary by state, but mandated reporters are required (not just encouraged) to notify the child welfare authorities when they have a reasonable suspicion that a child is being abused or neglected. *Reasonable suspicion* means that another professional who received the same information would suspect that child abuse may have occurred. Note that one does not need to be absolutely certain. If the suspicion of child abuse report turns out to be unsubstantiated, the mandated reporter is protected from any negative consequences as long as they acted in good faith without malice.

Many states have similar requirements for mandated reporting of abuse of elders (ages 65 and older) or dependent adults (ages 18–64) (Dependent adults are those with mental or physical disabilities that require them to rely on others for care.) Elder and dependent adult abuse can include physical, sexual, or financial abuse or neglect. Laws vary across states in terms of whether reports of elder and dependent adult abuse are required or simply recommended. Note that anyone in a community has the right (and, arguably, the moral responsibility) to report abuse of children, elders, or dependent adults at any time; but mental healthcare providers and other mandated reporters are often required to do so.

These reporting requirements can feel burdensome at times, but they are necessary for protecting vulnerable members of society and preventing risk of further harm. While the rules seem relatively clear, like so many issues in mental health, there is subjectivity in interpretation, which can be confusing. Let's say you are working with a 45-year-old woman who reports that her uncle touched her inappropriately when she was 15. She's never told anyone before. This uncle is in a nursing home now. He does not live with any minors, but there are frequent family visitors to the facility, including young girls. Your client is concerned that her uncle may abuse children again, but she is also reluctant to speak up now regarding events of 30 years ago. What do you do?

I have found it challenging to be a mandated reporter when working with families who use corporal punishment, such as spanking or paddling, as a disciplinary technique. Decades of research indicate that corporal punishment is not an effective disciplinary technique and can be harmful.[3] It's not easy to talk about this with parents who are simply practicing the disciplinary strategies their own parents used with them and following their own culturally accepted norms.[4] It gets even more difficult if they practice severe corporal punishment, and you need to explain that their disciplinary techniques are actually considered reportable child abuse.

I know many students feel nervous about working with parents when they've not been parents themselves and feel they won't have enough credibility. This can be particularly challenging when addressing suspected child abuse. Therapists worry that families won't return to therapy if a child abuse report is made. This is definitely something you'll face if you work with children, and you'll learn more about how to manage the conflicting tensions. Ethical codes offer protection to therapists when we need to take action that may be uncomfortable or unwanted by our clients.

Finally, at the other end of the developmental spectrum, imagine working with a family with an elderly father who has been diagnosed with early symptoms of Alzheimer's disease. He is really angry that his daughter has taken over authority for his investment decisions. She says she did this because he fell victim to a scam and lost half his savings; but he denies it, and you haven't seen evidence. He is accusing his daughter of theft and says that she took money from his account to use as a down payment on a new home. He wants you to report her for financial elder abuse. What would you do?

Suicide Risk and Reporting Requirements

Most mental health professionals will have the experience of assessing a client's risk for suicide, and, unfortunately, as many as one-fourth to one-half of all therapists will have a client who dies by suicide at some point in their career.[5] Working with clients who are suicidal can be very stressful, but you will learn how to evaluate the level of risk and what actions to take. One of the biggest responsibilities a therapist has is to assess a client's safety and to determine how to respond. While this is primarily a clinical issue, I've included it in the ethics chapter because assessing a client's risk of harm (to self or others) is a major factor in decisions about breaking confidentiality. For example, you may need to speak to a family about restricting a client's access to firearms or other dangerous objects or lethal substances. You may need to make decisions about referring a client to a psychiatric hospital even when they are adamantly opposed to it.

Imagine that you are working with a 13-year-old girl who is struggling with anxiety and depression. Her parents are successful business entrepreneurs, and she has an older brother who is an academic and sports superstar. She is an average student who feels like a "loser" in her family. She also happens to be adopted, whereas her brother is the biological child of the parents. You've been meeting with her for a couple months and sometimes with her parents. She has been opening up more and seems to value therapy with you. One day, she arrives very agitated and describes an incident of social bullying on social media the night before. She's very upset about it and makes statements such as "I'll show them, they'll be sorry when I'm gone." "Nothing is going to get better." "I hate it all and want out."

You ask follow-up questions to assess her risk for suicide and determine that she is at moderate risk. She feels demoralized and hopeless, and when asked about a specific plan for suicide, she is somewhat evasive, so you're not sure if she has a specific plan or not. You feel that taking the most cautious action of referring her to a hospital could just reinforce her sense of being a loser and add to pathologizing her in her family and among peers. However, she is definitely at some risk, so caution may be best. You decide to consult a trusted senior colleague to discuss next steps and collaboratively decide not to hospitalize her, but this decision weighs heavily on you for a week until you next see her.

These are common experiences for a therapist; you'll gain knowledge and skills to help you feel better prepared for making critical decisions, but these decisions will always weigh on you. While stressful, you will also have extraordinarily rewarding experiences when clients build resilience after a crisis that you helped them to manage. Some risk assessment decisions are crystal clear, but many are ambiguous and challenging. In our field we do not have blood tests or X-rays to identify clear diagnostic or treatment decisions. Becoming comfortable with some ambiguity is critical in this career.

Forensic Mental Health Practice

Someone who works in forensic mental health practice addresses legal or criminal issues. Thanks to popular television shows and movies, you may be intrigued by the fascinating work of criminal profiling. While some mental health professionals do collaborate with law enforcement agencies on profiling, it's a relatively small and specialized field. More commonly, mental health professionals will be involved in family legal issues, such as conducting child custody evaluations or assessments of individuals to determine their psychological competency to stand trial. Those who do this type of work need expert knowledge in the ethical codes for their discipline, as well as the law.

Forensic practice can also include working with clients involved in the criminal justice system. The adult prison system as well as the juvenile corrections system hire a lot of mental health professionals. In fact, in some cities, the justice system has been referred to as the "de facto mental health system" since so many individuals who are detained suffer from mental health challenges.[6] The criminalization of mental health problems and the lack of effective care for these individuals are major public health problems in the United States and globally. Working with this population can be quite rewarding.

Even if you don't choose to specialize in forensic practice, mental health professionals can be required to testify in court, and/or their records can be subpoenaed. As luck would have it, this happened to me during my very first year working as a therapist. I was a prelicensed intern working at a Veterans Administration hospital. I had conducted a comprehensive psychological evaluation on a veteran who had been a physician. Her medical license had been revoked due to erratic behavior and multiple signs of psychiatric illness. I met with her a few times and administered several standardized tests, as well as a comprehensive clinical interview. After scoring and interpreting all my findings and meeting with my clinical supervisor, I submitted a thorough written report supporting a diagnosis of a paranoid delusional disorder. A few weeks later I received a certified letter requiring me to testify in court. My client was suing to try to get her medical license back and to "clear her name."

As you might imagine, I was very anxious about having to testify in court. I anticipated being grilled by attorneys about my work and my relative lack of experience and hoped there might be a way to avoid this, but there was not. I remember sitting in the witness chair and answering a lot of pointed questions from a medical board attorney and from the client, who chose to represent herself. I had to defend my interpretations and clinical decision-making under pressure. In retrospect, this was a great professional growth experience, but at the time it was really stressful. I've carried that experience with me all these years, and when faced with an ethical decision, I ask myself, would I feel confident defending this decision in court? It's not an abstract question.

Ethics in Research and Teaching

Most of this chapter is devoted to the laws and ethics of therapy practice, but many of these same principles apply to research and teaching activities. As you likely know, researchers must have their studies approved by ethics committees, often referred to as *institutional review boards* (IRBs), established to protect the rights and welfare of human subjects. Some of the issues addressed in this chapter, such as confidentiality and requirements to report serious safety risks, apply to research as well as clinical practice. In addition, there is a great deal of attention to how participants provide informed consent with clear knowledge of the potential risks and benefits of participation in research. These ethical guidelines have evolved over time to reduce the risk of exploitation in research.

Ethics in academia also address confidentiality through regulations prohibiting sharing of student information, such as the Family Educational Rights and Privacy Act (FERPA).[7] More broadly, you are likely well aware of other ethical guidelines addressing academic integrity violations, such as plagiarism or other types of cheating. Most universities have academic integrity committees reviewing ethics violations such as these, as well as any type of research misconduct, like data falsification or misrepresentation.

Academic ethics and mental health practice ethics can intersect sometimes on college campuses. For example, there have been tragic cases reported in the media when students have died by suicide on campus, and their families were not aware they were experiencing serious difficulties.[8] FERPA restrictions and mental health confidentiality guidelines limit sharing information about adult students. There are actually some nuanced exceptions that allow sharing information with parents, but sometimes there is confusion about the laws and ethical codes. This is but one tragic example of the complexity and unintended consequences of well-intended ethical codes and laws. It's wise to contemplate these weighty issues as you enter the field so that you are not caught by surprise and overwhelmed by the significant decisions you'll be called to make.

Ethical Decision-Making

Given that we cannot anticipate all the potential ethical dilemmas we might face and ethical codes cannot provide answers to every conceivable circumstance, it is critical to develop an intentional strategy for ethical decision-making that can be applied to any given situation. The following universal steps in ethical decision-making have been identified by Anderson and Handelsman in their book titled *Ethics for Psychotherapists and Counselors: A Proactive Approach*[9]:

Step 1: Identify the problem.
Step 2: Develop and analyze alternatives using relevant codes, guidelines, laws, regulations, and policies.
Step 3: Consult other professionals.
Step 4: Choose, implement, and evaluate the decision.

I find these four steps to be excellent guideposts for decision-making. Each step can be more challenging than it may seem at first glance. For example, have you ever found yourself stressed out about a problem—maybe an interpersonal dilemma with a friend or co-worker—but you can't exactly pinpoint what that problem is? Sometimes ethical dilemmas are easy to define. But other times you may sense something is not right, and it will take some effort to clarify and define the problem (Step 1 of decision-making).

When I approach Step 2 of this decision-making model, I try to be as creative and open-minded as possible to generate a full range of alternative action steps, what many refer to as *brainstorming*. I find it useful to imagine even somewhat extreme or unusual options since they may help me bring the more reasonable options into focus. Let's say you are generating potential responses to an interpersonal conflict with your co-worker. One option is to show up at your supervisor's front door unannounced after work to complain about your co-worker. Another option is to quit your job immediately. Identifying these rather extreme (and probably unwise) options may give you some perspective to generate more reasonable ones.

Step 3 advises you to consult other professionals. Fortunately, when you are a trainee you will have ready access to your instructors and clinical supervisors. I've talked to many graduates who say that they only recognized in retrospect how lucky they were as a trainee to have lots of time with supervisors for consultation. Once you are an independent professional, it takes more initiative to seek consultation. Many providers build informal or formal peer consultation groups for this support. Professional organizations, such as the APA, ACA, or AAMFT, also often offer consultation for ethical dilemmas to members.

The final step in this recommended decision-making model requires you to choose your action and implement it and then to evaluate the consequences. One of the frustrations that I have felt at times is that after spending a great deal of time and energy deciding on the best action, I may never learn about the outcome. I've experienced this when I've made mandated reports about suspected child maltreatment. As a reporter, you will sometimes be informed about the consequences of your report but not always. I've had to get used to not knowing and accept that the consequences are often largely out of my control. My point is that we need to make ethical decisions and act on them regardless of our ability to control, or even learn about, the outcome.

Innovations Bring New Ethical Challenges

As noted by ethics expert Dr. Jeffrey Barnett, with new innovations come new ethical challenges that couldn't have been foreseen.[10] Good examples of this include the potential blurring of therapeutic relationship boundaries with social media connections. Should therapists and clients follow each other on social media? Does that represent a dual relationship? And should therapists even have a personal social media presence that is accessible to clients? What are the implications?

Likewise, increased use of remote platforms for therapy via phone, video, and text highlight new ethical dilemmas. Remote therapy improves access and can be effective, but it raises a variety of ethical questions.[11] It has been essential during the pandemic and is likely to be sustained beyond it. Yet confidentiality can be more challenging with remote technologies. What are the hacking risks? If therapy is conducted by phone, can the therapist and client be confident they are having a private conversation? Can a therapist even be sure of the client's identity, especially if on the phone without video? Another very serious issue regarding remote therapy relates to suicide or homicide risk: If the therapist does not know where the client is physically located, they cannot intervene—or send first responders—in an emergency. All of these issues and more are currently being addressed, but new ethical challenges will always emerge with new technologies.

In Chapter 13 I will highlight more innovative uses of technology in mental healthcare, such as mobile apps and virtual reality. These present yet more ethical dilemmas in terms of privacy, raising questions about data sharing and tracking. Likewise, there is no oversight of mobile apps or mental health video game technology. Developers are not required to address privacy, safety, or effectiveness when they introduce a new technology into the marketplace. It's great that our field is constantly evolving, but that means that our ethical codes must also evolve.

Consequences for Violating Ethical Codes

I'm sure there are unethical workers in every field: car mechanics who overcharge, investment managers who profit from insider information, or politicians who offer or accept bribes, for example. And while I would like to believe that those who choose to become mental health professionals are guided by particularly high ethical and moral standards, I've learned this is not necessarily true. Every year I see lists of mental health professionals whose licenses have been suspended or revoked due to legal or ethical violations. As noted, the most common violations are blurring of professional boundaries, but there are also egregious abuses of power and financial exploitation of clients.

Having been on IRBs at multiple institutions, I have also seen ethical violations in academia and research. Many violations seem to be unintentional, but others reflect malicious behavior driven by ambition or greed. As cumbersome as ethical reviews may be, they are clearly necessary to protect the public. And while it may seem to you that there is an overemphasis on legal and ethical issues in your training, you'll appreciate that emphasis when you are an independent practitioner faced with a weighty decision with significant consequences. Just remember that you will be supported by mentors and colleagues who will be pleased to offer consultation. You are not expected to manage these issues on your own.

Aspirational Ethics

How do we set our sights higher than the minimal expectation of not violating ethical codes to pursue more aspirational ethical ideals?[12] Aspirational ethics include a commitment to social justice and working to promote fair and equal access to mental healthcare.[13] Aspirational ethics also include a commitment to delivering high-quality, culturally sensitive care consistent with available research evidence. When we work to combat the destructive social determinants of health and mental health, such as poverty, racism, violence, and homelessness, we are pursuing aspirational ethics. The next chapter is devoted to exploring these issues in a mental health career.

I urge you to set lofty ethical ideals for yourself and aspire to become a well-respected role model and advocate for our mental health professions. You will be well positioned to contribute to causes you believe in. Find opportunities to apply your training to address the social ills, inequities, and injustices that you are passionate about. While it is true that we as therapists strive to be non-judgmental and open to our clients' diverse values and belief systems, that doesn't mean that we can't advocate for particular causes or values in our lives outside the therapy office. In fact, our empathy skills, communication training, and problem-solving strategies empower us to be effective social change-makers. I know and admire many mental health professionals who are effective crusaders for all types of social, environmental, economic, and political causes.

You may meet some mental health professionals and professors who think it is inappropriate for therapists to publicly advocate for social issues. While I understand the rationale in terms of maintaining a "blank slate" with your clients, I disagree with this approach. Who better to advocate for important social issues than those of us with lots of education about such issues?

I was fortunate to have a graduate school mentor, Dr. Edward Zigler, who encouraged mental health professionals to become involved in policy issues and social movements. He was a wonderful role model who believed that we need to share our expertise in child and family development, mental healthcare, and social issues, such as poverty and racial inequities with policymakers. He testified to Congress and partnered with policymakers to advocate for high-quality child development programs, namely Head Start, in underserved communities. He taught us to use our knowledge and skills to benefit whatever causes inspired us. I try to reinforce this important message whenever I can.

I hope that you will also use your skills and knowledge to advocate for whatever causes inspire you. Maybe it's Black Lives Matter, #metoo, climate change, immigration and refugee rights, LGBTQIA+ advocacy, global food security, animal rights, gun control/safety, reproductive rights, economic inequity, mental health advocacy, or something else. Mental health professionals have so much to contribute to social justice causes.

I'm excited about therapists beginning to step into the larger wellness/healthcare, business/organizational, social justice, and political conversations. I believe that systemically trained therapists have much to contribute. (Cassidy, therapist in private practice and instructor)

In Conclusion

While the weighty issues described in this chapter can be daunting, remember that you will not be facing them on your own. In graduate school you'll learn how to apply ethical decision-making, including consultation with peers and supervisors. And over time you will gain confidence, and you will be empowered by helping someone overcome a crisis.

This chapter included several brief examples of realistic ethical dilemmas you may face. The purpose was to illustrate that such dilemmas can be complicated and require good judgment. In graduate school, you'll learn more about what actions to take in these types of situations. For now, if you found these brief vignettes intriguing, it's yet more evidence that you are hooked for this career path!

8
Diversity, Equity, and Inclusion in Mental Health

> One of the joys, as well as the challenges of this career is the opportunity to work closely with people who have incredibly different experiences from yours. Even after 50 years, learning their stories never gets old. (Saul, therapist in private practice and retired professor)

The last chapter concluded with my call for you to pursue aspirational ethics of social justice in mental healthcare. This chapter expands on that call since it is devoted to themes of diversity, equity, and inclusion. These are prominent topics in our current social discourse as the United States and other countries continue to grapple with serious disparities in health and healthcare that were amplified during the pandemic tragedy, as well as racial injustice and the Black Lives Matter and other anti-racism movements. Race and ethnicity will be central themes in this chapter, but I will identify disparities based on other types of diversity as well, including gender, LGBTQ+, age, and ability. The purpose of this chapter is to raise awareness of how these issues are inextricably linked to mental health and mental healthcare and to suggest how you can become a culturally competent professional.

Personal Caveats and Lessons

The important topics addressed in this chapter call for ongoing personal reflection as well as openness to learning from others' experiences. Thus, it seems important for me to start by sharing personal reflections on experiences that shape my continually evolving understanding of diversity, equity, and inclusion. I am mindful of the sensitivities around these topics, including important concerns about perpetuating privileged voices over historically underrepresented perspectives. As a White, heterosexual, cisgender female, I am not claiming expertise regarding marginalized perspectives. I am working to practice cultural humility and openness. This is a work in progress, and no doubt, I will sometimes fumble in this effort. I could avoid the risk of fumbling by not confronting these critical topics directly, but that would be a "sin of omission," as well as a poor example for any aspiring mental health professional. So, with some trepidation, here it goes.

To start, the most meaningful experience for me is as a mother of a daughter who is of a different race than my own. We adopted our daughter from China when she was an infant, and she is now a young adult. My awareness of conscious and unconscious biases, attributions based on race, and complexities around ethnic identity and belongingness has been influenced by experiences we have had as a transracial family. More importantly, I have been influenced by what my daughter has shared with me about her own experiences navigating complex intercultural dynamics.

We are also a family with mixed spiritual, cultural, and socioeconomic backgrounds. My husband is a first-generation Jewish Canadian whose parents fled Eastern Europe due to persecution and poverty. Several of his family members, including two grandparents and an uncle, were killed in the Holocaust. He grew up in a crowded urban immigrant/refugee community, living with multiple extended family members in a small apartment. English was not his first language; it was Yiddish. Neither of his parents attended college. In fact, his father only completed the equivalent of a middle school education, and he was a wise, kind, and resourceful man. His mother was a very bright student who graduated from high school but did not have the opportunity to pursue higher education.

For contrast, I grew up in a comfortable Californian suburban home. Both my parents graduated from college. My father was a businessman and my mother a traditional housewife, conforming to the cultural norms at the time. My family's spiritual background is Protestant, and my ethnic heritage is primarily Norwegian and Scottish (i.e., very White or, as my daughter describes more accurately, pale pink polka-dotted). The differences between my husband's background and my own have enriched my life in numerous ways and shaped my understanding of historical discrimination and trauma, a particular type of immigrant experience, and privilege.

The contrast between my mother-in-law and my mother offers a lesson in bridging cultural diversity. These two women were incredibly different in their cultural backgrounds and in many other ways. My mother was tall and athletic until her death in her 70s. My mother-in-law was very short and stout; she abhorred exercise, yet she lived to age 101. She also disliked driving and never got a driver's license. In contrast, my mother spent much of her life driving her proverbial station wagon around the suburbs. Their political affiliations were opposite: My mother was conservative, whereas my mother-in-law advocated, and sometimes agitated, for far-left socialist policies. What could they possibly share in common?

In fact, the two women grew to love and respect each other quite quickly. They were both smart, strong, willful women and admired these strengths in each other. They also shared a great sense of humor and ability to laugh at themselves. (Writing this makes me realize how I miss their hearty laughter.) Although they never discussed it explicitly, they also shared the experience of cultural gender expectations limiting their career opportunities. No one who knew either of these women would doubt that they could have been successful CEOs or politicians in a different era. Instead, they found other ways to channel their considerable strengths. My mother-in-law supported her husband's business enterprises and was a community organizer for families of children with special needs. My mother channeled her ambitions into community volunteer organizations, ultimately being elected president of every community group she joined, whether it was a sports club, parent–teacher association, or charitable foundation.

I've taken a couple lessons from the contrasts of these two admirable women. First, despite divergence on most measurable characteristics, they found ways to connect and appreciate each other. Second, the gender expectations of their times powerfully impacted their lives. I'm aware that in just my own lifetime these expectations have shifted dramatically, yet inequities persist. As a child, I did not know one mother who worked outside her home in my community. Yet, for my daughter, virtually all her friends' mothers worked outside their homes. That's a huge shift over just one generation.

My extended family reflects diversity and shifting cultural contexts in other ways as well. My sister is married to her wife, and they have raised two terrific kids who are now young adults. They've been together for decades but were only legally allowed to marry a few years ago. Through my sister's experiences coming out in the 1980s and then raising children in a same-sex household, I have gained awareness of explicit and implicit discrimination as well as resilience in the LGBTQ+ community. I've also witnessed a generational shift in attitudes, although, of course, prejudices still exist. I do recognize that the awareness I've gained indirectly is not at all equivalent to the direct experiences of members of marginalized communities. But it has certainly shaped my evolving understanding.

My professional work has also helped me to gain awareness of diversity, equity, and inclusion in mental healthcare. I've conducted my clinical work in public mental health settings as opposed to private practice. The public settings primarily serve families with fewer economic resources where families of color are overrepresented. In addition, I've conducted research highlighting inequities in the mental healthcare system that result in children of color receiving fewer services. I'll discuss these types of disparities, including related disparities in education, corrections, and child welfare systems in greater detail in the "Disparities in Mental Healthcare" section of this chapter.

I've shared these personal and professional experiences for transparency regarding how my experiences have shaped my perspectives, in terms of both potential strengths as well as weaknesses or blind spots. I urge you to similarly think about how your awareness of diversity, equity, and inclusion has evolved over time and to reflect on experiences that have shaped it. This type of reflection will be essential in your ongoing journey as a mental health professional.

Key Concepts and Mental Health Implications

In this section I will describe the relevance of key diversity, equity, and inclusion concepts to mental healthcare. These are relatively brief introductions with just a few examples. You'll learn a lot more about all these issues in graduate school and beyond.

Culturally Competent Care

All mental health disciplines emphasize the importance of building culturally competent skills throughout your career. Different terms are used to describe these types of skills, including *cultural sensitivity*, *cultural responsiveness*, and *cultural relevance*; but the intent is similar. The goal is for mental health professionals to gain personal awareness, knowledge, and skills to work effectively with individuals from diverse backgrounds. To do so, mental healthcare providers need to appreciate the impact of culture and context at the individual, family, organizational, and societal levels. I have listed some key elements of cultural competence below, adapted from an original list by Cross and colleagues[1]:

 a. Valuing diversity and inclusion
 b. Understanding the importance of representation
 c. Having the capacity for cultural self-assessment, including exploration of conscious and unconscious biases
 d. Appreciating the history and the dynamics inherent when cultures interact
 e. Being aware of systemic factors that promote bias against certain groups and working to counter those biases
 f. Working collaboratively with individuals from diverse backgrounds to adapt services for different cultural contexts

This is not an exhaustive list, but it's a good place to start. It's very important to recognize that cultural competence is not an all-or-none skill. As defined by the Department of Health and Human Services, "striving to achieve cultural competence is a dynamic, ongoing, developmental process that requires a long-term commitment."[2] It's a work in progress for all of us and for the institutions in which we work.

Practicing cultural competence is essential for building effective therapeutic relationships (also referred to as *therapeutic alliance*) with individuals from diverse backgrounds. You may assume that it will be easier to build working relationships with clients who share your own basic sociodemographic characteristics, such as race, gender, sexual orientation, or age group. However, the results of research on the benefits of client–therapist match have been more mixed than you might expect. Specifically, while some studies have found a benefit for racial match between therapist and client for a stronger therapeutic alliance,[3] many more studies have been inconclusive.[4]

My interpretation of the literature suggests that, for many clients, meeting with a therapist of the same general demographic characteristics, such as race, can facilitate early alliance-building; but it is not crucial. What does seem to be essential is a therapist's openness to discussing issues such as race and ethnicity directly and respectfully with clients. Research confirms that open dialogue about issues of race and ethnicity in therapy promotes a more positive therapeutic alliance.[5] I believe that the same is true regarding other sociodemographic characteristics such as gender, age, sexual orientation, ability, spirituality, and socioeconomic status. Even when we assume that we share some of the same characteristics as our clients, it's important to remember that we may have very different life experiences. Thus, we must be comfortable discussing these important issues directly. We need to be open to learning from our clients, practicing respect, and valuing differences.

Cultural Humility

Cultural humility is described as "a lifelong process of self-reflection and self-critique whereby the individual not only learns about another's culture, but starts with an examination of her/his own beliefs and cultural identities."[6] By adopting a humble and curious approach, the goal is to redress power imbalances and to develop mutually beneficial working relationships with individuals from diverse backgrounds. A culturally humble and open perspective helps us to be more aware of our own biases and to challenge them, improving our ability to offer effective care for diverse individuals.

When therapists are practicing cultural humility, they adopt a "not-knowing" stance,[7] avoiding assumptions about someone else's experiences and the meaning of those experiences. This stance reinforces that the client is the expert on their situation, and we need to listen deeply and learn from the client. This is so important to remember whether we are working with individuals who seem similar to ourselves or those who seem very different.

Conscious and Unconscious Bias

You are likely familiar with these terms, but how do they relate to mental healthcare? Mental health professionals, just like everyone else, have biases about individuals or groups of people. Biases are complex and context-dependent; they can be positive or negative, but we'll focus on the biases that negatively impact care. Sometimes these biases are conscious and explicit, but often they are unconscious and unintentional. Yet they can powerfully impact judgment and behavior.

Many studies have documented how healthcare providers' biases impact healthcare delivery and outcomes.[8] In mental health, for example, clinicians tend to over-pathologize behavioral symptoms among ethnic and racial minorities. Specifically, African Americans are more likely to be diagnosed with a more severe diagnosis, such as schizophrenia, compared to White clients even when the behavioral descriptions are similar or even identical.[9] In fact, African Americans with mood disorders, such as depression, are more likely than other groups to be misdiagnosed with schizophrenia.[10]

These types of biased diagnostic disparities have potentially life-altering consequences. Consider the implications for two 8-year-old boys, one Black and one White, who exhibit exactly the same type of "acting-out" behavior problems, such as impulsivity and minor physical aggression. Let's assume they both actually have attention deficit hyperactivity disorder (ADHD). Research shows that the White child is more likely to be diagnosed and treated for ADHD, whereas the Black child is more likely to be diagnosed with conduct disorder, not ADHD.[11] The White child who is diagnosed with ADHD receives therapeutic and educational supports and accommodations, whereas the Black child diagnosed with conduct disorder does not. The Black child with undiagnosed, untreated ADHD is more likely to continue to struggle with academic achievement as well as with peer and family relationships. These struggles may exacerbate his frustration and acting-out behavior and interrupt his progress in school, resulting in all kinds of negative outcomes. Thus, biases in diagnostic decision-making can have significant long-term consequences.

There are diagnostic biases based on other characteristics as well. In their report on gender and mental health, the World Health Organization determined that providers are more likely to diagnose depression in women compared to men even when the reported symptoms are identical.[12] Women are also almost twice as likely to be prescribed psychotropic medications, and they are more likely than men to experience side effects.[13] There is also compelling evidence of diagnostic bias for individuals who identify as sexual minorities. For example, bisexual individuals are more likely to receive a diagnosis of borderline personality disorder.[14] In addition, ageism biases often inhibit diagnosis of mental health problems among older adults who are suffering, resulting in particularly high rates of untreated mental health problems.[15]

The point of these examples is to raise your awareness about how unconscious biases impact mental healthcare. Raising awareness of the prevalence and impact of unconscious biases is a first essential step in combating them, but it may not be sufficient to change our behavior. To override implicit bias, we need to boost motivation and build self-regulation skills to counter habits developed over a lifetime. Building empathy for the injustices of biases can help to boost motivation to combat them. Strategies to override implicit bias include focusing on individual characteristics and what we may share, as opposed to focusing on our group differences.[16]

As research on the damaging impact of implicit biases grows, many graduate mental health programs have reinforced efforts to help trainees become more aware of their own biases. As I said in Chapter 2, if your automatic response to that statement is something like "But I don't have any biases," I urge you to reassess. Everyone has inherent biases. You may want to explore an easy, self-administered assessment available online called the Implicit Association Test.[17] As you pursue this career path, it is critical that you remain open to exploration of how your own attitudes and preferences have developed and how they may impact your behavior as a mental health professional.

Social Determinants of Mental Health Problems and Mental Healthcare

When we talk about social determinants of mental health, we're talking about all the factors other than traditional psychological symptoms that can impact mental health. These include issues such as poverty; unstable housing; segregation; safety concerns in schools, neighborhoods, or workplaces; as well as interactions with the justice or child welfare system.[18] Likewise, exposure to all types of trauma is associated with mental health challenges. People of color and others in marginalized communities are more likely to experience these social determinants. In addition, macroaggressions and stigmatization build up, and discrimination is in itself a form of trauma.

All of these types of social determinants can contribute to the development of mental health problems and impact access to care. Research shows that the more adverse childhood events (commonly referred to as ACEs) a person has experienced, the greater the likelihood they will experience chronic health, mental health, and/or substance abuse challenges.[19] There is compelling biological and sociological evidence that prejudice and discrimination have direct detrimental negative effects on physical and mental health.[20] Factors that have been shown to protect against the negative impacts of these experiences include strong family and social supports as well as psychological optimism and mindfulness.[21] Of course, reduction of discriminatory experiences would be the strongest protective influence, which is why we should all advocate for social justice.

Disparities in Mental Healthcare

The term *healthcare disparities* refers to differences in access or quality of healthcare that are due not to actual health needs but rather to demographic, socioeconomic, or environmental factors. In an ideal world, we'd like to think that the only predictor of mental health service use is the actual need for that care. Unfortunately, we are far from that ideal.

Throughout this book, I've mentioned that many people who need mental healthcare do not receive it. Disparities in mental health service use are well documented across a wide range of marginalized groups. For example, among adults with mental illness, a federal report indicates that 48% of Whites received mental health services, whereas the rate for Blacks and Hispanics was only 32%, and for Asians just 22%.[22] Among all racial/ethnic groups except Native American/Alaska Native, women were more likely to receive mental healthcare than men.[23] Research also suggests that gay men experience particular disparities in access to continuing mental healthcare due to providers' discriminatory attitudes.[24]

I've been involved in research on racial and ethnic disparities in mental healthcare for children and have been struck by the persistence of these disparities. For example, the disparities cannot be explained by differences in the severity of behavioral or emotional problems or by differences in family income or insurance status.[25] It should concern all of us when there are persistent disparities resulting in greater unmet needs among people of color and other marginalized groups.

What are the barriers to mental health service use beyond demographic characteristics? I find it useful to think about these potential barriers as two different types. First, objective barriers are tangible factors, such as insurance coverage, finances, geographic distance, hours of operation, and language access. Even with services offered remotely, there are additional barriers in terms of digital devices and Wi-Fi access.

Second, subjective barriers are attitudinal factors, such as perceived stigma or shame, skepticism about the effectiveness of mental healthcare, or cultural help-seeking preferences that are not consistent with traditional mental healthcare, such as a preference for indigenous or faith-based healers. Some marginalized families may have concerns about accessing public services based on negative experiences or immigration status implications. Objective and subjective factors can interact to limit mental healthcare use among families of color and other marginalized individuals.

To better understand the relationship between mental health service needs and use, it is important to examine disparities in other related service sectors. For example, according to the American Psychiatric Association, Black children with mental health needs are more likely to end up in the juvenile justice system compared to White children with mental health needs; and this is due, in part, to disciplinary actions in schools that disproportionately impact youth of color.[26] Correctional facilities (i.e., jails and prisons) have been referred to as a de facto mental health system in the United States since, in many states, there are more individuals with serious mental illness in prisons and jails than in psychiatric facilities.[27] Estimates suggest that up to half of adult male prisoners and three-quarters of female prisoners experience symptoms of mental illness, yet only a minority of those who need treatment receive it.[28] Due, in part, to shortages in mental health staff, wait times for treatment can be up to a year.[29] Incarcerated individuals with untreated mental illness have an elevated risk for suicide and are more likely to recidivate.[30] People of color, particularly Black individuals, are significantly overrepresented in the corrections system[31] and thus more likely to face these barriers to mental healthcare.

There are also disparities in other service sectors including the child welfare and education sectors, which intersect with mental health services for youth. Specifically, Black and Native American/Alaska Native youth, and those from lower socioeconomic backgrounds, are disproportionately overrepresented in the foster care system.[32] In contrast, Asian American children are significantly underrepresented in the system relative to their proportion of the population.[33] LGBTQ+ youth are also overrepresented in foster care, with transgender youth at particularly high risk for out-of-home placements.[34]

Not surprisingly, rates of mental health problems are elevated among children in foster care, but there are disparities in their access to mental healthcare. I've been doing research on this for the past few decades and have found that White children in the system are more likely to receive psychotherapy and, once in treatment, to receive more sessions than other youth.[35] The type of maltreatment a child suffered also predicts how likely they are to receive mental healthcare, regardless of the emotional or behavioral problems the child is exhibiting. For example, children who had been sexually or physically abused are more likely to receive mental healthcare than those who experienced neglect, and yet the consequences for children who have been neglected are devastating.[36]

Inequities in the education sector have been well documented for decades, if not centuries. These include disparities in teacher expectations, support and enrichment service access, academic achievement, and behavioral discipline patterns.[37] Teachers' implicit biases have been shown to impact expectations for student achievement and recommendations for enrichment programs.[38] Likewise, biases impact student discipline patterns; for example, the school suspension rates for Black students are 2–3 times higher than for other racial/ethnic groups.[39] These differences cannot be explained by differences in socioeconomic status or observed behavioral problems.[40]

Teacher biases can have significant and lasting effects on students' mental health. As suggested by the earlier example about ADHD diagnostic disparities, when students with mental health problems are disciplined as opposed to assessed and treated, their challenges can be compounded over time, resulting in increasingly serious behaviors with tragic outcomes. For some, this has been referred to the "school-to-prison pipeline."[41] Fortunately, there are effective programs to reverse these trends. Teacher coaching programs have been shown to have lasting beneficial effects in reducing the disparities in disciplinary actions in schools.[42]

There are other ways that school culture can impact mental health. Certainly, marginalized youth are at higher risk for being bullied, which can contribute to the development of mental health problems. Both those who are bullied and those who do the bullying are at increased risk for a variety of mental health problems including depression and suicide.[43] Schools that foster a climate that protects sexual minority youth are associated with lower risk for suicide among students.[44] Schools that are particularly high-achieving and competitive can foster a culture that increases mental health risks for all students.[45]

The point of these examples is to highlight the linkages between mental health and other sectors and how experiences in one sector are associated with potential disparities in mental health problems and services. It's important to identify these disparities in order to address them and move closer to the ideal goal of delivering services based on need as opposed to demographic or socioeconomic factors.

Workforce Diversity and Representation

Like most industries and service sectors, the mental health workforce faces challenges in achieving full representation of the diversity of the US population. While there are variations across disciplines, overall Whites and women are overrepresented in the mental health workforce relative to their proportion of the population. In general, the workforce is becoming more diverse; but there is still underrepresentation of males, providers of color, sexual minority individuals, as well as individuals with disabilities. A fully representative, diverse workforce would likely reduce some of the service use disparities. Many potential clients indicate that they would prefer to see a provider who shares some of their own demographic characteristics or at least to visit an agency that reflects diversity in staff and is located in their community.

So what does the mental health workforce look like? A 2017 national report[46] confirms that women are significantly overrepresented compared to their proportion in the population; 75% of master's-level providers and 70% of doctorate-level providers are women. If you are a male who is interested in this career path, I can assure you that graduate programs are motivated to recruit well-qualified males to reduce this disparity.

Regarding racial and ethnic representation, among master's-level providers, Latinx, Asians, and Native American/Alaska Natives are underrepresented, whereas all groups of color are underrepresented among doctorate-level providers. Across disciplines, the largest representation of providers of color is in social work.

There are a variety of efforts to recruit and retain people of color into each of the mental health disciplines. The next section lists resources for each discipline that provide scholarships and other professional development supports targeting students from underrepresented minorities. If you are a student of color or you have fluent second language skills and cross-cultural experiences, please know that many graduate programs are highly motivated to diversify their student body, and they will welcome your prospective interest. If you don't perceive that welcoming attitude or don't see signs of commitment to diversity, equity, and inclusion ideals, I encourage you to keep exploring programs to find those that do embrace these ideals and offer specific supports (as described in the next section). You will find welcoming programs.

The representation of LGBTQ+ providers is not reported in national data, so I can't offer conclusive evidence about whether such individuals are underrepresented in the workforce. However, given that stigma, discrimination, and historic criminalization of LGBTQ+ individuals are associated with significantly higher rates of need for mental health services, there is a great need for providers who are well trained to serve this diverse community, whether they are motivated by academic interest, personal experience, or as well-informed allies. Most graduate programs recognize this need, so the advice I gave with regard to looking for programs that promote values of diversity, equity, and inclusion applies to LGBTQ+ individuals as well.

I do not have data on the representation of therapists with different types of disabilities. However, I can offer anecdotal evidence. I've been fortunate to work with extraordinary trainees who have physical, neurological, psychiatric, hearing, and vision challenges. All of these individuals brought unique perspectives on empathy, adaptation, and resilience to their work. They also served as inspiring role models for clients. Some had to advocate for necessary accommodations, and I imagine this was tiring (both literally and figuratively). I appreciate their perseverance and hope that with each experience our institutions become more accommodating. As a specific aside, there is a particular need for more mental health professionals with proficiency in sign language to meet the needs of those with hearing challenges.

Finally, regarding representation by age, the average age of counselors and social workers is about 42 years, and the average age of psychologists is 46.[47] Mental health professionals tend to retire later than people in many other professions. For example, in a report of retirement age by job type, psychologists were listed in the top 10 occupations for later retirement age, with a significant percentage working beyond age 66.[48] I speculate that this is due to multiple factors, including the fact that the educational path is long before people even start their professional careers, the job is less physically taxing than many others, and it is particularly fulfilling.

As I noted in the Introduction, trainees enter this field at different ages. In my experience, roughly half of all trainees enter directly after completing their undergraduate education. Among the other half, there is a wide range, from those who take just 1–2 years away from college to those who have been away for decades, sometimes in a different career or raising a family. Whatever your particular age, know that you will likely find people in a graduate program who are in a similar developmental stage. You will benefit from attending a graduate program with a diverse group of students, in terms of life experiences and cultural backgrounds.

Resources to Support Diversity, Equity, and Inclusion in Mental Healthcare Training

Most graduate programs and professional organizations are sincerely committed to increasing the diversity of the mental health workforce. This motivation is driven by both a recognition of the inherent value of diverse perspectives and experiences as well as the practical value of meeting the mental health needs of a diverse population. However, I understand that good intentions need to be backed up by actions and resource allocation. So what resources have been committed to building diversity in graduate education for mental health professionals?

There are a variety of resources across disciplines for students who represent different minority groups. Some offer scholarships; others offer dedicated mentorships or workshops and institutes. Individual universities also usually have their own unique scholarship or assistantship programs where students from underrepresented minority groups may have priority.

Each professional organization for the different mental health disciplines has scholarship and professional development opportunities for students from racial–ethnic minority backgrounds, as listed here:

Counseling: National Board for Certified Counselors Minority Fellows Program (www.nbcc.org/advocacy/mfp)

Marital and Family Therapy: American Association for Marriage and Family Therapy Minority Fellows Program (blog.aamft.org/minority-fellowship-program)

Social Work: Council on Social Work Education Minority Fellowship Program (www.cswe.org/Centers-Initiatives/Initiatives/Minority-Fellowship-Program.aspx)

Psychology: American Psychological Association Minority Fellowship Program (www.apa.org/pi/mfp)

Psychiatry: Substance Abuse and Mental Health Services Administration (SAMHSA) Minority Fellowship (www.psychiatry.org/residents-medical-students/residents/fellowships/available-apa-apaf-fellowships/samhsa-minority-fellowship)

Psychiatric Nursing: SAMHSA Minority Fellowship (apply.emfp.org)

In addition, the federal Health Resources and Services Administration (HRSA) funds behavioral health workforce education and training and opioid workforce expansion program grants for dozens of universities across the country. Universities compete for these grants that provide stipends to students and training enhancements to graduate programs. HRSA has also funded grants to universities for scholarships to disadvantaged students pursuing mental health practice degrees. Be sure to inquire about these opportunities in programs you are exploring.

The National Health Service Corps (part of HRSA) offers scholarships and student loan repayment assistance for mental healthcare providers who commit to working in underserved areas or with underserved clients. These resources are open to trainees from any accredited programs. All of these federal investments are designed to improve recruitment and retention of graduate students from diverse backgrounds and those who are committed to serving underserved communities.

There are also many different advocacy organizations for individuals who identify with specific groups, such as LGBTQ+, ability, and spiritual affiliations, within and across mental health disciplines. It may take a bit of searching, but you can find these advocacy organizations online, such as the National Latinx Psychological Association (www.nlpa.ws), the National Association of Black Counselors (www.nabcounselors.org), the Facebook group Black Men in Social Work (www.facebook.com/groups/BlackMeninSocialWork), and GLMA: Health Professionals Advancing LGBT Equality (www.glma.org). These are just a few examples. I urge you to find affiliation groups that can offer professional resources and support.

In Conclusion

As I noted in the beginning of this chapter, the topics of diversity, equity, and inclusion are prominent in our society and in most mental health training programs. Depending on your own background or educational focus, the examples of inequities and discrimination that I've highlighted may be well known to you or, alternatively, eye-opening. It's important to remember that we all are in different phases of reckoning with historical forces that have shaped current injustices, inequities, and disparities. No matter how much awareness we've gained, however, we need to remain open to new perspectives. We also need to translate awareness into action by holding ourselves accountable to ideals of justice and equity. As I've mentioned, this is a work in progress for me and many others I know. I hope to have sparked or reinforced your own motivation to grapple with these complex and critically important topics.

> Inviting historically traumatized, marginalized, and under-resourced community members to collaborate with us in addressing unmet needs brings hope, healing and transformation to all of us. This is the "magic" of psychotherapy. (Ana, professor)

9

Preparing for Success in Graduate School

> What surprised me most about grad school was not how much reading or writing there is, which there is a good amount of, but actually how much my genuine interest in what we discuss carries me through all the work. It feels so different from undergrad where the focus was much broader and not always so compelling. (Diana, graduate student therapist)

This chapter is designed to prepare you for success in graduate school. I'll highlight how graduate school is different from undergraduate and encourage you to shift your approach to education accordingly. I'll also preview course topics you can expect and suggest how to prepare for them if the topics are unfamiliar to you. Finally, I'll describe what to look for in terms of practicum experiences and how to maximize the career benefits of these opportunities.

Making the Shift to Graduate School

If you are thinking that graduate school is going to be an extension of your undergraduate experience, I'm going to challenge you to shift that mindset so that you can really capitalize on your graduate education. Graduate school is qualitatively different because it is focused on your professional training, which is much broader than an exclusive focus on academic achievement. The purpose of graduate school is to build your knowledge, skills, personal awareness, and professional network to launch your career. Academic coursework is certainly one part of this professional training, but personal development, practical training, and networking are equally important. The purpose of this section is to help you make this important shift to thinking about graduate school as the foundation for your professional career.

In order to be a competitive applicant for graduate programs, you need to focus on your grade point average (GPA) as an undergraduate. This means paying lots of attention to each course's grading criteria, assignments, and exams. Your attention to grades is essential not only for earning your undergraduate degree but in order to demonstrate that you have the academic ability to succeed in graduate school. Good grades reflect more than just acquired knowledge; they reflect a strong work ethic and organizational skills.

Once you enter graduate school, I'm suggesting that you shift your attention away from grades as your major focus and toward a focus on learning and professional development. Are you surprised to read this advice from a professor? My colleagues may be concerned about my statement, but I feel strongly that graduate professional training is about so much more than your GPA. I've met too many graduate students who do not make this mindset shift, and consequently, they do not capitalize on the full professional training benefits of graduate school. They remain overly preoccupied with each course's grading criteria, unnecessarily stressed about the difference between an A and an A– as if that will determine their career success. A sole preoccupation with grades can prevent a more rewarding, well-rounded professional training experience in graduate school.

Before I risk getting fired as a professor, please note that I'm not advocating for you to slack off of your study skills or disregard course assignments. Grades in graduate school do matter, and you will benefit from positive professional relationships with your instructors, which depend in part on your engagement and performance in their courses. I'm just urging you to keep grades in perspective and not allow them to obscure the other critical aspects of professional training.

Your GPA is not likely to be the crucial link to a job opening, but a positive relationship with a clinical supervisor in your community may be that link to a desired job. Graduate school is the beginning of your professional networking. Remember that your fellow students and instructors are likely to be professional colleagues when you complete your training. Faculty members, clinical supervisors, and peers will share potential job opportunities and referrals for clients with you.

It's all, once again, about balance. Yes, you want to learn as much as you can from your classes and apply that knowledge to course assignments, exams, and, ultimately, practice. But you also need to attend to the enriching personal development opportunities where you'll gain the maturity and self-awareness that are critical for a therapist. You'll find that most graduate programs push you to challenge some of your biases and stretch your preconceived opinions to work effectively with people from diverse backgrounds. This can be hard work; but it is absolutely essential, and it is not necessarily reflected in your GPA.

What are some other ways in which graduate school differs from undergraduate? There are often practical differences in how courses are delivered. Graduate courses tend to meet fewer times per week. But there will be more reading, writing, and other project-based work outside of class time. You may encounter more collaborative assignments, working in partnership with other students to prepare you for collaborative work in the field. As noted previously, your courses will likely be smaller, which builds a higher expectation for discussion. You will be expected to participate actively in debates and in role-playing learning experiences. You may also find that there is a stronger emphasis on sharing your personal or family experiences with classmates when relevant to the academic content. I encourage you to seek out opportunities for more in-depth discussions with faculty members outside of class too, during office hours or as part of any extracurricular group events or meetings. Students have often told me that the extracurricular opportunities, in honors clubs, in affinity groups, or in global travel courses, are the most meaningful of their training. These types of opportunities help you feel more connected to your fellow students, and that peer support is essential in graduate school.

Social life in graduate school also differs from undergraduate. Graduate students are not as likely to live on campus, for example. And they often have busy lives outside of school with family or work obligations. There may be fewer built-in opportunities to make friends compared to your undergraduate experience. However, you will find many students who want to connect to study or socialize. Students often use social networking apps such as WhatsApp or GroupMe to connect for social and academic purposes. So while there is not the same built-in social scene as in undergraduate years, you can build your own social network to fit your own individual needs. Many students form lifelong friendships. Needless to say, it's particularly valuable to have a group of peers who can understand the stress of grad school and support each other.

Regardless of what type of student you were as an undergraduate, whether you were passionately involved in extracurricular activities, buried in books all the time, working to pay the bills, or partying, you'll have an opportunity to reset your student identity in graduate school. My advice is to get involved in clubs or activities that foster friendships, fun, or meaningful connections that expand your horizons. Consider a volunteer position if you have any spare time and the luxury to gain experience without getting paid. Or look for on-campus employment opportunities as a graduate assistant or research assistant. These are particularly important if you want to pursue doctoral studies. Like most things, graduate school will be most rewarding if you push yourself to fully explore and engage in a range of opportunities.

Course Topics

In this section, I'll describe the array of course topics usually included in mental health graduate programs. There will certainly be variability in course requirements across disciplines, degree programs (master's vs. doctoral), and accreditation status; but there is actually a great deal of overlap given that these topics are considered essential for all mental health professionals. Please note that my list of common course topics is not a prescriptive list of courses that programs must include but rather an overview of topics likely to be found in graduate programs. I've based this list on my knowledge of multiple programs, as well as an online review I conducted examining curricula in multiple programs across disciplines in the United States.

I've listed the foundational courses first, followed by courses that are more specialized. Note that even if you've taken courses on the same topic as an undergraduate, you will likely need to take the graduate-level course since it will be more advanced and more specifically targeted to your degree program. For each topic, I offer a rationale for why the topic is important to mental health training and suggest how you can become more familiar with it if it is new to you. I also give examples of some variations you may encounter.

Foundational Courses

Human Development Across the Lifespan

This type of course addresses normative development from birth through death. The course may cover a range of types of human development including cognitive, social, emotional, moral, career, personality, sexual, and physical development. It will likely emphasize key developmental challenges at different life stages and may highlight how these challenges can be affected by other identity variables, such as gender, race and ethnicity, sexual orientation, socioeconomic status, family composition, ability, or health challenges.

Gaining knowledge about normative human development is critical. You need to know the normal range of behavior at a particular life stage in order to accurately evaluate if someone's behavior is outside the norm. This is perhaps most important during the rapid developmental stages of childhood and adolescence. Weekly tantrums in public should be evaluated very differently for a 2-year-old compared to an 8-year-old. Examples later in life may be more subtle but are important too. For example, lack of motivation to work should be interpreted differently for a 25-year-old compared to a 75-year-old.

One of the important roles of a therapist is to help educate clients or family members about normative developmental expectations. You might be surprised how often parents have unrealistic developmental expectations for their children's behavior and how much conflict this can cause a family. Think about a mother who is worried that her 3-year-old daughter is developmentally delayed because she doesn't always dress herself appropriately for the weather and the social context. (If you've spent time with any 3-year-olds, you've likely noticed that they tend to have creative fashion choices, and the weather forecast is rarely a factor.) I've also met parents who are angry if their adolescent seeks greater privacy by locking a bathroom or bedroom door. I've had to discuss why this is actually a healthy developmental expectation as opposed to a problem. Having a good understanding of this normative developmental shift is important for helping families navigate the tensions that often arise as adolescents seek greater independence.

Many students will have the necessary baseline familiarity with human development from their undergraduate education. (Although I understand you may be worried that you've forgotten everything, but the important concepts will likely come back.) For each of the course topics mentioned in this chapter, it's important to understand that you are not expected to have mastered the details prior to entering graduate school. Just having some basic familiarity with the topic will help you to learn more detailed information when you take a graduate course. If human development concepts are completely new to you, consider doing some web browsing. You could read a bit about a few of the major theorists, such as Jean Piaget, Sigmund Freud, Erik Erikson, Albert Bandura, Lawrence Kohlberg, Carol Gilligan, John Bowlby, or Urie Bronfenbrenner. Again, you do not need to know details prior to entering graduate school, but introductory familiarity with some of these theorists will help.

Variations

Many programs will have a devoted course in child and adolescent development, given how much there is to cover in these life stages. Likewise, with increasing recognition of the mental health needs of older adults, some programs have added courses devoted to aging or geriatric issues. In addition, you may see courses devoted to specific domains of development, such as a specific course on cognitive or personality development.

Multicultural Issues/Diversity and Inclusion

Most programs will have a course devoted to multi- or cross-cultural issues, diversity, and/or inclusion. These courses are designed to raise your awareness of how culture impacts all aspects of our lives. While discussions of race and ethnicity will be prominent in such courses, other types of diversity are likely to be addressed, including socioeconomic status, gender identity, sexual orientation, ability, and spirituality. These courses sometimes stretch you beyond your comfort zone and can be challenging for some students. As uncomfortable as it might feel sometimes, stretching beyond one's comfort zone is essential to prepare you to work with diverse clients.

As I emphasized in the last chapter, mental health professionals need to work with individuals who come from a wide variety of backgrounds and embrace different identities and value systems. Therapists need to gain self-awareness of how their own life experiences and identity have shaped them. They also need to work continually to recognize their own conscious and unconscious biases. Exercises in classes like this will challenge you to recognize your own biases in your journey to gain deeper self-awareness. The most important preparation for a course like this is to be mindful of your own background and how it affects you and to be open and curious about learning from others.

Variations

Some programs may have specialization tracks for specific cultural groups, with corresponding courses devoted to Latinx, African American, Asian American/Pacific Islander, or Native American communities or to the LGBTQ+ community, for example.

Theories of Counseling or Psychotherapy

These types of survey courses provide an overview of the major theoretical orientations in mental healthcare. You'll learn about theories including psychodynamic, behavioral and cognitive-behavioral, family systems, humanistic, narrative, postmodern, feminist, and integrative theories. You'll be introduced to specific subtheories within these broad categories as well; for example, there are multiple variations on psychodynamic and family systems theories. You'll also gain a historical perspective about how psychotherapy approaches have evolved over time, and you'll learn about some of the founding fathers and mothers in the field.

Most students who enter a graduate mental health program have some basic knowledge about a few of these theories through undergraduate coursework or explorations in the field. You will not be expected to have deep, comprehensive knowledge when you enter graduate school; but if you don't have a clue about the basic differences between psychodynamic, behavioral, and family systems theories, for example, I urge you to do some preliminary independent research. It will be much easier to learn details if you have some basic familiarity with the big theories in advance.

Theory courses provide the essential foundation for understanding how and why psychotherapy works. You'll be able to compare and contrast theories to determine which ones resonate most strongly for you. As you progress in graduate school, you'll be encouraged to choose a theoretical orientation that you rely upon to guide your work. In practicum and job interviews, you may even be asked to identify your preferred theoretical orientation and to explain why you chose it. Yes, that means this is a critical course for your career advancement.

Variations

Most graduate programs offer comprehensive coverage of multiple theories, but specific programs may emphasize some over others. For example, marital/couples and family therapy (MFT or CFT) programs will emphasize family systems theories and thus devote courses to in-depth learning of different subtheories within this orientation. You'll still learn about other theories, but the emphasis will be on family systems. Likewise, some, but not all, psychology programs emphasize cognitive-behavioral theory. Be sure to investigate whether there is a particular emphasis in programs before applying so that you'll know if the program is a good fit for your interests.

Psychopathology

Some people who pursue a mental health career were originally hooked in college while taking a course in abnormal psychology. I confess that this course, describing different mental health problems and how they develop, was definitely a major draw for me. Even if you took such a class as an undergraduate, you will take a more advanced version as a graduate student. You'll learn about the *Diagnostic and Statistical Manual*[1] (DSM) and the specific symptoms that characterize major psychiatric disorders. If you are unfamiliar with the DSM, I suggest you take a look at it prior to graduate school to familiarize yourself with the general concept of psychiatric diagnoses. Having some general familiarity will help when you need to learn details about specific diagnoses in graduate school.

In addition to reviewing diagnoses and their symptom criteria, a psychopathology course should help you to understand how mental health problems develop; namely, what are the causes? Learning about what causes or exacerbates mental health problems is essential for identifying how to intervene to help. Knowledge about causes is complex and always evolving. You'll learn about a range of factors as varied as sociodemographics, family experiences, trauma, thought processes, brain chemistry, and genetics. Appreciating all these diverse factors can be described as taking a comprehensive *biopsychosocial* approach to mental health.

Variations

Many graduate programs have a specialized course in developmental psychopathology focused on how mental health problems develop in childhood and adolescence. This is important because the majority of mental health problems emerge prior to adulthood.[2] Some programs, particularly psychology and psychiatry, may also infuse neuroscience content into a psychopathology course; or they may have a separate neuroscience course focused on learning about brain structure and function.

Research Methods

The majority of students entering master's-degree programs in counseling, MFT/CFT, and social work want to devote their careers to practice as opposed to research. I've met many students who are less than thrilled to learn that they need to take a research methods course to earn their master's degree. If this sounds like you, please keep an open mind. The goal is not to train you for a career as a researcher but rather to teach you how to be an informed consumer of research. This is essential if you are going to be an effective mental health professional who delivers evidence-based practice (more on this in Chapter 12).

Research methods courses in master's-degree programs are designed to help you evaluate and interpret research designs and research findings so that you can apply this knowledge to practice. You'll learn about the importance of reliability and validity in measurement, concepts that are directly relevant to accurately assessing clients' difficulties. And you'll learn how to evaluate the effectiveness of mental health interventions. In fact, sometimes these courses are called "program evaluation" to emphasize the focus on evaluating outcomes of interventions. In addition, there is a lot of evidence demonstrating that when therapists use valid measures to track their clients' progress in therapy, clients show greater improvement.[3]

A research methods course will help you sort through the voluminous scientific literature more efficiently. Technological innovations (e.g., Google, and digital university library catalogs) have made it relatively easy to find research articles, but how do you judge the credibility of the research? Or the relevance to your specific question? What about the ethical implications? Or attention to diversity implications? A good research methods course will address these questions and provide guidelines for sorting through research more efficiently, preparing you for lifelong learning as a therapist.

If you are entering a doctoral program, you will definitely have more research courses, including advanced courses in research design and statistics. Some programs may also have courses in qualitative data collection and analysis. In fact, one of the biggest differences between master's and doctoral programs is the approach to research training. In a doctoral program you are being trained to conduct research in addition to training in how to be an informed consumer of research.

Variations

Some research methods courses at the master's-degree level may require you to come up with a proposal for a research project, and you may or may not be expected to actually collect the proposed data and complete the project. Sometimes just coming up with a proposal is sufficient for learning about research ideas and designs. Also, some programs require or offer an option to complete a master's thesis. A thesis project may be a field-based research project or a literature review project. Depending on your own motivation to pursue research, be sure to investigate the research project expectations when you are applying.

Gaining experience with research or program evaluation can also enhance your job qualifications. I've known many students who proudly talked about their research project in a job interview, and they felt that this distinguished them from other candidates. I believe that participating in a research project is incredibly valuable for your career even if you don't want to be a researcher. It helps you to learn to ask good questions and follow a disciplined plan to answer them. These are great skills to gain no matter what your career direction.

Laws and Ethics

Every mental health graduate program that I'm aware of includes a course on that particular discipline's laws and ethical codes. Some programs combine this with an orientation to the discipline. Such a course will delve more deeply into the types of issues raised in Chapter 7, including the risks of dual relationships, the importance of confidentiality and when it can or should be broken, as well as reporting laws for child or elder abuse and homicidality. Additional topics in this type of course may include the scope of practice for particular disciplines, expectations for marketing or advertisement of services, as well as record-keeping and billing. Increasingly, ethical issues in technology use are also being addressed.

I probably don't have to persuade you about the importance of this course. We all want to be ethical providers. But there are practical implications as well. Most states require you to pass an exam on laws and ethics to get licensed. Violations of laws and ethics also carry serious consequences throughout your career. So take good notes in this course; you'll be returning to them often.

Variations

The specifics of a law and ethics course will differ according to each discipline's ethical codes, but there is a lot of overlap across disciplines. Also, some programs combine a law and ethics course with forensic topics and/or risk assessment for issues such as suicide. As I mentioned in Chapter 7, some students can find these topics somewhat daunting without any introduction. Browsing through your chosen discipline's ethical codes, which are available online, will be good preparation. But you do not need to memorize details until you take the course.

Introductory Counseling Skills

Most programs across disciplines will have an introductory course on basic counseling skills. This course may have different titles, such as Helping Skills, Clinical Interviewing, or Basic Psychotherapy Skills. In such a course you will learn how to build a strong therapeutic alliance with diverse clients by using reflective listening skills and open-ended, exploratory questioning. This important course is designed to give you the foundational skills for all types of therapy and counseling.

Most students love this course because it is often their first hands-on experience practicing in the role of therapist. Courses like this usually rely on active role-playing exercises, which may include recording yourself practicing these skills with peers and then reflecting on how you can improve. The recording and feedback from peers and instructors can feel intimidating, but it's really important to be non-defensive and open to improvement. This is the type of course where you may get to know your fellow students in a deeper way and where you can all support each other in this journey.

Given that this is a skill-building course, it's not necessarily one that you can study for in advance, like a theories course. However, you might find it useful to explore psychotherapy demonstration videos online, where you will find a diverse array of therapeutic styles. If you do seek out such examples, I urge you to look at lots of different types so that you can get a sense of variation as opposed to simply following one specific example. The same advice goes for following the style of a therapist you have seen as a client. It's great to have a respected model in your mind but also important to seek out a variety of examples. Remember that each therapist develops their own unique style based on their particular strengths as well as preferred theoretical orientation.

Variations

An introductory skills course may or may not coincide with your first practicum experience. Some programs start students early with limited practicum responsibilities such as conducting intake interviews or practicing co-therapy with an experienced clinician. There are many variations to the sequencing of practice training.

Programs also vary in the specificity of skill-building courses. You may have separate courses for building group counseling skills versus individual versus family and couple skills. Some programs with a child focus may offer a specific course addressing alliance-building with children. Alternatively, all modalities may be included in a comprehensive course. This will depend on the emphasis of your program.

Advanced or Specialized Courses

The course topics listed in this section are more advanced or specialized. I will not provide as much detail about these courses because you will not be expected to have background preparation when you enter graduate school. In many ways, the foundational topics I've just described provide the necessary background for these more advanced courses.

I am providing a brief summary of these course topics so that you can test your assumptions about what you'll be learning in graduate school. It is my hope that this preview will boost your motivation to pursue the work of getting into graduate school.

Assessment or Psychological Testing

An assessment course will teach you how to use valid and reliable measures of mental health. You'll learn about questionnaires and scales that help with diagnosing mental health problems, personality strengths, behavior patterns, relationship patterns, and other psychological phenomena. Such a course will introduce you to a wide variety of assessment tools and teach you how to administer them, score them, and interpret a client's responses. You'll also learn about how cultural factors can impact assessment.

Most disciplines will include a course in assessment, but psychology programs will have courses devoted to learning how to administer and interpret psychoeducational tests given that this is an area of emphasis in psychology. If you are particularly interested in psychoeducational testing or neuropsychological testing as a career, the psychology discipline is likely the best fit for you.

Psychotherapy Approaches/Evidence-Based Practices

These courses may be called many different things, but they will all be designed to teach you more about specific psychotherapeutic approaches, including individual, family, couples, and group therapy models. You may have separate courses for each of these modalities. Increasingly, programs are emphasizing training in therapeutic approaches that are supported by strong research evidence; thus, they may label these courses "evidence-based practices." You'll learn more about the importance of evidence-based practices in Chapter 12.

Trauma

Trauma will be a prominent topic in many of your graduate school courses given that trauma and mental health issues are inextricably linked. You'll learn about all sorts of trauma, including child maltreatment, military conflict, relationship, domestic and community violence, as well as natural disasters, medical and brain trauma, and refugee trauma. It's critical for mental health professionals to know the risks of trauma exposure, the impact of trauma on an individual's mental and physical health, and how to work with individuals who have experienced trauma. You may have a specific course devoted to trauma in graduate school, or this topic may be integrated into your other courses. Some programs may have a specific course devoted to child maltreatment, elder abuse, or domestic violence.

Throughout this career journey, you will encounter people who have experienced significant trauma, and this can be emotionally overwhelming. The next chapter addresses the risk of secondary, also known as *vicarious*, trauma for therapists. You'll learn strategies to mitigate this risk. Fortunately, you'll also learn how inspiring it is to work with traumatized individuals, who demonstrate remarkable resilience.

Crisis Assessment and Intervention

Crisis assessment and intervention may be incorporated into a trauma course or a law and ethics class, or it may be offered on its own. You'll learn critical skills, such as how to assess for suicide or homicide risk, how to diffuse a volatile situation with clients, and how to respond when you suspect a client is experiencing current abuse or violence. In a course like this you may also learn psychological first-aid skills to use immediately following a crisis event. It's absolutely essential that you have some background in crisis assessment and intervention before entering practice so that you are prepared for emergencies.

Addictions

Given the high rate of addiction in our society, most programs include a specific course that addresses risk factors for addiction, the mental and physical impact of addiction on individuals, and established treatment approaches. Note that substance abuse will be a prominent topic in such courses, but other types of addiction will likely be addressed as well, including gambling, internet-related addictions, sexual addictions, and food addictions. Even if you do not choose to specialize in working with individuals who are struggling with addiction, you will encounter these struggles among individuals who seek mental health treatment for other problems. There is a high rate of *comorbidity* (i.e., the simultaneous presence of two or more problems) for addiction and other psychiatric disorders.

Human Sexuality

Many programs offer a course devoted to sexuality given that sexuality concerns often arise in therapy. Such a course covers the full range of normative sexual development and sexual expression, as well as types of sexual dysfunction and effective treatment approaches. A course like this may push you to expand your awareness about the diversity in people's experiences, as well as to raise your self-awareness to challenge any biases or blind spots you may have.

Psychopharmacology

Even though psychiatrists and psychiatric nurse practitioners are the only mental health professionals who can prescribe medications, a course on psychopharmacology is often included in other disciplines' requirements. There are important practical reasons for learning about psychopharmacology even if you can't prescribe. As a mental healthcare provider, you will often need to decide if a referral to a medical doctor or nurse practitioner is warranted; it is important for you to know what type of referrals are appropriate. In addition, many clients who are in therapy are on medications, and therapists need to have some understanding of the effects of those medications on their clients. I find that there is a lot of misinformation out there about the effectiveness and potential risks of a variety of psychoactive medications, so a course like this is quite valuable.

Neuroscience

There is considerable variability across programs regarding the emphasis on neuroscience in the curriculum. Some programs do not address neuroscience at all, whereas others have required courses addressing the brain, focusing on the anatomy and biochemical processes and how these relate to behavior, emotions, and cognition. Psychology and psychiatry programs are most likely to have required courses in neuroscience, but they can be found across disciplines. Many psychology programs have courses addressing neuropsychological assessment for issues such as memory, traumatic brain injury, or learning differences.

Prevention or Positive Psychology

While the majority of mental health training focuses on identifying, diagnosing, and treating problems, many trainees are interested in learning more about how to prevent such problems at the outset. There is considerable research on prevention programs that aim to build personal strengths and resiliency to reduce the risk of mental health problems. These types of programs include, for example, social skill-building programs in elementary schools designed to boost all children's social and emotional strengths to reduce risks for depression, anxiety, or substance abuse. For parents, there are positive parenting education programs to reduce risks of child maltreatment, and there are communication skill-building programs for premarital couples.

There is also growing interest in the field of positive psychology that focuses on how to cultivate happiness and fulfillment as opposed to how to identify and treat problems. If this emphasis interests you, look for programs that offer a course in prevention, health promotion, wellness, or positive psychology. These may be programs that incorporate a public health perspective or partner with a school of public health since prevention is a focus of this discipline.

Organizational Systems, Policy, or Advocacy Issues

I've grouped a few topics here that may or may not be combined into a single course. In reviewing curricula across disciplines, I found courses with these labels offered most often in social work but sometimes in other disciplines as well. These topics address big picture issues such as the organizational structure and funding of mental health and social services as well as policy issues that impact service delivery. These are particularly important topics to learn about if you want to pursue a career as an administrative leader of an organization. Some programs also include a course on advocacy, which may include policy advocacy as well as advocacy for individual clients and/or specific communities.

Health Psychology or Integrated Behavioral Healthcare

This is another specialty topic that can be found in some programs. Psychology programs are most likely to have a course in health psychology, but you will find related topics such as medical family therapy or integrated behavioral healthcare in some MFT/CFT programs. These types of courses address the intersection of medical and mental health issues, in terms of how they influence each other and how providers coordinate patient care for both. Some programs offer specialized training in integrated behavioral healthcare, preparing students to work in medical settings in partnership with medical providers. You'll read more about the value of integrated behavioral healthcare in Chapter 13 since it is a growing service delivery model for the future.

Group Dynamics or Group Therapy

Many programs across disciplines devote a course to understanding group dynamics and learning how to lead therapy groups. I've encountered many students who find a group therapy course to be one of their favorites. There are specific models of group therapy to learn and specific skills to gain as a group leader. Some group therapy courses incorporate an experiential component, which is another way to accelerate your own personal growth and self-awareness.

Even though it happened decades ago, I'll never forget an intensive group training workshop I attended in graduate school. It was an immersive 4-day experience involving hours of meetings with a small group of strangers discussing personal issues and getting direct feedback. This group experience gave me a dramatic firsthand introduction to group dynamics such as scapegoating and alliance-building. The raw emotions expressed made an indelible impression on me regarding the power of group dynamics.

Career Counseling

Most counseling programs will have a course addressing career development across the lifespan. It is rare for other disciplines to have a course devoted to career counseling. Such a course covers theories of career development, career resources and the labor market, career assessment and planning, and career counseling. A career development course may also address work–life balance and how to approach this common challenge with clients. If career counseling is a major interest of yours, the counseling discipline is likely the best fit for you.

Computer and Technology Applications for Mental Health

When I reviewed curricula across disciplines for this chapter, I was pleased to find some programs, albeit just a few, offering a course on the use of technology in mental health. As you'll read in Chapter 13, this is a booming topic as there are thousands of mental health apps flooding the digital marketplace, as well as therapeutic virtual reality programs and video games. I think it's great that some graduate programs are offering training on this. While it is rare for a program to devote a full course to this topic, many programs are incorporating it into other classes. I predict that courses addressing uses of technology in mental health will become more common in coming years.

Practicum Training

Practicum training is arguably the most important part of your graduate education. For the vast majority of students, it is both incredibly exciting and somewhat terrifying. As I noted in the Introduction to this book, I vividly remember what it felt like to finally meet with my first client in practicum, after so much classroom learning. I was thrilled, and I was also anxious. Every student I know feels some variation of these emotions when they begin practicum training.

There are multiple terms that are used for this supervised practice training, including *fieldwork*, *internship*, and *residency*; but I'll use the term *practicum* to refer to supervised practice with actual clients (as opposed to role-play practice with peers). The timing and structure of practicum training differ by discipline and degree program, but it is required across all disciplines for graduation and for licensure or certification. There will be specific requirements for the type of mental health practice, the number of hours of practice, and the ratio of hours of practice to hours of clinical supervision, depending on your discipline and licensure path. The next section of the chapter highlights a few things to think about when looking at graduate programs and evaluating how they operate practicum training.

On-site placements Versus Community Placements

Some universities have on-site training clinics serving the university community, and students are required to work in that clinic. Other programs rely exclusively on placement partnerships with clinics, hospitals, or schools in the surrounding community as training sites for students. In doctoral programs, you may have the opportunity to work in both an on-site university training clinic and a community placement. There are advantages and disadvantages to all types of placements, and these are factors to consider as you explore graduate programs. Most programs will provide lists of their practicum sites; check to see if they offer sites of interest to you.

Finding Your Own Placement Versus Program-Facilitated Placements

This is a particularly consequential distinction I urge you to investigate. Some graduate programs require you to find your own practicum placement and make all the necessary arrangements for clinical supervision and meeting the required hours.

Other programs will facilitate your placement into one from a set of preselected practicum placements with which the program has partnered previously. These preselected practicum placements have been vetted, assuring that they meet program standards for training quality and clinical supervision expertise.

Having to seek out your own practicum placement is often difficult and may result in a poor training experience. However, it is not impossible, and many students succeed despite the challenges. But I believe it is far preferable to have placements facilitated by the program. It is very important to have a placement where staff members are familiar with trainees' needs and requirements. Even if you feel like the preselected options are not necessarily the perfect fit for the population you want to work with, it will be more important to have a quality training experience than it will be to work with a narrowly defined specific population.

The Importance of Clinical Supervision

Clinical supervision is perhaps the most important part of graduate and postgraduate training. Learning how to use clinical supervision effectively, without defensiveness, is essential. If you are particularly sensitive to critical feedback, you'll need to work on that because the purpose of supervision is to critically review your practice and to provide constructive feedback—often in a group setting. High-quality supervision requires that you share video or audio recordings of your practice (with client consent). This can be intimidating, but remember that you are not alone. Most of us are anxious about sharing our work on video. After decades of doing this, I still cringe when I see how many times I say "um" or begin sentences without finishing them. But I also appreciate that I need to get direct feedback to improve my skills. Therapy is a very private experience, and there are limited opportunities for others to observe your work in this career, so it's critical to be open to supervision feedback when you have it.

Another challenging aspect of clinical supervision is the fact that you'll likely have supervisors who give you somewhat contradictory advice. I remember when I had one supervisor who told me I shouldn't ask so many questions of a client and another who kept suggesting more questions I should ask. Sometimes I got tied up in knots about this contradictory feedback. No doubt, this can be frustrating when you are a beginner looking for instructions about what to do. But, over time, you'll see that it is actually valuable to get multiple perspectives, to recognize that there are multiple options for delivering effective care. As you advance in your career you'll figure out how you want to incorporate different aspects of each supervisor's feedback as you craft your own therapeutic style.

I believe the quality of supervision in training is more important than the specifics of the clinical population or type of setting in which you are working. I know students who select a practicum placement because they are passionate about the particular clinical population regardless of the quality of clinical supervision. While

I understand that choice, these students I've known have sometimes regretted it. There will be plenty of time in your career to seek experience with a specific clinical population; but your graduate training is one of the few times you'll have the luxury of intensive clinical supervision from experts, and you want to have supervisors you respect.

How do you judge the quality of the supervision offered at a site? First of all, ask students who have worked with the supervisors about their experience. Don't assume that a critical supervisor is a bad supervisor; you'll learn more from someone who pushes you to improve than you will from someone who offers only a smile and a pat on the back. Ask if supervisors review video or audio recordings of practice—as I've noted, this is a key element of good supervision. Try to find out if the supervisor is someone who enjoys teaching or not. This may be apparent in an interview. Does the supervisor seem interested in your interests? Do they speak fondly about previous trainees and their accomplishments? If a supervisor isn't keen on supervising, they may resent the time it takes and do a cursory job. Organizations that value training provide support to supervisors such as reducing their required clinical service hours as compensation. This fosters an investment in quality supervision.

Professional Networking Opportunities

Your practicum placement is important as the launch of your professional career. You'll make connections to peers, staff, and supervisors that may open doors to job opportunities. Remember that you are building your professional reputation beginning with an initial interview at a site. Be aware of the impressions you are making from day 1. It's common to be anxious when you first start practicing, but managing this anxiety is really important for building a strong professional identity. Remember that conscientious work habits are as important as stellar clinical skills, so completing paperwork details and being on time to meetings matter, as does building strong therapeutic relationships with diverse clients. Ethical practice is also imperative. Beginning your practicum training can feel overwhelming because of all these new responsibilities, but you won't be alone.

> I feel lucky to have met several close friends in my cohort. I can tell them how I really feel—sometimes totally overwhelmed—and they get it. (Anonymous, graduate student therapist)

In Conclusion

Since you are still reading this book after the initial chapters designed to help you determine if this career path is a good fit for you, I'm going to assume you are either already "all in" or at least leaning strongly in that direction. I hope this chapter helped to solidify your decision by previewing what to expect in graduate school. If you find yourself intrigued by the course topics and practicum training, that's a great sign. If none of the course topics spark your interest, you may need to re-evaluate or look into other helping professions outside of mental health.

This chapter provided suggestions to help you prepare for an optimal graduate school experience. Graduate school provides unique and life-changing opportunities for personal and professional growth. It is also a significant investment of time, money, and energy. My goal is for every student to derive maximum benefits from that investment.

10

Occupational Hazards and How to Manage Them

> I've had really challenging days when I see many clients who are in extreme distress and I do not have time to process what I have just experienced. . . . If you want to become a therapist, ask yourself, do you have supports in your life—supportive people, good self-care, etc.—to ensure that you will stay emotionally stable while surrounded by emotional chaos? (Marcia, therapist in schools and private practice)

Being a therapist is an amazing privilege and a weighty responsibility. This chapter addresses some hard truths by highlighting occupational hazards. You'll learn about the risks of career burnout due to the stress of being a therapist. I'll discuss related challenges such as compassion fatigue, secondary traumatic stress, and vicarious traumatization. And while this may sound discouraging, rest assured that I will also share proven strategies to prevent or minimize the symptoms of burnout. The goal is for you to have realistic expectations and to be well equipped to protect yourself from the harmful effects of these occupational hazards.

You'll learn about the importance of peer support, self-care, and self-compassion. In addition, I'll suggest ways that you can gain essential self-awareness as a necessary foundation for this career journey. You'll learn why many practicing therapists urge you to do your own work in therapy before becoming a therapist. Finally, I'll end by offering an optimistic note about the potential for rewarding experiences of vicarious resilience and compassion satisfaction to counterbalance the risks of vicarious traumatization and compassion fatigue.

Sources of Stress for Therapists

Every career brings its own unique rewards, to be sure, but also its own types of stress, whether it is physical, intellectual, interpersonal, or emotional. A mental health career can be particularly emotionally stressful. To do this job well, mental health professionals need to tap into their own psychological resources, namely, compassion, empathy, and resilience. The strengths that draw many people to this career, such as the ability to empathize with other people's pain, are exactly the characteristics that place us at risk for stress and burnout. In other words, our work requires us to be good at feeling others' pain, but this very skill is what can also weigh heavily on us. This is a tricky balance: We must be genuinely and deeply empathic toward our clients but not so much so that we become overwhelmed by these feelings.

In this section I'll describe major sources of stress for therapists. I've adapted much of this from the book *On Being a Therapist*[1] by Dr. Jeffrey Kottler.

Client-Associated Stress

Therapists are often witnessing and experiencing high levels of emotional arousal. We empathize with our clients' intense emotions, which can include anger, despair, panic, hate, suicidal thoughts, violent urges, etc. Clients also share distressing traumatic experiences with their therapist, who soaks in all these stories and images. Therapists need to remain calm and model the ability to manage intense emotions that clients may express.

Worrying about our clients' well-being also adds stress, as Carolyn articulates so well here:

> The most challenging part is worrying about patients who are potentially suicidal. I really lose sleep over this. I work hard to keep my patients from seeing this anxiety as it is best to keep suicide from taking on too much meaning in the context of the therapeutic relationship. (Carolyn, professor and therapist in a hospital)

When we are worried about our clients' safety, we may feel like we need to be available to them all the time. Most of us understand intellectually that it is unreasonable and unhealthy to be available to clients 24 hours a day. Most agencies and treatment centers have emergency on-call procedures, with clinicians sharing coverage responsibilities. We're taught to communicate the boundaries of our availability by phone, text, or email so that clients have clear expectations at the outset of therapy. All this makes good sense; but when you are worried about someone, it's not always easy to enforce those limits, and enforcing the limits can be stressful too. In your graduate training, you'll hear a lot about boundary-setting, why it's so important and how to practice it.

> One of the major challenges is turning off the work day. Clients reach out at all hours of the day, all days of the week. It is not always necessary to respond immediately but it is difficult to learn boundaries. This is only getting worse over time with more technological access to therapists via text, email, etc. (Mary, professor and therapist in private practice)

Work Environment Stress

This type of stress includes the administrative and financial pressures I addressed in Chapter 6, such as burdensome paperwork requirements or productivity demands for billable hours. Many therapists report that these types of pressures add more to their stress than the client-associated factors. And even though one would like to think that mental health professionals are all wonderfully collaborative, unfortunately, mental health organizations, schools, and hospitals can have the same petty work politics and occasional poor leadership as all other workplaces. While the vast majority of people I've met in this field are wonderful colleagues, I've certainly experienced frustrations ranging from trivial squabbles over procedures to bigger concerns about inequities and unethical behavior in organizations. These work environment issues are not unique to mental health contexts but can definitely contribute to therapist stress.

> The biggest challenges include intense productivity demands, lack of appreciation for seasoned staff and supervisors, uninformed and clueless management practices and leadership. (Barry, therapist and clinical supervisor)

Event-Related Stress

Therapists may face unexpected life events outside of their work roles that can dramatically impact their overall stress. These could be personal or family health challenges, other family transitions (marriage, divorce, etc.), financial crises, or even global pandemics! (Prior to 2020, that would have sounded like science fiction to me.)

For example, a major life event, even a positive one such as having a baby, can be very disruptive and leave a therapist with limited emotional or physical resources to manage common client- or work-related challenges. I have many colleagues who struggled with returning to work after welcoming a new child. I can still picture one incredibly competent young colleague crying in her office, totally depleted by lack of sleep plus the complicated feelings of placing her infant in child care. I remember similar stress when I became a parent. Likewise, when my mother was struggling with a terminal illness, it was extremely difficult to devote the needed emotional and physical energy to my work in between taking her to chemotherapy appointments. Not surprisingly, research suggests that therapists are at increased risk for major stress and career burnout if they are experiencing a life event or personal or family challenge.[2]

Internal Personal Stress

This type of stress includes psychological stress such as excessive self-doubt, mental health or addiction challenges, or an inability to take care of oneself. In addition to the stress of a mental health or addiction problem itself, a therapist may experience the compounded stress of feeling like a hypocrite for succumbing to behaviors that they help others to avoid.

Some internal stress and self-doubt is normal. Many therapists experience the *imposter syndrome*, where they feel like a fraud when others are looking to them for expertise. I have certainly had this feeling at times throughout my career—often when my professional and personal lives overlap a bit. For example, when I wasn't able to offer effective assistance to a friend who struggled with a painful parenting challenge, I felt both personally and professionally inadequate. At other times it's been more comical, such as when my daughter was very young. Given that I'm supposed to have some expertise in child mental health and behavior, it was slightly embarrassing when my own child behaved in normal but not particularly flattering ways, like refusing to join a preschool activity or having an emotional meltdown at school drop-off. I've joked with other colleagues about this phenomenon. If our own children misbehave, it suggests not just that we're fallible parents but perhaps that our professional skills are lacking as well. Being a parent is a humbling experience, as is being a therapist.

Timing Stress

There are also specific phases of therapy that can be particularly stressful for therapists. For some, this can be at the beginning, when one may feel pressure to have all the answers right away. It is stressful to conduct a thorough and timely assessment and build a good working relationship immediately to ensure that the client will return. For others, myself included, it is the conclusion of therapy that is most challenging. Endings can be difficult for a variety of reasons. Sometimes clients just stop attending, and we may never know why. Other times, there are financial or administrative reasons therapy has to end, even if it is going well. Even planned endings can bring up mixed emotions.

> One of the most challenging issues for me is termination. We develop intimate relationships with our clients, and if we've done our jobs well, this ultimately means saying goodbye. (Jill, therapist in private practice)

As Jill notes, a planned termination of therapy can be emotionally challenging. Therapeutic relationships are very unusual in that they can be intense; and yet they are time-limited, and the end is a definitive end. When we say goodbye to our clients, we do not keep in touch following the completion of our work. At times, I have found it difficult to say goodbye, and I've caught myself wondering how clients are doing many years past our time together. However, I do respect the ethical need for the firm boundary when our therapeutic relationship ends. This is one of the many important ways in which the role of therapist is very different than the role of friend or mentor.

The boundaries around the therapeutic relationship are important to maintain (as discussed in Chapter 7).

Inability to Help Stress

Another source of stress for therapists is the fact that no matter how strong our efforts, therapy will not always be successful. In fact, estimates suggest that about 20% of those who enter psychotherapy will have negative outcomes.[3] It can be demoralizing to recognize the limits of our ability to make a difference for some of our clients. It's possible that it isn't the right time or that the therapeutic relationship just isn't a good fit and the client will have more success with someone else. It's also important to acknowledge that our clients face all kinds of challenges outside of our influence.

> I find it hard to recognize the limits of my role as a therapist. Sometimes, I wish I could do more to create change, but I have also learned (and am still learning) to cultivate acceptance for what I cannot change. (Angela, therapist in a hospital and instructor)

Angela articulates an occupational challenge that I have experienced. At times, I've felt powerless to address some of my clients' needs. For example, I've worked with families who desperately needed stable housing; I have done my best to connect them to resources but have sometimes been unsuccessful. I have felt extremely frustrated in situations like this, knowing that families struggle with essential basic needs that are more consequential than whatever I can offer as a therapist. I know many colleagues who similarly struggle with anger, sadness, and frustration about inequities and injustices our clients often confront. Caroline expresses these sentiments very well:

> It is difficult to witness firsthand the effects of poverty and injustice on individuals' health and to run into barriers helping clients access resources that could vastly improve their health and well-being. (Caroline, professor and therapist)

Burnout

When do the stresses of this career build up to a dangerous level to impair a therapist or make them consider quitting? What are the warning signs that someone is experiencing burnout? Three classic signs have been identified by Christina Maslach,[4] as follows:

> *Emotional exhaustion:* Therapists feel totally psychologically or physically depleted by the perceived demands and needs of their clients, as well as by the demands of their organizations or co-workers. *Depersonalization:* They may develop

cynical, pessimistic, or negative attitudes toward clients or colleagues. This could look like a detached or aloof demeanor, lacking compassion and empathy.

Decreased sense of accomplishment: Individuals experiencing burnout often feel ineffective and inadequate. They may have a pessimistic attitude, and their job performance may deteriorate.

How common are these experiences? Several research studies have measured the prevalence of these signs of burnout among practicing therapists. Estimates range from a minimum of 21% to a maximum of 67%.[5] If we take the middle-range estimate, it means that approximately a third of therapists experience symptoms of burnout at any given time. Emotional exhaustion is the most commonly reported symptom.

Therapist burnout has direct detrimental effects on therapists themselves as well as on their employers and their clients. For therapists, burnout symptoms are associated with poor physical and mental health, including depression, anxiety, sleep problems, gastrointestinal distress, and substance use. Burnout is also a problem for organizations since it is associated with poor work performance and higher staff-turnover rates, thus requiring more frequent hiring. Research also confirms what you might expect, that therapists who feel burned out deliver poorer care for clients.[6]

Burnout is not unique to the mental health field. It occurs across professions and across cultures. Other professions known to be at high risk include teachers, criminal justice workers, nurses, and other healthcare providers. During the coronavirus pandemic, we have heard tragic stories of traumatized healthcare workers who experienced many of these negative effects, including some who have died by suicide.[7]

Compassion Fatigue, Secondary Traumatic Stress, and Vicarious Traumatization

While *burnout* may be the most familiar term for the types of occupational hazards addressed in this chapter, you may also hear about three closely related concepts: compassion fatigue, secondary traumatic stress, and vicarious traumatization. *Compassion fatigue* is a particularly apt term. It means exactly what it sounds like, emotional and physical fatigue related to empathy for helping others in distress.[8] I think many people can relate to this sense of depletion at times. It's important to know that experiencing some compassion fatigue is normal; the critical issue is to recognize and manage it before it impairs our ability to function. In the next section I will offer strategies to manage these challenges.

Secondary traumatic stress and *vicarious traumatization* are different terms which refer to the indirect effects of clients' traumatic experiences on therapists. Research has established that indirect exposure to clients' trauma—and empathy for that trauma experience—carries a risk for significant emotional, cognitive, and behavioral impact on the therapist.[9] In severe cases, therapists experience some of the symptoms of post-traumatic stress disorder, such as intrusive images, hyperarousal, and distressing emotions, through secondary exposure to trauma.

While I have not personally experienced severe symptoms of vicarious traumatization, I have experienced more mild symptoms. Years ago I worked with a family whose 11-year-old daughter was involved in a fatal stabbing incident. It was a terrible tragedy, impacting traumatized witnesses and family members. I worked hard to keep my own therapeutic composure while empathizing with the family, but I was deeply affected. I definitely experienced intrusive imagery of the scene they described to me, and I was preoccupied and distracted by my feelings about this horrible event for several weeks. I sought consultation for this painful work, and as a result, I gained skills in compartmentalizing my own feelings in order to better serve the clients. I was reminded by the senior colleague that I wouldn't be able to help this family if I couldn't manage my own distress. She used the metaphor of the oxygen mask on a plane. We are advised to put our mask on first before we try to help others; we won't be of any use to anyone else if we are in distress ourselves.

I have seen the toll of compassion fatigue and vicarious trauma build up over time in insidious ways. I'm thinking specifically about someone I knew who worked with children in the foster care system. She spent many years doing important work and listening to horrific stories of child abuse and neglect. Early in her career, she channeled her outrage toward advocacy for these children. Over time, however, I believe this work wore down her spirit. She fit the description of burnout, becoming less empathic, more cynical, and more pessimistic. There is no question that the weight of the stories of trauma and frustrations with aspects of the system that she could not change built up like toxins. If we aren't careful and self-aware, the symptoms of burnout can sneak up on us before we even know it.

I hope that I haven't scared you too much about the occupational hazards of this field. My intent is to make sure you have realistic expectations regarding the challenges. The detrimental effects of burnout are actually most likely when therapists' expectations about this career do not match up with the realities. So it's important to prepare yourself for the stress associated with empathizing with others' struggles. It is also important to know that you will be exposed to truly painful glimpses of humanity in this career. These are simply unavoidable. Nevertheless, you can help protect yourself with coping skills. Moreover, if you prepare yourself well, you can even thrive by experiencing the power of vicarious resilience as described in the last section of the chapter.

How to Protect Yourself Against Burnout

Take care of yourself, keep your life balanced and adopt a daily practice of self-care including exercise, social connection, and quiet time. (Carrie, therapist and supervisor in hospital and private practice)

One of the biggest challenges of this career is balancing self-care while also being present and available to your patients who often have overwhelming needs. (Jo Ellen, professor and therapist in private practice)

Self-Care

Experiencing some symptoms of burnout is common for mental health professionals, so it's unrealistic to expect that we can avoid these experiences entirely. However, it is critical that we recognize early signs and take appropriate steps to manage the stress. One proven strategy to prevent serious burnout is to emphasize therapist self-care.[10] Specifically, therapist self-care includes common-sense health and wellness practices: good nutrition, exercise, adequate sleep. In addition, creative and/or spiritual activities personalized to the therapist's particular interests are essential. Social support is another critical aspect of self-care, including peer support from other mental health professionals.

Take a few minutes to think of what types of creative, spiritual, or social activities are most relaxing or reinvigorating for you. Obviously, these will differ for each of us, and it's important for you to know what works for you. One person may love training for triathlons, while another enjoys marathon movie bingeing to destress. You'll want to keep your self-care strategies in mind so that you can remind yourself even when you are under significant stress. It's at those times when it's often most difficult to have the energy and insight to initiate a self-care activity.

There are also things that organizations can do to support self-care and limit staff members' burnout. Some organizations foster a work culture that promotes open discussion of the value of self-care and encourages leaders to model their own self-care. Organizations may also offer workshops on warning signs of burnout and self-care strategies to combat it.[11] Given that professional isolation can lead to burnout, mental health professionals need to look out for each other. Self-monitoring for symptoms of burnout is critical; but when someone is struggling, their own judgment may be impaired, so we may need to identify signs a colleague is struggling and offer support.

Studies also indicate that when mental health providers learn new, effective, evidence-based approaches to mental health treatment, they report lower symptoms of burnout.[12] This important research reinforces the value of continuous learning throughout our careers. In addition, burnout risk can be decreased when we feel confident about the effectiveness of the help we offer our clients.

Self-Compassion

What has surprised me is that the thing that I feel the most scared to say or do with a client is often where the most potential for growth lies. Also, that trauma is very prevalent and deeply impacts mental health. And, how difficult it is to practice self-compassion since most of us are much harder on ourselves than anyone else. (Caroline, professor and therapist)

Research on therapist well-being and burnout prevention increasingly promotes the importance of self-compassion.[13] As therapists, we need to extend to ourselves the same compassion that we give to our clients. Again, this seems like common sense, but we often need to be reminded. As Caroline notes, most of us are harsher in criticizing or judging ourselves compared to others. Practicing self-compassion also encourages us to take a broader perspective, focusing on our sense of shared common humanity. It is related to the popular concept of improving our mindfulness: holding our painful thoughts and feelings in balanced awareness, not overjudging or identifying with those thoughts and feelings.[14] Among its many benefits, mindfulness training has been shown to reduce stress and negative emotions such as anxiety.[15]

Mindfulness is a ubiquitous concept now. One can find books, mobile apps, podcasts, and workshops to support mindfulness practices, promising all kinds of wellness benefits. I know friends and family members who feel that mindfulness training has transformed them in wonderful, healthy ways. The term *mindfulness* has become so popular that it may mean different things to different people. For some, it refers to the benefits of meditation or deep breathing exercises; for others, it reflects a relaxed and centered physical sensation achieved through yoga or other exercise; and still others find that immersion in a creative artistic pursuit brings similar benefits.

Alternatively, some people don't resonate with the concept of mindfulness, but they do recognize the value of pursuing preferred activities to reduce their own stress and worry. Think about what this is for you; maybe you love the concept of mindfulness and have reaped the benefits of mindfulness training and meditation. That's wonderful and will serve you well. Alternatively, maybe you prefer other ways to achieve similar benefits. Perhaps it's playing or listening to music, swimming, playing with a pet, baking, practicing a martial art, painting or drawing, walking in the woods, sweating through a spin class, getting lost in needlepoint, gardening, hip-hop dancing, reading or writing poetry, or building cabinetry. The point is that stress-relieving activities are different for all of us.

Unfortunately, I think we do ourselves a disservice when we suggest that there are specific self-care and self-compassion activities that are the "right" ones for everyone. No matter what yours are, please do be intentional about seeking those out to prevent burnout symptoms as you enter graduate school and throughout your career.

Gaining Self-Awareness

Working on one's own issues is an essential part of being a therapist in order to be able to do the work in the best interest of the client. While assisting others in facing life's challenges and crises, you inevitably face your own. (Larry, therapist in private practice, instructor, and business consultant)

One of the major rewards of this career is the opportunity to gain deeper self-awareness, but this requires hard and sometimes painful work. If you approach this journey with an open mind and genuine curiosity, you will learn so much about yourself; but the lessons won't always be fun or easy. You'll learn about your biases and blind spots as well as behavior patterns in relationships that you may not have noticed before. Perhaps your peers or supervisors will call you out on subtle nonverbal communication habits that could be interpreted as annoying or disrespectful to others. Maybe you'll need to question long-held beliefs about how people fall in love or the "right" way to raise children. Hopefully, you'll gain amazing insights into how you became you, why you have struggled with some aspects of your identity or sense of belongingness, how you fit in your family system, what your spirituality (or lack thereof) means to you, etc. Gaining greater self-awareness is an enriching perk of this career, but it takes work, often in the form of your own therapy.

> Go to therapy. You probably have a few personal experiences that will influence your effectiveness as a clinician. Experience the "other side" of the relationship. (Barry, therapist and clinical supervisor)

> If you think you can be effective without having done "the work" yourself . . . forget it! (Leita, therapist in private practice and retired instructor/supervisor)

Some graduate mental health programs actually require students to participate in their own therapy to earn their degree. Others simply recommend it. Most of the therapists surveyed for this book strongly recommend that you gain experience as a client in therapy prior to becoming a therapist. This is very sound advice. Most importantly, you need to be aware of how your own background and beliefs may impact you as a therapist, identifying trigger issues and biases. Also, experience on the other side of the relationship, as Barry notes, is valuable for empathizing with what your own clients may experience.

Can One Be a Good Therapist Without Having Been in Psychotherapy?

I imagine you may have already had experience in therapy and can relate to the value of it. You know how important it is to feel like you can trust your therapist because you have felt nervous about being judged or worried about confidentiality. Hopefully, you have a sense of that intangible, hard-to-describe feeling of true, meaningful connection with a therapist. Or alternatively, you know the disappointment over the lack of a genuine connection. Perhaps you know the frustration of wishing that your therapist would just give you explicit advice about an important decision; maybe you've also experienced the recognition that it was necessary for you to make the decision yourself. Or you know how valuable some specific evidence-based therapeutic strategies have been for you to make real changes in your life.

So while it is possible to become a therapist without ever having been in psychotherapy, it is not recommended. There are so many ways that being a client in therapy can help you to become the therapist you want to be.

Self-Awareness Versus Self-Absorption

As Jeffrey Kottler notes in his book *On Being a Therapist*, there can be a fine line between self-discovery and self-absorption. Is this yet another tension to balance in this career? Self-reflection and discovery are essential, but can they go too far? An occupational hazard for therapists can be the risk of becoming "psychological hypochondriacs,"[16] preoccupied with assessing our own psychological and relationship functioning. This is a real risk, particularly for students first learning about clinical disorders but also for anyone prone to anxiety about symptoms. Have you experienced anything like this while learning about various types of psychological problems or dysfunctional relationships?

It's a natural and healthy inclination to wonder how what you are learning may or may not apply to you. The problem arises when this self-referencing dominates everything that you are learning. Likewise, you won't win over many friends if you are constantly evaluating or pathologizing their behavior (i.e., diagnosing problems). Ideally, your advanced education in mental health will give you deeper appreciation for the amazing variability in how people live, love, and work. Using it to critique others will not serve you well.

There is a related risk that in our efforts to gain self-awareness, we prioritize looking inward at the expense of directing our attention to others. Too much *navel-gazing* (i.e., "self-indulgent or excessive contemplation of oneself or a single issue at the expense of a wider view"[17]) can be another occupational hazard. I've met people (very few) in this profession who seem much more interested in their own thoughts and feelings than in their clients'. Like so much of what I've discussed in this book, the challenge here is to find some balance. Self-examination and reflection are absolutely necessary and beneficial in this career, unless they impair our ability to fully attend to others, including clients, co-workers, family, and friends.

Vicarious Resilience and Compassion Satisfaction

The most rewarding aspect of being a therapist is watching people grow, change, and survive situations that are beyond what I would expect a human to have to endure. (Carrie, therapist and supervisor in hospital and private practice)

While exposure to trauma can be overwhelming, witnessing strength and resilience can be incredibly inspiring. Recovery from trauma fosters resilience in clients and their therapists.[18] Our clients literally model strength and resilience for us, and this fuels us to keep working hard. Playing a role in someone's recovery and personal growth is an absolutely awesome experience. Helping someone overcome despair, panic, hopelessness, or loneliness and get to the other side of a crisis gives us a sense of compassion satisfaction, to counter the inevitable experiences of compassion fatigue. Jeffrey Kottler describes the experience of successful therapy as the "Helper's High," bringing a sense of inner peace and well-being, thereby contributing to our own mental and physical health.[19]

Imagine working with a family to reduce chaos and conflict in their home, helping a child learn to make friends, supporting a group of bereaved widowers to find new meaning in their lives, helping an individual released from prison successfully transition into a social work career, partnering with a patient in treatment for a terminal disease to manage pain, or helping a couple successfully cope with their unfulfilled dream to have children. In this career, you will have these types of opportunities and so many others that you can't even imagine.

In Conclusion

As promised, you've read about the weighty occupational hazards of this career and should consider yourself forewarned. Realistic expectations are critical to success in any career. You've also read about the ways you'll be able to manage the challenges. Advice about the value of self-care, self-reflection, and self-compassion will serve you well no matter what direction your career path takes. To counter the stress of this career, you will have the opportunity to be inspired by clients' resilience and will be fortified by these experiences.

> I'm fortunate that burn-out hasn't been a problem for me. The clinical work has been thoroughly rewarding. I remind myself repeatedly of how grateful I am to have this career. (Kathy, professor and therapist)

11

Inspiring Hope and Change

Anxiety and despair can be lethal; confidence and hope, life-giving.
— Jerome Frank[1]

I've begun with a poignant quote from an author whose work inspires this chapter. Jerome Frank wrote the first edition of his landmark book *Persuasion and Healing* in 1961, and many of his assertions about what makes psychotherapy work have been reinforced over the decades. He drew a connection between psychotherapy and other healing traditions, emphasizing the importance of boosting a client's hope for relief from suffering. And he asserted that the quality of the relationship between the client and the therapist can be a powerful healing force. These elements of psychotherapy, namely the power of expectations within the context of a strong healing therapeutic relationship, are referred to as *common factors* because they are essential ingredients for all types of therapeutic approaches and theoretical orientations.[2] I consider these common factors the necessary foundation for all effective therapy.

In the first chapter of this book, I wrote that effective therapy capitalizes on both the power of the healing arts and advances in science. This chapter is devoted to understanding the healing art of therapy, whereas the next chapter addresses science. I'll dive deeper into the common factors of therapy to highlight how therapists inspire hope and change. I will discuss the essential role of expectations and challenge you to confront assumptions you may have about the meaning of the placebo effect. And I'll discuss how the relationship between the therapist and the client is essential to inspiring hope and change in therapy, offering recommendations for how to build strong relationships.

These last few chapters of this book represent a bit of a shift from the practical information presented in previous chapters. In these remaining chapters, I'll be raising big picture perspectives on mental healthcare, including how and why it works and how it may evolve in the future. The purpose is to get you thinking about deeper implications of this career, setting the stage for you to find your place in this field and thrive.

The Importance of Expectations

> Favorable expectations generate feelings of optimism, energy, and well-being and may actually promote healing, especially of those illnesses with a large psychological or emotional component.
>
> — Jerome Frank[3]

Whenever I begin a new course with students, I warn them that they are often going to hear me speak about the importance of expectations in therapy. I blame Jerome Frank for my obsession with this topic. When I read his book as a graduate student, it made a big impression. I found his arguments about the power of expectations compelling. And I appreciated learning how psychotherapy is connected to a rich tradition of the healing arts. I like how Mary Pipher reinforces this point in her book *Letters to a Young Therapist*: "We therapists are small potatoes, but we are connected to an ancient and beautiful idea. Since time began, humans have needed shamans, curanderos, and tribal healers."[4]

Boosting Positive Expectations About Benefiting from Care

Expectations play a central role in the healing arts, dating back to indigenous healing rituals led by shamans. Societies imbue healers and healing rituals with special powers that are reinforced through shared belief systems and folklore, thereby building the positive expectations of those hoping to be healed. Psychotherapy has evolved from these healing traditions. When clients have positive expectations about benefiting from therapy, they are more likely to benefit.[5] Yes, this seems obvious. But it goes deeper, as I describe in this section.

How do therapists instill positive expectations? Fortunately, clients often come into therapy feeling hopeful about getting better, so this is a good start. Others who feel helpless and hopeless may need stronger persuasion that therapy can help to ease their suffering. Either way, therapists need to build the client's confidence that they have the knowledge and skills to help relieve suffering. This can be challenging.

Beginning therapists sometimes struggle with instilling confidence in their clients because their own confidence is shaky at best. As I shared in the Introduction, I certainly struggled with this, and the students I teach often struggle too. It's difficult to project confidence, especially when one is nervous about one's own lack of experience. For many of us, our tendency is to lower expectations if we are not feeling confident. That can work well in some circumstances. For example, I tend to lower expectations when preparing a meal for friends because I'm not a very confident cook. Then, if the food is decent, I've exceeded expectations and everyone is happy. But this is not a helpful approach in the role of therapist. It is not in our clients' best interest to express doubts about our ability to help them. We need to do the opposite, which means that sometimes we need to "fake it till we make it" in order to build and reinforce positive expectations.

Therapist confidence is one way to build positive expectations, but confidence without some rationale for how we can help will fall short. We also need to be explicit about how and why we believe that a particular therapeutic approach will help someone. We need to discuss the rationale and the evidence behind the approach to boost the client's expectations of benefiting from it. Think about it this way: If you sought couples counseling due to serious conflict in your relationship, how optimistic would you feel if your therapist said, "I think that I can help you and your partner" versus "I feel confident that I can work with you and your partner to identify the sources of conflict and help you build proven communication skills to more safely and effectively address your issues."

Both examples express some optimism, but only one boosts positive expectations by expressing confidence and providing a persuasive rationale for the treatment approach. Explicitly discussing the rationale for the effectiveness of the therapeutic approach also helps the therapist to feel more confident. Research confirms that when clinicians have more positive beliefs about the effectiveness of the treatment, clients are more likely to achieve positive outcomes.[6]

The power of expectations is apparent even when clients are placed on a waiting list for treatment. You might think (as I did originally) that clients would always feel worse when therapy is delayed. However, many studies have shown that, on average, clients who are placed on a waiting list report slight improvement in their mental health even before seeing anyone.[7] Why? Perhaps they are feeling some optimism about getting help, and this hope provides some relief. I want to emphasize that I'm not advocating for denying or delaying treatment; clients who receive evidence-based care show greater improvement than those on a waitlist. But this somewhat counterintuitive research finding reinforces the role of expectations.

As further evidence for the power of expectations, cognitive behavioral therapy, one of our best-researched psychotherapeutic approaches, emphasizes the value of educating clients about the rationale for its effectiveness at the outset of therapy. When a client enters therapy feeling demoralized, it can be very reassuring if the therapist offers reasons to be optimistic about the potential effectiveness of their therapeutic approach. When clients feel that the treatment approach being offered is credible, they are more likely to benefit.[8]

Addressing Expectations About What Therapy Entails

In addition to expectations about the effectiveness of therapy, a client's specific expectations about what will happen in therapy and how long it will take are important. Some clients are not sure what to expect, while others may enter treatment with specific expectations. Imagine a client who has read about traditional psychoanalysis, watched movies depicting it, and grown intrigued by dream analysis. This client is experiencing serious anxiety and depression after losing her job. She is convinced that dream analysis will cure her anxiety and depression, and she's been diligently keeping a dream journal for weeks. She finds a therapist who takes her health insurance and has good ratings online and she makes an appointment. She is a bit nervous about starting therapy but also very hopeful about finally getting the help she desperately needs.

Upon entering the therapist's office, she is somewhat surprised to see a few comfortable chairs but no sofa to lie upon as she expected, based on her image of psychoanalysis. The therapist greets her warmly and proceeds to ask her a variety of questions about what brings her into therapy. He asks questions about her mood, her social activities and relationships, and her work and even probes for details about her daily habits including sleep, appetite, and exercise. He confirms that she does seem to be struggling with classic symptoms of social anxiety and depression. When he says it's time to wrap up and schedule a second visit, she is quite disappointed that he's not asked anything about her dreams. She gets up the courage to ask him if they'll discuss her dreams next time and proudly shows him the dream journal. He laughs heartily and tells her that's not a valid way to practice psychotherapy. She leaves feeling embarrassed and unmotivated to return or to seek therapy elsewhere.

Even though this client had positive, hopeful expectations about therapy's potential benefits, the encounter was unsuccessful. I'm using this rather blatant example to illustrate why attending to specific expectations is so important. It's critical for therapists and clients to talk about their expectations for therapy at the outset and to find some mutually agreeable plans and goals. It's great if the therapist and client are on the same page from the beginning, but if not, they can negotiate to reach some mutually agreeable plans and goals. Reaching general consensus on expectations for what will happen in therapy and how long it will take is associated with a more positive relationship between the therapist and the client as well as better outcomes for the client.[9]

In my example, the anti-dream-analysis therapist didn't seem interested in the client's expectations about therapy, and even worse, he ridiculed her expectations. How could he have negotiated this initial session better? He should have asked the client earlier about what she was expecting or looking for in therapy. When she mentioned dream analysis, he could have maintained a curious and respectful attitude, learning more from her about why she was so intrigued by it and how she thought it could work for her. Then he could have engaged in a more collaborative discussion about other therapeutic approaches that he believed would be more effective, sharing the rationale and maybe even research findings to build her confidence. While he worked to persuade her about the effectiveness of his preferred approaches to treating anxiety and depression, he could still have expressed openness to learning more about the meaning of dreams to the client. Hopefully, they would have found a mutually agreeable balance moving forward. If not, he could have referred her to a provider who might be a better fit.

The Power of Expectations

What makes expectations so powerful? Expectations are fueled by our hope and faith in something better. Think about what has inspired you to tackle a difficult challenge. What about people you admire—what inspires them? Chances are you and your role models are strongly motivated by faith, either religious faith or secular faith in humanity or the pursuit of justice. Faith in something better is the ultimate positive expectation. Someone I greatly admire said, "I have always believed that hope is that stubborn thing inside us that insists, despite all the evidence to the contrary, that something better awaits us as long as we have the courage to keep reaching, to keep working, to keep fighting." This could've come from a psychotherapist, but it was actually part of President Barack Obama's victory speech in 2012. One of the most valuable things we can do for clients is help them find their source of hope and nurture it in every way we can. When it is lost, it's very difficult—but not impossible—to build it back.

Optimistic expectations are both inspirational and practical. When someone expects something to work, they may put forth more effort to succeed. In other words, a person who believes that therapy can be effective may be more fully engaged in the difficult work of therapy. In general, we tend to work to confirm our initial beliefs. So a client who believes in a therapist and a treatment approach at the outset is motivated to prove that they were right all along. This is somewhat like a self-fulfilling prophecy; when someone believes something to be true, their behaviors align to fulfill the belief.

The Healing Power of the Placebo Effect

The placebo effect is another great example of the power of positive expectations. *Placebo effects*, defined as beneficial effects of inert treatments, have been demonstrated for many medical and mental health issues. You may assume that only gullible individuals would respond to a placebo. However, the truth is that most people respond positively if the provider builds positive expectations and administers the placebo in a context that the client expects to be healing. In a very interesting article aptly titled "What if the Placebo Effect Isn't a Trick?," Gary Greenberg presents evidence demonstrating that the placebo effect is, in fact, a biological response just like our response to other medical treatments.[10] He reviews evidence of how the placebo response operates on the same biomedical nervous system pathways as other medical treatments. Similarly, Ted Kaptchuk, director of Harvard University's Placebo Studies and the Therapeutic Encounter Program, has called the placebo effect a biological response to an act of caring. Think about what this means; positive expectations fostered in a caring relationship translate to actual biomedical healing processes in our bodies and our minds.

Building positive expectations within the context of a caring therapeutic relationship provides the foundation for all therapy. Adding specific effective interventions on top of that foundation accelerates healing. Imagine that you have a stiff neck and consider the role of building positive expectations and creating a healing context by comparing two different scenarios for acupuncture treatment.

In Scenario 1, you find an acupuncturist online who is offering a big discount for neck pain relief. You immediately arrange an appointment and go to her "office," which is actually just a small apartment. She says the discount is offered because she is lacking some of her usual tools in this location. She lets you know she doesn't have much time and immediately asks you to lie down on the table. She doesn't describe the procedures she'll be performing before simply inserting a few needles in your back.

In Scenario 2, you call an acupuncturist recommended by a trusted friend who says she "worked miracles" on her sore shoulder. Appointments are hard to get, so you have to wait a week for your visit to the well-appointed professional office. You are asked to complete an intake questionnaire about your pain history and any other medical issues. The acupuncturist greets you warmly and professionally; she sits down with you to discuss your pain and shows you a detailed diagram while describing her treatment rationale and its effectiveness. Then she proceeds to implement her treatment plan by inserting needles in the targeted spots on your back, speaking to you throughout the procedure about how the needles are working and reassuring you that your muscles are responding really well.

Which scenario boosted your confidence for recovery? In which scenario do you think your pain is more likely to be relieved? Let's assume that the actual treatment interventions were identical, that the needles were inserted in the same locations on your back. Isn't it interesting how expectations and context can shape your confidence about recovery? You might prefer to believe that these contextual factors don't matter—all that matters is the treatment intervention itself—but research suggests that expectancy and context factors can powerfully impact outcomes. Everything comes together to foster healing: confidence and trust in the provider, positive expectations about the treatment approach, contextual stimuli (e.g., detailed questionnaire, professional office space), and the actual treatment (insertion of the acupuncture needles).

How the Power of Expectations Can Be Counterproductive

By now I hope I've persuaded you of the importance of expectations. Now I'll add some critical caveats. Research suggests that when expectations for therapy are unrealistically high, that can backfire because clients will experience demoralizing disappointment. Imagine a 35-year-old man who has struggled all his life with interpersonal relationships. He's never dated or had a close friendship. He finally has a job with benefits covering mental healthcare, and he enters therapy with great optimism.

He expects to solve his social challenges within 1 month and to be enjoying an ideal romantic relationship within 2 months. How might his unrealistically high expectations about therapy backfire?

Expectations for a rapid "cure" are usually unrealistic, and clients can be demoralized when improvement is slower than they expected. They may even quit therapy. It's important for a therapist and client to collaboratively set treatment goals and timelines that are optimistic but also realistic. Think about this hypothetical 35-year-old man. Gaining critical insights into his interpersonal relationship challenges, identifying necessary changes, and actually making those behavioral changes will be difficult and will take time. There is no question that psychotherapy can help him meet his goals but likely not within 2 months.

Another important caveat relates to how "healers" sometimes exploit the power of positive expectations in unhelpful or even dangerous ways. The COVID-19 pandemic offers current examples. While the public desperately looks for reasons to be optimistic about treatments to ease the suffering, nefarious businesses are attempting to profit. By mid-2021, the Food and Drug Administration website listed about 185 fraudulent products that claimed to prevent, treat, diagnose, or cure COVID-19.[11] These products ranged from teas, herbs, and essential oils to vitamins and minerals to precious metals and amniotic fluid, just to name a few—and this is likely just a fraction of these types of products in the marketplace. This is a sobering reminder that while clients' hopeful optimism can be harnessed for good outcomes, it can also be exploited for malevolent purposes. Unfortunately, as noted by Mary Pipher, the mental health field also "has its share of space cadets, strange agents, and woo-woo practitioners."[12] My goal is to provide sound advice in this book that will steer you away from the woo-woo path.

This dark side of profiting from clients' hopeful expectations has a long history. You've likely heard the term *snake oil salesman*, used to refer to a con artist selling fraudulent products as miracle cures. In the 19th century, US traveling salesmen advertised cure-all tonics for a wide variety of problems. Many of these tonics were actually made from snake oil, but over time the term has been used for any type of fraudulent hoax advertised to cure all sorts of problems. I'm encouraging you to build your clients' positive expectations for the benefits of therapy but not by selling them on unsupported practices.

Healing is most effective when it relies on the power of expectations plus scientifically valid treatment interventions. It is unethical to exploit clients by raising false hopes not backed up by science. We want to embody our privileged and powerful healing role in the most responsible way.

The Therapeutic Relationship

I am most surprised by how simply sitting and listening to a patient for four to five sessions is often enough to help patients feel much better. I wholeheartedly believe Jerome Frank's claim that psychotherapy is based on common factors that help restore a patient's morale. (Carolyn, professor and hospital therapist)

The final topic in this chapter is near and dear to every therapist's heart, namely, the healing power of the therapeutic relationship between clients and therapists. The therapeutic relationship is also referred to as the *therapeutic alliance* or the *working alliance*. I'll be using these terms interchangeably as they all refer to the strength and quality of this relationship. Decades of research emphasizes the critically important role of the therapeutic alliance in the effectiveness of psychotherapy.[13] Not surprisingly, when clients and therapists rate the alliance as strong, the clinical outcomes for the client are likely to be more positive.[14]

What Contributes to the Therapeutic Relationship?

The elements that contribute to the therapeutic relationship include the following:

a. Agreement on goals
b. Agreement on the tasks to achieve those goals
c. The emotional bond between therapist and client(s)[15]

I've already covered the importance of explicitly discussing goals and expectations about treatment processes (the actual tasks of therapy) in this chapter. But I haven't discussed the emotional bond between the therapist and client. This sounds so important, but what does it mean? Therapists and their clients are not supposed to have a social relationship or friendship, so what is an ideal emotional bond for this unusual type of relationship? Is it about liking each other? Trusting each other? Is it related to the therapist's ability to convey sincere warmth, compassion, and empathy? Is it their sense of humor? Or their calm emotional stability and wisdom? Their ability to make a client feel heard, understood, and safe? How about the therapist's flexibility to adaptively meet the unique needs of each client? Or their ability to respect clients from diverse backgrounds, including racial, ethnic, sexual orientation, gender identity, religious, abled, and socioeconomic backgrounds?

I believe the answer is yes to all the above. The strength and quality of the alliance between the therapist and client are likely related to all these factors, plus others that may be harder to define. There will always be intangible reasons for why some people feel a strong healing connection and others don't. That's one of the mysteries of therapy that makes it so fascinating. As much as I love the science of therapy, I also love that there is a magic to human connection that we'll never be able to define or measure. That's the inspiring healing art of therapy.

What about you? If you've been in therapy, what made you feel you could benefit from working with a particular therapist (or not)? Did you feel you needed to like the therapist's personality? Or were there other qualities that mattered more? Did you know from the start, or did the relationship evolve over time? Many factors influence the connection that clients feel to their therapist, some more consequential than others. I knew someone who said that she could tell immediately if a therapist was a good match for her based on the shoes the therapist wore. Others care a lot about the "vibe" they get from a therapist's office. Some of the ingredients of a strong therapeutic relationship have been identified by experts, but there will always be some mystery as to why some people develop a healing human connection and others don't.

For me, one of the essential ingredients for a strong therapeutic relationship is trust. Clients need to trust that their therapist has their best interest at heart. If so, they are more willing to pursue the hard work of change. Think about how you determine if someone is trustworthy. I think of characteristics such as integrity, reliability, and honesty as signs of trustworthiness; but you may think of other ways to judge trustworthiness. Think about how you'll convey trustworthiness when you become a therapist.

Compassion is another essential ingredient for a strong therapeutic relationship. As I've written in Chapter 2 of this book, many people choose this career because they are naturally caring and empathic. There are many different ways that therapists demonstrate these qualities. Some therapists have a classically compassionate demeanor, radiating warmth and caring; they are emotionally expressive. I've known other wonderful therapists who are more emotionally stoic. They express their compassion in different ways, perhaps through their serious approach to delivering the most effective therapeutic interventions for each client or through their sense of humor that can lighten despair. Think about people you know who are compassionate. How do they convey that?

How to Build a Strong Therapeutic Relationship

As you embark on the path to becoming a therapist, please consider how you will build healing relationships with clients from diverse backgrounds. It is essential that you tailor your therapeutic approach to the unique needs and background of each client. We need to respect our clients' backgrounds by communicating interest in each individual's beliefs, values, traditions, and social experiences. Studies show that an open dialogue about issues such as race and ethnicity promotes a stronger therapeutic alliance.[16] I believe this is true for clients' race and ethnicity, as well as family composition, gender identity, spirituality, sexual orientation, age, socioeconomic status, and even political perspective. As noted in Chapter 8, in order to build strong working relationships with diverse clients it is essential for you to gain awareness of how your own background and identity influence your assumptions and behaviors toward others. Gaining this self-awareness is critical, and it is an ongoing process for all of us.

Building strong working relationships with clients is not just about our personal characteristics and attitudes; there are skills to learn. Regardless of what discipline you choose to pursue, you'll learn about alliance-building and the work of Carl Rogers. He was particularly influential in advocating for the important role of the healing therapeutic relationship.[17] Rogers suggested there were three core conditions therapists need to provide for a growth-promoting experience for clients[18]:

a. *Unconditional positive regard*: Therapists shouldn't be judgmental; they should express acceptance, caring, and support for all clients.
b. *Empathy*: Therapists should demonstrate and communicate understanding of the client and what the client is feeling.
c. *Congruence*: Therapists should relate to the client with authenticity and openness.

Rogers' theories about how to promote psychological healing through the power of a nonjudgmental, empathic, and genuine therapeutic relationship are still widely endorsed. He wrote about basic therapeutic skills that you will learn to build caring relationships with your clients. One of those skills is active listening (sometimes called *reflective listening*). This skill is used to convey empathy and to help clients feel understood. You'll learn how to listen deeply and then to reflect back to the client what you are understanding about their experiences and feelings using paraphrasing and other techniques. It may sound easy, but there are lots of important nuances that you'll learn in graduate school. Active listening is essential for helping clients to feel truly heard and validated. (And, as a perk, it can be quite valuable in relationships outside of therapy too.)

What else contributes to a strong therapeutic relationship? Not surprisingly, when clients feel they are improving, they are more likely to rate the therapeutic relationship more positively.[19] This may sound a bit like a "chicken and egg" problem. Specifically, a positive therapeutic relationship is associated with better clinical outcomes, and improvement in clinical outcomes is associated with a more positive therapeutic relationship. Which comes first? Frankly, the answer isn't too important since it wouldn't change how therapists work. The important implication is that we need to be working on building a positive therapeutic relationship and helping the client solve problems to meet their clinical outcome goals at the same time.

Some older approaches to psychotherapy divided up these two goals, assuming that therapists needed to spend considerable time, as in many weeks, building a strong relationship prior to actually attempting to address any of the specific clinical problems that brought the client in. I don't believe that we need to separate these goals. Yes, we need to be building trust and rapport from the outset, and we need to nurture it as we progress. And, yes, we need to help our clients relieve pain in their lives from the outset. As a therapist, I've found that one of the best ways to strengthen a working alliance with a client is to work together on strategies to reduce chaos or despair in their lives from the start.

As an example, I worked with a single mother whose young son was referred by the school due to impulsive and aggressive behavior. She was absolutely exhausted from working two part-time jobs and trying to manage a household with three young children. Attending therapy sessions was just one more demand on her limited time and energy, but she did it so that her son wouldn't be expelled from school. I really empathized with her and communicated my respect for all she was managing. She was initially skeptical that therapy could work, but in our first session, I helped her prepare a schedule for the kids' morning routine. We discussed the importance of consistency and structure, as well as the value of praising good behavior. She practiced how she would present this to her kids with me and built her confidence. She returned the following week with more optimism. While the schedule didn't work perfectly by any means, it helped to reduce chaos at home just a bit. Thus, our therapeutic relationship was built on (a) my empathy and validation for all her stress and (b) my help in some basic early problem-solving. This was a good start to deeper and more complicated therapeutic work over time.

Many clients (but not all) report relief of distress and a reduction in problematic symptoms after just a few sessions of psychotherapy.[20] Why would this be when the actual work of therapy has barely begun? Jerome Frank suggested that the initial connection with a caring professional helps to free up the client's own coping strengths. I think this is true for many people. We gain strength by feeling cared for and understood. The humanistic approach to psychotherapy suggests that our burdens feel less overwhelming and that we can utilize our strengths when we feel supported. We can reach our potential and become more self-actualized when we know someone cares about us. This is an inspiring and valid perspective on the healing power of the therapeutic relationship.

Without a doubt, a strong therapeutic relationship is the foundation of all therapy; it is necessary but not sufficient. We need to build on that foundation by employing therapeutic strategies supported by science to help clients reach their goals. This is what the next chapter is about.

In addition, it is important to remember how the therapeutic relationship is distinct from other relationships or friendships. Unfortunately, I've known therapists who are motivated solely by being liked by their clients, and this can limit the effectiveness of therapy. Being liked is not necessarily the most important goal for a therapist. The bond between therapist and client can be exceptionally strong and therapeutic even if it is not always easy.

In her popular book about psychotherapy *Maybe You Should Talk to Someone*, Lori Gottlieb wrote that therapy will inevitably be uncomfortable. As a therapist, she said, "Our work is an intricate dance between support and confrontation."[21] Here we are with yet another balance for therapists to manage. We need to be empathic, compassionate, and nonjudgmental, while also confronting clients to recognize hard truths and coaching them on how to make difficult changes. It's definitely an important balance to achieve. And when it all comes together, there is that healing magic.

In Conclusion

> The most rewarding aspect of my career is the chance to witness hope and change. It truly feels like an honor to be invited into someone's life during their most vulnerable transitions and moments. (Cassidy, therapist in private practice and instructor)

Psychotherapy has evolved from an ancient tradition of healing arts, which harness the power of clients' hope for relief of suffering and the benefits of a caring relationship. The common factors of psychotherapy have been shown to account for much of the clinical effectiveness, and they are the essential foundation for all specific psychotherapy models. When you experience the power of a healing connection with a client, it is an absolutely awesome experience. It is life-affirming and protects us from the frustrations and disappointments we will also face in this career. There is a certain indescribable magic in these types of human connections. We are fortunate to be in a field that offers opportunities to experience that magic in our day-to-day work.

12

Embracing the Science
of Mental Healthcare

Science knowledge only adds to the excitement, the mystery and the awe.

— Richard P. Feyman[1]

The last chapter celebrated the healing art of therapy, and this chapter celebrates the science. One of the reasons I love this field so much is that it inspires us to embrace both the humanistic healing arts as well as innovative science, thus fully engaging our hearts and our minds. For inspiration, I conjure up the image of a warm, supportive spiritual guide who also thinks like a scientist, maybe a wise Zen master who consults scientific texts and deploys a calculator to track data. In other words, a kind, empathic professional well trained in scientifically supported mental health practices who objectively evaluates the effectiveness of their work.

We are most effective when we draw on the power of a healing human connection in combination with practices supported by rigorous research. A healing human connection and adherence to research evidence may seem unrelated, but they complement each other. Relying exclusively on one or the other would limit our impact. Throughout this book I've emphasized the need to balance potentially conflicting priorities, and this may be the most important example. Figure 12.1 illustrates the balance we should aspire to as mental health professionals. On the left, you see the key elements of the healing art of effective therapy; namely, the client's expectations and the therapeutic relationship, as described in the previous chapter. On the right, you see the scientific factors of effective therapy, including evidence-based practices and measurement-based care, described in this chapter.

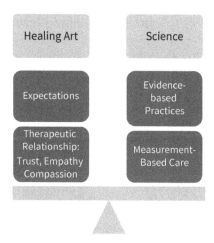

Figure 12.1 Balancing the Art and Science of Mental Health Care

Mental Health Professionals as Clinical Scientists

Do you think of yourself as scientifically minded? Perhaps you are motivated to pursue this career path because of a fascination with neuroscience discoveries or experiences you've gained with a research team. That's terrific and will serve you well. But some who pursue this career path do not think of themselves as scientifically minded. If that includes you, I'm hoping to persuade you to embrace scientific thinking. Maybe you imagine scientists as cold and calculating, more interested in data than in human emotions and relationships. I've known many therapists who dismissed the importance of science because of this perception. Likewise, some students have made comments such as "I'm a people person not a science person," as if these are mutually exclusive self-identities. I want to challenge this type of dichotomous thinking. The truth is, a "people person" will be most effective in helping others when using strategies supported by science.

The previous chapter highlighted the humanistic aspects of mental healthcare, including the awesome and sometimes intangible healing power of human connections. How do we reconcile that with a scientific approach? Some people worry that applying scientific methods to therapy, dissecting and measuring it, will detract from that intangible healing essence. But I don't see it that way. There will always be an element of healing magic about psychotherapy that will never be fully measured or explained by science. I am inspired by that mystery. At the same time, I am inspired by how science has given us tremendous insights into the most effective ways to help people. As reflected in the opening quote by Richard Feyman, science adds to the excitement and awe. It does not detract.

Respecting science does not require us to dismiss phenomena that can't be fully explained by science. Quite the opposite. Listen to a great scientist speak about their field of study; there is often a poetic or reverentially spiritual tone about intangible mysteries. For example, Albert Einstein wrote,

> The most beautiful thing we can experience is the mysterious. It is the source of all true art and science. He to whom this emotion is a stranger, who can no longer pause to wonder and stand rapt in awe, is as good as dead: his eyes are closed.[2]

At the risk of getting too philosophical, the point I want to make is that science, as well as art, illuminates human mysteries and realities. Scientific discoveries and artistic expression give us tremendous insights into the human condition. We can and should respect knowledge gained through scientific methods and apply it within the healing context of human relationships. That idea doesn't sound cold and calculating to me. It sounds both inspirational and aspirational.

As mental health professionals, we need to think like scientists in our scholarly work as well as in our clinical practice. First of all, the objectivity of scientific thinking can help to minimize the inevitable biases in our judgment. Second, in research and in practice we develop hypotheses about what's going on and then test those hypotheses. To test hypotheses we need to come up with incisive questions, collect relevant data, and evaluate them in order to determine if our hypotheses are supported or refuted. We also generate and test alternative explanations for the evidence and revise our hypotheses accordingly, repeating the data collection and analysis cycle to draw closer to confident conclusions.

This approach to scientific thinking is likely familiar to you when we're talking about a research project, but how does it apply to clinical practice? Let's say I am conducting an assessment with a 14-year-old girl named Maya whose parents have referred her due to concerns about (a) a recent significant drop in her grades, (b) her reported "moodiness" and "snarky" oppositional attitude with them, (c) her "secretive" communications and meetings with friends, and (d) her poor sleep patterns. I learn that Maya's parents immigrated to the United States from the Philippines a few years before Maya was born and that most of the parents' friends are from the Philippines. Maya entered a large, diverse urban high school 6 months ago and has a few friends from diverse backgrounds.

Based only on this information, I need to develop hypotheses about what might be going on with Maya. There are many possibilities. For example, perhaps Maya is struggling with depression or an anxiety disorder and/or substance abuse. Alternatively, maybe her parents have gender and developmental expectations based on their cultural context that are very different than Maya's emerging identity and current social environment. Perhaps Maya is striving for greater independence and engaging in developmentally appropriate teenage activities, but the culturally divergent expectations are causing significant problems. It is also possible that she has experienced a trauma or is the victim of bullying. Or that she has a medical issue related to hormonal changes in puberty that are driving some of these reported behaviors. Perhaps she has an undiagnosed learning disorder causing more academic challenges now that she's entered high school. Each of these hypotheses could explain the initial presentation.

These hypotheses will guide my clinical interview with Maya and her family. As I collect more data from their responses to my questions and to standardized diagnostic questionnaires, I'll need to narrow down my hypotheses. And just like a scientist, I'll need to test for alternative explanations about the conclusions I'm drawing. Keeping an open mind about alternative conclusions is very important due to common biases in our judgment. If I can think like a scientist, while also building a healing therapeutic relationship with Maya and inspiring her expectations for success, I'm likely to be most effective in figuring out how best to help her and her family.

Mental health professionals also need to be well-informed consumers of research to identify assessment and treatment approaches that are most effective. As I noted in Chapter 9, you'll learn more about how to identify and critique the credibility of research in graduate school courses. You'll also learn about online resources to identify evidence-based practices at the end of the section on evidence-based practices. Developing this kind of scientific literacy to find and critically evaluate research is valuable in many areas of our lives. It's how we learn to differentiate valid evidence from fraudulent claims. Thinking like a scientist is not just useful; it is imperative to providing ethical, effective care.

What Is Evidence-based Practice?

Being committed to evidence-based practice means that you value interventions that have been shown to work. There have been so many exciting treatments developed over the past few decades and I am glad that I got exposure to a lot of them in my graduate training. I love the freedom that I have to pull in practice elements from different interventions and individualize treatment for each youth. I would not be able to do that if I weren't trained in multiple evidence-based treatments and encouraged to be flexible in my thinking. (Jennifer, therapist in community and private practice)

The term *evidence-based practice* has become fairly common in public discourse, and I've already used it many times in this book. In this section, I'll delve deeper into the origin and definition of this term as well as the controversy it has inspired in our field. It's no exaggeration to say that the promotion of evidence-based practice has incited a bit of a revolution in mental health.

The term *evidence-based medicine* was first popularized by David Sackett and colleagues in the 1990s. Dr. Sackett defined evidence-based medicine as the integration of the best research evidence with clinical expertise and patient values or preferences.[3] This full definition has been obscured over time. Consequently, some people assume that evidence-based practice refers exclusively to research support. I appreciate the original definition because while it highlights the value of scientifically derived evidence, it also acknowledges the value of clinicians' expertise and patients' values, beliefs, and preferences. So here we are again, returning to the theme of integration and balance of potentially conflicting priorities so that they become complementary.

The original focus on evidence-based medicine has since expanded to evidence-based practice across multiple disciplines, including all the mental health disciplines. The promotion of evidence-based practice is now common. In fact, the majority of US states offer incentives to mental health agencies to deliver evidence-based practices.[4] This may sound logical to you; wouldn't you want providers to deliver care that is supported by evidence of effectiveness? As logical as it sounds, this push for evidence-based practice created tension in our field.

Initially, many mental health professionals resisted the pressure to deliver evidence-based practice, arguing that such practices were rigid and mechanistic, that a focus on research evidence devalued the healing art of therapy and interfered with the all-important therapeutic relationship. As a result, a significant tension developed in our field between the scientists who were promoting rigorous research to identify the most effective treatment approaches and some clinicians who were skeptical about the relevance of this research to their actual practice. Clinicians criticized researchers as detached ivory tower dwellers, clueless about the realities of frontline practice and the complex diversity of their clients. Scientists criticized clinicians as resistant to change and uninterested in learning about research that would improve their practice. One author described this tension as "psychological warfare between therapists and scientists."[5] That's a very hyperbolic statement, but it certainly reinforces my point about the tension.

It is unfortunate that our field suffered this disconnect between science and practice, which you may hear referred to as the *science–practice gap*[6] or the *laboratory-clinic gap*.[7] The truth is that scientists and practitioners share the same goal, to improve clients' lives. Increasingly, scientists and practitioners are recognizing this mutual goal, and they are working together to bridge the gap between science and practice. Many scientists are working collaboratively with clinicians to conduct applied research with maximal rigor and relevance. Clinicians are helping to pose relevant research questions and to translate research findings into practice. A new discipline of "implementation science" has arisen to tackle the challenges of bridging science and practice.[8] Our field needs more people who respect both science and practice to be effective in translating across this gap. If this challenge motivates you, look for mentors who are bridge builders, who seek to integrate science and practice.

The identification and delivery of evidence-based practices are central to bridging the science–practice gap. While there are hundreds of mental health treatments that have been tested in research studies and determined to be more effective than other approaches, many clinicians still aren't using the more effective evidence-based approaches in routine care. There is a long time lag between research discoveries and common application. Estimates suggest it takes up to 20 years from the initial development and testing of an evidence-based practice to the delivery of that practice in routine care.[9] This is not unique to mental healthcare. It's not easy to change routine practices. Providers believe in the approaches they have been using and may not be highly motivated to change. They also tend to be very busy people and do not necessarily have the time or financial resources required for retraining in new practices. As noted, they may be skeptical about the benefits of new, research-based practices and the relevance of these to their own practice.

Many evidence-based practices require providers to deliver more directive, skill-building therapeutic strategies. This is in contrast to less directive strategies such as empathic listening and support, which some clinicians may be more comfortable relying upon. This distinction between active, directive, evidence-based approaches and non-directive empathy and support is another tension in the field. To illustrate this distinction, imagine that Steven has been referred to therapy because of anger outbursts at work. A directive therapist will use empathy to build a trusting relationship and will work with Steven to build his anger-management skills, using modeling (i.e., therapist demonstrates the skills) at first and then active role-playing exercises with coaching feedback (i.e., Steven practices the skills in session). The non-directive therapist will also use empathy to build a strong trusting relationship. However, they will follow Steven's lead in therapy. They'll likely ask him some questions about his angry feelings and ask him to share how he feels, but they will not necessarily focus on building any particular skills using the modeling or role-play practice strategies. This is admittedly an oversimplified example to emphasize the contrast, but as the following comment from Mary reveals, the tension between a directive and a non-directive approach to therapy is real.

> I continue to be surprised by the huge amount of time spent following the client's lead and asking questions in most therapeutic sessions rather than using directive, evidence-based teaching methods, especially since the shared ingredients across the evidence-based models are structure, directive teaching/didactic lessons, modeling techniques and in-session practice. (Mary, professor and therapist in private practice)

The benefits of evidence-based practice include better clinical outcomes and satisfaction for clients as well as better outcomes for providers. When providers are supported in learning a new evidence-based practice, they actually report lower levels of emotional exhaustion compared to providers who are unsupported.[10] So learning how to deliver evidence-based practices can actually prevent therapist burnout by building therapists' confidence in the effectiveness of their interventions. Continuous learning protects against burnout. But how do you determine exactly what the evidence-based practices are?

A full review of what is and is not an evidence-based practice is beyond the scope of this book, and no one would expect you to have comprehensive knowledge about this at this early stage in your career. (Many practicing therapists are just learning about this.) I will describe some variations in how interventions are designated as evidence-based practices. If you wish to learn more, several good resources that identify evidence-based practices are listed at the end of this section.

Approaches to identifying and implementing evidence-based practices are evolving all the time. For example, the original and still most common approach to identifying evidence-based practices is to test specific individual treatment models, also referred to as *empirically supported treatments*. You may have heard of some of these such as dialectical behavior therapy (DBT), prolonged exposure (PE) therapy for post-traumatic stress disorder (PTSD), Coping Cat for childhood anxiety, brief strategic family therapy (BSFT) for youth behavior problems and substance abuse, and many versions of cognitive behavioral therapy. There are literally hundreds of treatments meeting the criteria for evidence-based practices.

In more recent years, complementary approaches to identifying and implementing evidence-based practices have been developed to support greater flexibility desired by some clinicians. These include approaches that are called *modular*, whereby clinicians select specific treatment modules based on unique client needs, as opposed to the original standard of delivering a treatment program in its entirety.[11] This has some similarity to a "common elements of evidence-based practice" approach my own research group has promoted.[12] We have advocated for identifying practice elements that are common across evidence-based treatment models and training clinicians to deliver these flexibly. Finally, there is growing support for *transdiagnostic* treatment models for children and adults; these are treatment elements effective for multiple anxiety and mood disorders (hence the *transdiagnostic* label, meaning that they cross multiple diagnoses). I believe these and other exciting innovations to come will inspire more clinicians to adopt an evidence-based approach to practice.

When you are exploring graduate programs, I urge you to look for a commitment to training in evidence-based practices. You will be able to find programs in each discipline that share this commitment, but it is not universal. This priority is important because you want to learn the practices that are most likely to benefit your clients. Evidence-based practice is ethical practice. It's also beneficial for your career aspirations because many employers want to hire providers who know how to deliver evidence-based practices. If you want to learn more about what types of practices are evidence-based, you can consult a variety of website resources. I've listed several, some of which have search capacity for locating specific treatment models for specific types of clinical problems. The resources are listed in alphabetical order, not necessarily in order of preference.

Website Resources on Evidence-Based Practices

Association for Behavioral and Cognitive Therapies: www.abct.org/Help/ ?m = mFindHelp&fa = WhatIsEBPpublic
California Evidence-Based Clearinghouse for Child Welfare: www.cebc4cw.org

Cochrane: www.cochrane.org

Evidence-Based Behavioral Practice: ebbp.org

Evidence-Based Programs for Positive Youth Development: www.blueprintsprograms.com

Oxford University Press: Treatments That Work series. https://www.oxfordclinicalpsych.com/page/307/%20Treatments%20That%20Work

PracticeWise: www.practicewise.com

Society of Clinical Child & Adolescent Psychology: www.effectivechildtherapy.com

Society of Clinical Psychology, Division 12 of the American Psychological Association: https://div12.org

Substance Abuse and Mental Health Services Administration's Evidence-Based Practices Resource Center: www.samhsa.gov/ebp-resource-center

What Is Measurement-Based Care and Why Is It Important?

Measurement-based care refers to clinical decision-making informed by assessment. When practicing measurement-based care, clinicians use valid assessment tools, such as standardized questionnaires and rating scales, to measure clients' symptoms and functioning at the outset of treatment and throughout to assess progress. They adjust treatment strategies depending on progress toward the desired outcomes. Similar concepts and terms include the use of measurement feedback systems and routine outcome monitoring. The important point is that clinical decisions, such as diagnoses and treatment strategies, are made using actual data as opposed to relying exclusively on subjective perceptions. Likewise, data are used for evaluating treatment progress and impact. Multiple research studies demonstrate that clients are likely to benefit more from treatment if the clinician utilizes a measurement-based care approach.[13]

Once again, you may be thinking that this makes logical sense and wondering why I'm advocating for something so obvious. For example, if you injure your arm, wouldn't you want your doctor to take an X-ray to determine if it's broken and if so, to pinpoint the type of break to determine the specific treatment plan? After a few weeks you'd want a follow-up X-ray to check if the bone is healing properly and to determine when you can get back to your usual activities. This measurement-based approach sounds a lot more effective than a physician simply using their judgment (without benefit of an X-ray) to make decisions.

This broken arm example is admittedly a slightly unfair analogy to mental health because it is more difficult to measure mental health problems as precisely. However, I am using this example to highlight how we expect healthcare providers to use established measurement tools even if they are fairly certain of diagnosis and treatment based on clinical perceptions. I could cite other examples, such as blood tests to identify infections, skin biopsies in dermatology, or EKGs in cardiology. Responsible providers use valid measurement tools in their repertoire to confirm or challenge their clinical impressions. As mental healthcare providers, we need to do the same.

Even though our measurement tools in mental health are not necessarily as precise as an X-ray or a lab test, we do have hundreds of reliable and valid measurement tools to assess psychological symptoms, substance use, mental health wellness, trauma exposure, family relationship conflicts, parenting styles, cognitive ability, and other relevant constructs. Established measures undergo multiple steps of psychometric testing to demonstrate reliability and validity. Increasingly, they are tested with diverse samples of participants to identify potential bias in interpretation by cultural background, age group, gender, language skills, etc. In graduate school, you'll learn more about the details of psychometric testing and how to select measurement tools that are reliable, valid, feasible, and culturally responsive.

The push for measurement-based care is another source of tension in our field. Unfortunately, some clinicians don't use standardized measures to inform their decision-making. Seeking to understand the reasons behind this, my colleagues and I surveyed practicing clinicians from multiple disciplines many years ago, and the majority were skeptical about the benefits of using standardized measures.[14] More recent studies suggest there has been some shift in clinicians' attitudes about the use of standardized measurement, but the majority still do not routinely use such tools.[15]

In addition to general skepticism, our research and that of others points to several reasons clinicians may be reluctant to use standardized measures. Many clinicians feel that such measures are infeasible due to costs and the time required to administer and score the measures. Some also point to cultural and literacy challenges for their clients. Interestingly, clinicians assume that clients don't like to fill out questionnaires, but there is not a lot of evidence to support this perception. Most of us expect that when we see a healthcare provider, we'll need to complete forms regarding health history. Some clinicians feel that structured measurement tools may interfere with getting to know a client interpersonally—although there is no compelling evidence for that perception either.

Nevertheless, some of the criticisms of standardized measurement have merit. It's true that many measures are too lengthy, and some can be costly. Also, our field continues to grapple with multicultural relevance and validity in assessment. However, just like in the case of evidence-based practice research, there have been improvements in both feasibility and multicultural validity of assessment. While our measures are not perfect, the limitations should not be a reason for avoiding the use of measurement tools altogether.

I find it frustrating that many clinicians who are skeptical about the use of standardized measurement tools don't have any skepticism about their own judgment. Clinicians' overconfidence in the validity of their clinical judgment has been called out as a major problem in our field.[16] I've experienced this firsthand with clinicians telling me that they don't need to use any sort of measure because they know best about how their clients are doing or feeling; some have said that they know better than the client themselves. Oh, to have such unshakable confidence!

Mental health professionals have fallible judgment just like all other humans. We have blind spots and biases, such as paying more attention to data that confirm our opinion than to any evidence to the contrary. Even with all the best intentions, if we base our clinical decision-making on our judgment alone, we will make mistakes. Standardized measures offer a more objective data source to balance our judgment. I'm all for paying close attention to our intuition as one important source of information, but we must complement it with standardized measurement.

In this field we are often called on to make judgments that have serious consequences for people's lives. For example, we assign diagnoses that can have vocational, financial, educational, and even legal implications. Although there's been significant progress in efforts to define diagnostic criteria more objectively, subjective judgment still plays a big role. In addition to diagnostic judgments, we make consequential treatment decisions, such as placing an individual in a psychiatric hospital. Forensic mental health practitioners make judgments and recommendations with life-altering implications about issues like competency to stand trial, likelihood of guilt or innocence, impact of a crime on a victim, and advisability of parole. Relying exclusively on subjective clinical judgment for all these types of decisions is irresponsible and unethical.

Relying on clinical judgment alone to assess progress and success in therapy is also irresponsible. Research has demonstrated that therapists are not necessarily accurate judges of how well therapy is benefiting their clients. We may assume all is well if the client keeps coming back, but that is not an adequate indicator. Clients also have conscious and unconscious biases of their own that can obscure how things are really going. For example, the social desirability bias may lead a client to give the therapist positive feedback regardless of whether they are actually making progress toward their goals. I see this pattern frequently. Clients don't want to disappoint their therapist, so they agreeably indicate that things are going well when, in fact, they may not be. Similarly, you may remember learning about cognitive dissonance in an introductory psychology class. The theory also has relevance in this context. Since clients are investing time and money, as well as emotional energy, in therapy, they are biased toward seeing that investment as worthwhile. Judging that investment as useless would create cognitive dissonance.

In general, clients' ratings of their satisfaction with therapy are usually rather high, which is great. However, I've been disappointed to learn that satisfaction ratings are not strongly correlated to actual clinical changes.[17] It seems like satisfaction with treatment should be very strongly correlated to meeting treatment goals and demonstrating real change—in behavior, emotions, relationships, self-esteem, substance use, etc. But the data suggest this is not always true.

So what's going on? Imagine yourself as a client; you feel satisfied because your therapist is very kind and supportive, empathizing with you about difficult people in your life and reassuring you that you are doing fine. Yet, what if your addiction challenges persist or you can't seem to commit to a relationship or you continue to avoid the situations that make you anxious? Satisfaction with therapy is one indicator of its impact but not a sufficient sign of clinical effectiveness.

A measurement-based approach can assess both satisfaction and actual behavior or symptom change. It can also raise alarms when things aren't going well during treatment. Measurement feedback systems can alert a clinician when a client is exhibiting high-risk signs for suicidal behavior or treatment dropout. Sometimes clients will reveal thoughts and feelings on a questionnaire that they have difficulty discussing. Sophisticated measurement feedback systems also collect data on the treatment strategies delivered by the clinician and the client's response, so it is possible to look for patterns regarding what seems to be working best. Experts argue that these types of systems are imperative to help clinicians learn about which interventions are having the desired impact and to improve the effectiveness of mental healthcare overall.[18] Measurement feedback systems can also help to sustain and improve evidence-based practices.[19]

In addition to shifting clinicians' attitudes about the importance of measurement-based care, we need to address feasibility challenges. Collecting all of these data sounds time-consuming and costly. Fortunately, innovative researchers and clinicians are working together to develop software to facilitate mental health measurement. Clients can respond to standardized assessments remotely, and client data can be shared with their clinician in advance of sessions to inform care. These types of remotely accessible data collection and communication platforms may become more common now that the pandemic forced clinicians and clients to communicate remotely. A few systems have been implemented and have demonstrated a positive impact on client outcomes.[20] These types of systems offer clinicians an online "dashboard," highlighting important client data for clinical decision-making. I imagine that we will see exciting developments in this area in the near future, likely utilizing mobile devices.

In Conclusion

As I read through this chapter, I imagine you saying, "So, tell us what you really think." My opinions about the value of science in mental healthcare may be lacking in subtlety. During the early years of the evidence-based practice movement, when I spoke to groups of students or clinicians about the value of science, I often felt like a proselytizer or a particularly passionate salesperson. I faced a lot of skepticism and had to be very persuasive. So many mental health clinicians had dismissive attitudes about science and its relevance to therapy. I'll never forget the respected therapist who told me that if she were required to use a research-based measure of treatment outcome, she would have to "throw her heart out the window." These experiences have motivated me to work hard to break down this false dichotomy between the science and the healing art of therapy. I've tried to humanize and demystify the science while also respecting the heart and soul of the healing art.

After more than 20 years of teaching and writing about these issues, I'm happy to see a significant shift in attitudes, especially among students entering the field. The majority are eager to learn more about how science can improve their ability to help clients. This is so promising because it reflects that we are experiencing an essential shift in the culture of mental healthcare, normalizing research-based approaches to practice. I hope you'll contribute to building on this momentum into the future.

13
The Future of Mental Healthcare

I believe there are many exciting opportunities in the world of technology and artificial intelligence. I just hope that our field can maintain the value of real human to human connection. (Cassidy, therapist in private practice and instructor)

In this opening quote, Cassidy summarizes a common sentiment among therapists and previews one of the major themes in this chapter: What are the exciting innovations in our field, and how might these expand and improve mental healthcare? Are there potential unintended consequences of such innovations? Should we worry about therapists being replaced by robots?

By speculating about the future, I am hoping to help you prepare for long-term success. A psychotherapy career in 2040 is likely to look very different from a psychotherapy career today. This chapter highlights four emerging developments in mental health: (1) technological innovations; (2) neuroscience applications; (3) integrated healthcare delivery, and (4) global mental health, with particular emphasis on technological innovations.

Technological Innovations

Technology has provided some of the coolest things for the mental health field. We are able to personalize what we deliver to patients at the click of a button. Results, risk concerns, and generated notes are all possible because of technology. In addition, we are able to deliver incredible treatment through various forms of technology, all with the goal of improving patient lives. (Nick, therapist in hospital and instructor)

In this section you'll learn about the growing use of remote therapy, as well as mobile applications (apps), wearable technology, and therapeutic video games. I'll introduce exciting developments in the use of virtual reality, artificial intelligence (AI), and precision medicine. These innovations carry great promise to expand access to needed mental healthcare and improve our ability to personalize effective treatment. However, as is common with innovations, we must consider the potential risks and ethical challenges. There are significant trade-offs; many therapists are concerned about how increasing use of technology in mental healthcare will minimize the focus on real human connections that are so important to our work. Overall, I am very optimistic about how these developments will advance our field, but I am also cautious, recognizing that technological innovations often come with excessive hype and unrealistic expectations.[1]

At the start of this chapter I posed a provocative question: Should we worry about robots replacing therapists? It's not as crazy a question as it may seem. There are robots named *Ellie* and *Pepper* who are being used therapeutically with veterans, older adults, children with autism, and individuals with sexual dysfunction.[2] So should you embark on this career path if robots will be taking over your job? It turns out that there is actually a website that calculates the odds of various jobs becoming obsolete due to automation (see Will Robots Take My Job? at willrobotstakemyjob.com). The good news for all of us is that this site evaluates a mental health career as "totally safe" from automation risk.[3]

Even if our jobs are not at risk, it would be foolish to ignore the potential impact of technological innovations on our field moving forward. Many of the therapists I know are concerned about the proliferation of technological innovations, such as AI, virtual reality, and mobile apps. They assume that such innovations will negatively impact mental healthcare, and many are reluctant to even learn about them. I'm concerned that this avoidance strategy is unwise. Although robots are not going to replace therapists in the foreseeable future, I predict that the therapists who do not learn how to effectively use technology to enhance therapy will be replaced by those who do!

Creative mental health professionals are using technological innovations to expand their reach in numerous ways. Some produce YouTube videos, podcasts, or blogs addressing a wide range of mental health topics. Talented therapists have posted TikTok videos tackling a wide variety of topics including intergenerational trauma and healthy ways to express rage.[4] These outreach methods offer education to the public and can also serve as a marketing strategy to generate potential referrals. Like much of what is discussed in this chapter, the possibilities for expanding impact are exciting, but these platforms are unregulated; the effectiveness of these innovative communication methods is unknown, and some may even have unintended consequences.

As you learn more about the technological innovations described in this chapter, consider how they can be used along a continuum ranging from technologies that are designed to be used as stand-alone therapeutic interventions to those that are used to support or extend therapy with a human clinician. It's exciting and daunting to be in the early stages of a significant evolution in how therapy is delivered.

Remote Therapy and Internet Therapy

I worry about an increasing trend toward overvaluing and/or overselling the powers of teletherapy. The depth and breadth of nonverbal connection, the information it provides, and the simple experience of being in a room with another cannot be replicated by therapy via text, phone, Skype, etc. (Leita, therapist in private practice and retired instructor/supervisor)

Remote therapy refers to psychotherapy conducted by phone or video conferencing. The majority of therapists I know shared the sentiments Leita articulates in this quote, which was submitted before the COVID-19 pandemic. However, despite their misgivings, the pandemic's physical distancing restrictions required therapists and clients alike to adapt to remote therapy very quickly. Most therapists had minimal experience with telephone or video therapy, so the learning curve was steep—all during a time of increased stress and need for mental health support.[5] Yet, in just a few months, regular use of remote therapy among psychiatrists, for example, rose from 2% pre-pandemic to 85% during the pandemic.

While the pandemic did not inspire the invention of remote therapy, it certainly pushed it to the mainstream. Professional organizations, ethics boards, and funders adapted very quickly by offering teletherapy training to therapists and demonstrating uncharacteristic flexibility to reduce barriers across state lines. I am very proud of our professions for adapting so quickly to meet clients' needs during this crisis.

Multiple research studies indicate that remote therapy can be as effective as in-person therapy, and it offers clear advantages in terms of access and convenience.[6] While most therapists and clients likely miss the in-person connection, I've heard from many who are pleasantly surprised by how well remote therapy has gone despite their initial worries. Unexpected benefits include a glimpse into the client's "real-life" environment. Plus, a minority of clients seem to actually open up more in remote therapy, with the distance perhaps adding to a sense of safety to express difficult emotions or experiences. Of course, there are exceptions; some therapists chose not to embrace remote work, and they may find themselves out of work. Others report many frustrations with glitchy technology—perhaps similar to technological glitches you may have experienced in remote education and all other types of remote work and socializing.

Additional concerns about remote therapy include disparities in reliable internet and device access, ethical issues having to do with maintaining confidentiality, as well as the ability to immediately intervene when there is a risk to a client's safety. The physical boundaries of a therapy office help to reinforce confidentiality and often provide a comforting ritual of entering the therapy space. These may be more difficult to achieve remotely. In addition, there is no doubt that remote therapy can obscure important non-verbal communication. Telephone (i.e., non-video) therapy is particularly challenging due to the lack of visual cues for facial expressions, body movements (e.g., fidgeting, wringing hands, and tearing up), and even the surrounding environment. Modalities such as group and family therapy may be difficult due to the logistics of multiple people involved. Likewise, it can be difficult to keep children engaged in sustained remote therapy sessions.

As you are reading this book in a (hopefully) post-pandemic world, the long-term sustainability of remote therapy will be clearer. During the pandemic, I think it is fair to say that remote therapy has been life-saving for clients, as well as career-saving for therapists. Once the restrictions of the pandemic are lifted, it will be very interesting to see if remote therapy retains its popularity. My guess is that given the advantages for access and convenience, remote therapy will remain a popular option in the post-pandemic future, despite its inherent challenges.[7]

Internet therapy is a variation of remote therapy where interventions are delivered via a website. These interventions have been available for over a decade, and more than 100 studies have demonstrated that internet-delivered, evidence-based therapy can be effective for both adults[8] and children.[9] Most studies find that outcomes are better when internet-based therapy is guided by a human therapist, as opposed to self-guided by the client. Therapists can use the internet to deliver treatment content that includes text messages, audio, and/or video content. Internet-based cognitive behavioral therapy (CBT) has been used effectively to treat children and adults with a variety of mental health and somatic problems including depression, anxiety, headache, and other pain issues. This delivery method has all the same potential access and convenience benefits of remote therapy, as well as the same potential technological and ethical challenges.

Mobile Apps

Estimates suggest that there are approximately 325,000 health-related apps available,[10] and at least 15,000 of those are mental health–related.[11] Most people who have a mobile device have downloaded at least one health-related app. Some of the most common mental health–related apps are designed to support relaxation, deep-breathing exercises, and meditation. But there are apps designed to address a variety of specific mental health issues as well, including anxiety, depression, sleep disorders, post-traumatic stress disorder (PTSD), childhood behavioral problems, and eating disorders. While some apps offer strategies consistent with evidence-based practice elements, many do not.[12] Mental health apps have the potential to dramatically and efficiently extend access to mental healthcare, but more research on effectiveness is needed.[13]

Unlike traditional mental healthcare which is highly regulated through licensing boards and ethics reviews, there is no oversight of the effectiveness, safety, or utility of mobile apps. Anyone can create and market an app whether or not they have mental health training. Across the roughly 15,000 available apps, there are likely many that are unhelpful and some that may even be harmful.[14] Some may also carry security risks for personal data and confidentiality breaches that have not been adequately addressed. How are consumers or therapists supposed to figure out which apps may be effective, safe, and user-friendly?

When you search for an app, perhaps you rely on customer ratings. For games or entertainment, that's likely sufficient. However, subjective and easily manipulated customer ratings are not likely the best way to identify a therapeutic app. Fortunately, there are services, such as PsyberGuide (OneMindPsyberGuide.org) that offer helpful reviews of apps by mental health experts. This site allows you to search by clinical problem area or type of intervention. I highly recommend checking it out to learn more about the range of available apps and the extent to which they have been evaluated for effectiveness, safety, and security, as well as user-friendliness. PsyberGuide is a trusted and objective resource for identifying and evaluating the vast array of mental health apps.

One of the most sophisticated mental health apps currently available is Woebot.[15] Clients interact with Woebot through instant messaging with a chatbot. According to the website, in September of 2020, almost 5 million text messages were exchanged through the app every week, and 75% of users reported feeling better after their first use. The app uses AI to deliver CBT-based treatment elements. The team of developers includes mental health professionals partnering with tech entrepreneurs and AI specialists. Research on the effectiveness of Woebot is promising, with demonstrated reductions in depression and anxiety symptoms among a group of college student clients.[16]

So should we worry about Woebots replacing therapists? I think we need to shift away from this replacement question to more nuanced questions about how these types of innovations can optimize care. How can we human therapists utilize these innovations to make therapy more helpful, supporting clients in between sessions or collecting useful real-time data on moods and thoughts throughout the week to discuss with a therapist. One of the limitations of traditional therapy is that contact with a therapist is usually just 1 hour a week, at best. That represents less than 1% of a person's week. There is growing evidence that when used in conjunction with a human therapist, apps can extend therapy's effectiveness.[17]

In addition, I believe we need to pay more attention to matching the severity of mental health needs to the type of intervention. These technological innovations can definitely help with that. Think of this like triaging in medicine.[18] Perhaps people who are struggling with mild symptoms of anxiety or depression could be helped with something like Woebot with only minimal contact with a human therapist. Alternatively, individuals struggling with severe anxiety or depression likely need more intensive assessment and treatment from a skilled human provider. Better triaging would help us redistribute valuable mental health resources so that those in greatest need receive the most intensive help. I am hopeful that your generation of mental health experts will advance our knowledge of which types of interventions are most clinically effective and cost-effective for which types of clients.

Wearable Technology

Wearable technology devices include smart watches, sensors, and patches worn on the body. Referred to as *ecological momentary assessment* devices, they provide real-time personalized data collection in naturalistic environments. These devices have been used for years in research to assess frequency of physical movement and have become more sophisticated. For example, some researchers have been able to identify people's mood differences based on movement patterns,[19] and others have used geo-positioning data to identify socially anxious students who tend to avoid public spaces.[20] Analysis of a person's gait has been used to estimate blood alcohol level.[21] These are just some of the interesting ways that wearable technology is being used to assess mental health–related issues.[22]

The use of wearable technology to deliver treatment elements (as opposed to assessment of problems) is even more innovative. One basic common example may be my own smart watch that vibrates and recommends that I get up and move around at least once an hour. It also prompts me to follow its guided deep-breathing exercise at different times during the day. Frankly, I'm not certain if these deep-breathing prompts are random or prompted by data on my heart rate, but they are effective. I'm afraid this may be an example of the technology being "smarter" than the user.

There have been a few efforts to deliver interventions for depression via wearable technology, but the research is limited.[23] A proposed study presents a good example of the possibilities: Individuals could be coached, via device, to practice a deep-breathing or progressive muscle relaxation exercise and then asked to rate their mood. The device could track their response, and something called a *bandit algorithm* could figure out which exercise was most effective for that individual. That information would then be used to prompt them with the best exercise in the future.[24] Adding this element of personalized data collection and feedback seems particularly important for more targeted effectiveness.

Of course, the technologies described in this chapter can be combined. For example, mobile apps may use wearable technology data for assessment or intervention. I am still marveling at my ability to have a telephone or text conversation by speaking to my smart watch, but I know this is just the tip of the iceberg in terms of the possibilities for wearable technology. Your generation of mental healthcare providers will discover marvels that we can't even imagine now.

Video Games

Most of us don't think of video games as therapeutic interventions. In fact, it's usually just the opposite. Excessive video gaming has been associated with mental health problems such as low self-esteem, aggression, and symptoms of depression and anxiety; *internet gaming disorder* is now a psychiatric diagnosis.[25] But could the immersive, fun experience of video gaming be harnessed for therapeutic benefit? The answer is yes. Smart, creative mental health and tech experts have been working together, capitalizing on the appeal of video gaming to deliver effective mental health interventions.

EndeavorRx is the first Food and Drug Administration–approved video game for children with attention deficit hyperactivity disorder (commonly referred to as ADHD) that can be prescribed by doctors.[26] Preliminary research demonstrates that youth who play this game show improved attentional control. SPARX (Smart, Positive, Active, Realistic, X-Factor Thoughts)[27] is an interactive fantasy game delivering CBT elements to adolescents suffering from depression. The player chooses an avatar who pursues a series of challenges to restore balance in a fantasy world, working to master coping skills at each of the seven levels. There is a guide within the game that provides some education, assesses the player's mood, and reviews homework exercises. A paper workbook is used in combination with the video game. Rigorous research found that the outcomes for youth using SPARX, which was entirely self-guided, were similar to outcomes for youth receiving usual community-based mental healthcare. The majority of youth also reported enjoying the game.[28]

Another innovation combines the convenience of a mobile app with video game engagement. One study gave 75 adults with anxiety access to a "gamified" version of a scientifically supported therapeutic intervention called *attention-bias modification training*. You play by following two characters on your mobile screen, tracing their paths as precisely and quickly as possible. Participants who played this game reported feeling less nervous after just 25 minutes of play, and after 45 minutes, their attention biases that are associated with anxiety shifted in a positive direction.[29]

While these two emerging examples offer promising results based on sound research, mental health video games carry some of the same risks and challenges of other technological innovations. There is no regulation for these games. Research on effectiveness and safety is limited, and some may not be based on scientifically supported therapeutic principles.

A different type of problem can occur when games are created by mental health professionals without gaming expertise, resulting in games that may not be as much fun.[30] The most successful innovations are those that involve strong partnerships between mental health professionals knowledgeable about evidence-based practices and gaming experts who know how to make the games fully engaging.

Virtual Reality

Virtual reality (VR) interventions have been developed to treat a variety of mental health issues, most notably anxiety, PTSD, and substance abuse.[31] This technology has existed since before 2000, but until recently, the high costs made it infeasible for widespread use. Now the hardware and software are more affordable.

The benefits of VR for treating someone with a specific phobia, such as a fear of heights, spiders, or flying in a plane, are clear. The best-established evidence-based treatment for a phobia is exposure therapy. With exposure therapy, the therapist teaches the client coping skills to use before gradually exposing them to increasingly challenging images and experiences with the feared object or behavior. Without VR technology, therapists must rely on either (a) having the client imagine the feared object or experience or (b) conducting real-life exposures (i.e., experiences such as visiting a tall building, touching a real spider, boarding an actual airplane, etc.). VR is an effective way to simulate exposure to feared stimuli in a safe and controlled environment. Sophisticated VR technology incorporates sight, sound, motion, and even scent senses to simulate reality.

Imagine you have a fear of flying. With VR, a therapist can help you overcome this fear by simulating each step: entering the airport and going through security, boarding the plane, buckling your seatbelt, hearing the safety instructions, feeling the rumble of engines for takeoff and even smelling the jet fuel, or encountering unexpected turbulence. The VR experience can be personalized to the client's unique circumstances, offering a far more potent intervention than simply imagining it. VR exposure therapy is also more practical than conducting actual exposure therapy at an airport, although one could imagine the final step of therapy to be an experience like that.

VR has also been used effectively to treat military veterans with PTSD. The technology can replicate the sights and sounds of bomb explosions, including vibrations felt through a vest, to help veterans cope with recurrent traumatic memories.[32] The potential applications for this technology are expanding to include issues such as body image disorders, cognitive rehabilitation after a stroke or traumatic brain injury, and substance abuse. To treat alcohol addiction, for example, clients are placed in a VR high-risk environment, such as a bar; an attractive person offers them a drink, and they have the opportunity to practice sobriety skills.[33] Can you imagine how much more effective this could be than simply talking about this potential scenario?

Research on the effectiveness of VR for treatment of anxiety is strong, and evidence for many other applications is growing; but the technology has not yet been widely adopted.[34] It does require an investment in hardware and software, and therapists need training to use VR effectively. One of the unanticipated risks is that VR is so effective it can result in generating false memories. In one study, young children participated in a VR experience in which they saw themselves swimming with whales. When questioned later, many reported that they had, in fact, swum with whales.[35] This particular false memory is not necessarily problematic (unless they feel empowered to jump into the orca tank for "another" swim on their next visit to Sea World). However, one could imagine unethical misuse of this technology to create false memories regarding witnessing criminal behavior, etc. This is a great example of how innovations reveal new ethical challenges in our field.

AI and Precision Medicine

Some of the innovations already described, such as mobile apps and therapeutic video games, utilize AI, identifying patterns or relationships in data and using those data to prompt the next step; this is also referred to as *data-mining*. *Machine learning* is a common type of AI that uses algorithms to learn from data and make predictions. Think back to the examples of how an app like Woebot can identify effective coping strategies based on a user's responses to mood-tracking data. AI is a rapidly expanding field that has the potential to revolutionize many aspects of our lives, including health and healthcare.[36] I'll just offer a few interesting examples of applications to mental health, but if you want to learn more, I recommend reading the comprehensive article about this by Leonard Bickman.[37]

Data-mining strategies are being used in interesting ways to identify individuals with mental health challenges. For example, social media data (specifically Facebook and Twitter) have been used to identify individuals with depression.[38] Machine learning has been used to analyze conversational speech patterns to identify individuals with psychosis[39] and to identify risk for the development of PTSD among injured children.[40] And, as noted, movement data from wearable technology have been used to identify individuals with social anxiety. These examples represent important ways that AI can be used to predict or identify individuals who need mental healthcare, but what about informing us on how to effectively treat them? This is where the field of precision medicine comes in.

Precision medicine refers to the "customization of healthcare, with medical decisions, treatments, practices or products being tailored to the individual patient."[41] The hope is that precision medicine will lead us to deliver exactly the right treatment to the right person at the right time. It's a contrast to the one-size-fits-all approach. AI is applied to big data sets to find associations between patient characteristics and treatment outcomes. For example, think about when multiple hospitals contribute patient data to a registry on cancer treatment. AI can be used to identify patterns associated with good and bad outcomes.

This all sounds very promising, but applying precision medicine to psychotherapy is somewhat of a distant fantasy. Identifying the precise treatment for a cancer patient based on the genetic profile of their tumor cells is challenging, but it is still infinitely more straightforward than identifying the precise psychotherapeutic approach for a client. We don't have biomarkers or X-rays to identify the treatment targets. Our treatment targets, such as thoughts, feelings, behaviors, relationships, communication patterns, and social skills, are multi-determined and much harder to measure precisely.

As with all innovations, the use of AI in healthcare has also presented new ethical challenges. When patients' detailed personal health data are included in big data sets, is their privacy always well protected? It is relatively easy now to get genetic information through popular DNA home testing services such as 23andMe or Ancestry.com. How secure is the information? What are the implications for customers who choose to get their health risk data? There are many ethical dilemmas about these data beyond the issue of privacy. What are the implications for knowing that you are at increased risk for something like bipolar illness or Alzheimer's disease? How much do we know about the accuracy of such a prediction that could have a major impact on your life decisions? These are just some of the big questions that are raised by these innovations.

Neuroscientific Applications

As I noted in the beginning, the bulk of this chapter is devoted to technological innovations. But in the remaining sections, I will summarize other important trends likely to significantly impact the future of mental healthcare. The first of these is advances in neuroscience. Over recent years, we've seen growing evidence of how effective psychotherapy results in measurable changes in the brain. This is an amazing advance for our field. For too long, skeptics could argue that talk therapy didn't have any signifi-cant measurable neurological impact. No longer, since we now have multiple studies demonstrating how psychotherapy can impact brain structure, brain chemistry, and brain function.[42]

In recent decades we've learned a lot about the neurobiological bases of psycholog-ical phenomena, such as memories, emotions, and thoughts. We can now pinpoint specific areas of the brain that are activated for different tasks. Many have hoped that these advances would lead to more accurate diagnoses of psychological phenom-enon. Could we use brain scans to identify homicidal or suicidal risk? Or risks for bi-polar disorder, depression, or anxiety? Might a blood test provide a valid and reliable indicator of risk for schizophrenia or dementia?

While there have been exciting advances in understanding brain development for disorders such as autism,[43] the high expectations for major discoveries in diagnosis have not been met yet. Efforts to translate basic neuroscientific discoveries into valid diagnostic tools and effective psychotherapeutic interventions are just barely begin-ning. Greater integration of neuroscience with psychotherapy is potentially trans-formative, but it is in its infancy right now.[44]

I can only speculate about what some of the innovative applications of neuro-science to psychotherapy might be, but I'll describe a few emerging possibilities. First, over recent decades we have learned a lot about how traumatic experiences, such as child abuse, violence, profound loss, or neglect, can impact brain devel-opment and functioning. We've learned how trauma can "reset" people's brains, making them more vigilantly wary of threats.[45] We know that children who have been maltreated often exhibit neurobiological signs of chronic stress.[46] And ad-verse childhood events (referred to as ACEs) such as these are associated with higher risk for a variety of health and mental health problems in adulthood.[47] So while our knowledge of the impact of trauma on brains, bodies, and spirits has grown dramatically, our ability to translate this knowledge into effective treatment is just beginning.

There are many directions this work might go. For example, there is growing ev-idence that very young children who exhibit significant emotional dysregulation (constantly irritable and unable to manage strong emotions like fear, anger, or sad-ness) are at much higher risk for developing mental health problems.[48] Most toddlers and preschoolers gain emotional regulation skills over time, but those who have con-tinued difficulty are at higher risk for problems ranging from anxiety to aggressive behavior.[49]

How might neuroscience address this? Perhaps neurobiological markers will be discovered that help us better identify children who are prone to these challenges. Then, we may learn how to target therapies to reduce these kids' risk for problematic outcomes. Perhaps the discoveries will identify genetic, prenatal, trauma exposure, environmental, or family factors to target. Who knows? My point is that there will likely be advances in coming years that will help us to more precisely identify those at risk and point us toward effective therapies to minimize the risks.

I mentioned emotional regulation in this section because it relates to so many of the challenges bringing people into therapy. Many of our current evidence-based psychotherapeutic approaches seek to improve a client's ability to manage their emotions. One relatively new treatment approach called *emotion regulation therapy*[50] has been used to treat problems such as generalized anxiety and major depression in adults. This treatment draws largely from CBT as well as mindfulness interventions. It helps people gain skills to manage negative emotions, counteracting excessive worrying and self-criticism. Clients have demonstrated improved flexibility in their thinking and ability to adapt to conflict, as well as improved ability to sustain attention to goal-directed activities. (Who couldn't use some of these benefits?)

Why am I introducing this therapy in the neuroscience section? Because there is exciting research demonstrating that clients who engaged in this therapy demonstrated changes in their brains along with their improved psychological symptoms. Specifically, brain scans revealed improved connectivity in participants' brains that was associated with reductions in their symptoms of anxiety and depression. This is just one example of how neuroscientific and psychotherapeutic expertise can be combined to benefit individuals struggling with mental health challenges.

The growing and complex field of psychoneuroimmunology highlights more exciting possibilities. This field examines the interaction between our brain, our immune system, and psychological functioning. During the pandemic, we have heard a lot about immune system functioning, but did you know that researchers have identified clear links between inflammatory factors (signaling immune system functioning) and problems such as depression? Many studies show that treatments such as CBT have significant positive impacts on participants' depression symptoms and their immune system functioning.[51] Now the challenge—and opportunity—is to translate basic neuroscientific and immunological findings into effective personalized treatments targeting inflammatory mechanisms to treat depression.[52] This exciting field reinforces the fact that good psychotherapy impacts the mind, brain, and body in profound ways.

I've saved some of the most innovative developments for the end of this section. In what sounds like the plot for a science fiction movie, Elon Musk and others are developing "brain-reading" and "brain-writing" technologies. These include non-invasive models like a helmet that uses infrared light to read brain activity, designed by Facebook's Reality Labs division. Other groups are developing invasive, surgically implanted devices like Musk's *neuralink*, a small implant with hair-like filaments, and *neurograins*, developed by a company aptly named BrainGate.[53] These types of inventions are being used to help those who suffer from traumatic brain injury, stroke, or neurological conditions such as Parkinson's disease. They can also help people with different forms of paralysis and speech limitations. Robert Juste, a neurobiologist at Columbia University, suggests that feasible, non-invasive brain-reading and brain-writing technology could "change humanity" but that our society is not ready for the implications.[54]

Imagine how these innovations could be applied to therapeutic interventions for mental health problems. Maybe a device could pick up early signs of emotional overload and then electronically zap some neurons to manage those emotions. How precise could this be? Can we zap homicidal or suicidal urges, or deep despair and terror, while making sure to retain triumphant joy, overwhelming pleasure or love, and astonishing wonder? The extent to which we want our emotions to be neutralized is a profoundly important ethical and philosophical question. Just ponder that one for a while.

These devices could potentially address impulse control challenges related to substance use or eating behaviors. Maybe this technology will help to manage debilitating symptoms of psychosis or bipolar disorder with targeted assessment (brain-reading) and neurological intervention (brain-writing). The possibilities to ease suffering sound promising, but the ethical concerns about devices that can read our brain activity and/or change our brain activity are mind-boggling. The ways in which such technology could be misused are frightening.

As you imagine all the possibilities in neuroscientific development, it's also important to recognize long-standing tensions in our field. Over many decades, we have sometimes embraced scientific diagnostic and therapeutic methods that we now recognize as totally invalid, harmful, and often barbaric. These include phrenology (diagnosing based on the shape of the skull) and the hysteria diagnosis, trepanation (drilling holes in the skull), lobotomies, and electroshock therapy, just to name a few. If you are interested in this history and how it relates to current challenges in mental health, I recommend the book *Mind Fixers* by Anne Harrington.[55] This book highlights how we have often looked to neuroscience, genetics, and psychopharmacology to identify miraculous cures for mental health problems. Despite the many amazing discoveries from these disciplines in recent decades, miracle cures are still elusive. The basic scientific advances have not always translated well to effective treatments for psychological problems.

There are many innovative treatment approaches showing promise now, ranging from micro-dosing of psychedelic compounds to transcranial magnetic stimulation. We'll see if these innovations become accepted as best practices over time and what new innovations are discovered. I hope your generation will capitalize on neuroscientific advances to improve actual care for people struggling with psychiatric disorders. We need ethical, compassionate, and creative mental health professionals to lead these efforts.

Integrated Healthcare Delivery

Integrated care refers to the blended delivery of behavioral healthcare and physical healthcare in one clinical setting. It relies on collaboration between behavioral healthcare providers and medical providers. (The term *behavioral health* is more common than *mental health* in integrated care contexts.) The goal is to care for the whole person, recognizing that physical and behavioral health issues are interrelated. Sometimes this is called *collaborative care* or *primary care behavioral health*, but all labels refer to this integrated model.[56] Efforts to better integrate medical and behavioral healthcare are not new, but they have gained visibility in recent years. This model is a key part of the "advanced patient-centered medical home" model promoted in the Affordable Care Act, also known as Obamacare.

There is a lot of research demonstrating the benefits of integrated care, including better access to behavioral health services and financial savings, as well as overall positive health outcomes.[57] By offering behavioral healthcare in a primary healthcare setting, the goal is to reduce barriers. All the patient's needs can be met under one roof, and the providers will be able to coordinate care more effectively. This model makes care more efficient, saving both time and money. It can also reduce the potential stigma associated with seeking mental healthcare, given that virtually everyone uses primary healthcare.

Integrated care makes good sense. Think about how connected chronic health problems are to behavioral health issues. We know that stress is linked to many different medical conditions; likewise, common challenges such as substance use, chronic pain, and obesity may require both medical and behavioral health interventions. Medication compliance for chronic conditions such as diabetes often has behavioral health implications. And many people with depression or anxiety experience their distress physically with headaches, stomach aches, fatigue, and appetite or sleep issues, for example. Finally, patients often discuss significant life events with their primary care doctor, and in integrated care settings these doctors can connect the patient to behavioral healthcare providers to discuss issues such as trauma, relationship stress, parenting difficulties, bereavement, identity challenges, etc. In traditional nonintegrated healthcare settings, physicians may be aware of these needs, but they do not have time or often the expertise to address them.

You may be thinking, "So why don't we have integrated care everywhere?" It's a great question. My best answer: Anything that requires major shifts in policy and funding, as well as workforce training, is really difficult to implement. While there are currently lots of locations that offer integrated care, it is still considered an innovation and is not necessarily standard practice. However, given all the compelling research on the clinical and cost-effectiveness of integrated care, I believe it will continue to grow. If this model appeals to you, be sure to look for graduate programs that offer training and practicum placements in integrated (or collaborative) care settings. It will be valuable for you to gain experience in medical settings, learning how to collaborate with medical providers.

Integrated care offers proven strategies to address the major public health problem of unmet need for mental healthcare. It can also help to reduce unjust racial, ethnic, and socioeconomic disparities in access to needed care. Integrated care is considered a modern innovation, but the goal of treating the whole person, recognizing the connection between body, mind, and spirit for holistic physical and mental health wellness, reflects common beliefs held by ancient and indigenous cultures. Some of our current approaches to mindfulness similarly draw from ancient cultures. It's interesting to think about how modern approaches to effective care reflect some of these core ancient values.

Global Mental Health

Global mental health is the last future trend that I will review in this chapter. Evidence of the global impact of mental health problems has been gaining attention in recent years. The World Health Organization now recognizes depression as the leading cause of disability around the world.[58] Think about that. A mental health problem causes more disability than any other health issue, including cancer, heart disease, or obesity. In case you needed any more motivation to pursue this career, here it is.

Throughout this book I have mentioned the public health problem of unmet need for mental healthcare in the United States. Unfortunately, this problem is even worse in low- and middle-income countries, where very few people with mental health challenges receive any care at all.[59] There are multiple reasons for this, including limited healthcare resources, limited number of mental healthcare providers and treatment settings, and cultural barriers such as the stigma about mental health. The good news is that there are growing efforts to address these barriers across the globe with promising results.[60]

Innovative service delivery models have been developed to meet the challenges of resource limitations and diverse global cultural contexts around the world. Many models rely on *task shifting*; this refers to shifting basic care responsibilities to non-professional health workers in the community.[61] These individuals are not licensed healthcare professionals (they are often called *paraprofessionals*), but they are usually well-respected members of the community, supervised by professionals.

Empowering community health workers extends care beyond the limited professional workforce and reduces the stigma of seeking professional mental healthcare. For example, imagine a young mother in a South American village who may be struggling with postpartum depression, although not necessarily recognizing it as that. Even if some professional care is available, she is more likely to speak to a respected woman in the village about her challenges. There have been many successful variations of service delivery using task shifting for a variety of health and mental health problems.[62]

I have experienced how rewarding international work can be by partnering with an amazing team in Ethiopia. The group I work with is led by Dr. Menelik Desta in Addis Ababa, and it's called the Ethiopian School Readiness Initiative (www.ethiopianschoolready.org). Dr. Desta and his team have developed a comprehensive program designed to (a) prepare young children for success in school, (b) encourage parental engagement in education and positive parenting practices, (c) provide empowering vocational opportunities for mothers, and (d) screen children for early signs of health or behavioral health problems that could interfere with their success.

My role as a volunteer with this organization is to help the group write grants to support the program and collaborate on research evaluating the impact of the program. While this has been a bit of a "side gig" for me, it has definitely been one of the most rewarding activities of my career. Visiting the programs in Ethiopia, meeting the enthusiastic children and impressive staff, was a major highlight.[63] I'll never forget being in a packed classroom of young children proudly reading aloud and singing, asking me to help them with their English pronunciation and helping me to understand their native Amharic. Frankly, I've never seen a group of children so happy to be in a classroom setting, and I've visited a lot of schools in the United States.

You may recall that toward the end of the chapter about ethics (Chapter 7), I urged you to think about aspirational ethics, that is, pursuing social justice and equity in mental healthcare and addressing the social determinants of mental illness. This is highly relevant to global mental health efforts. International leaders in this field Vikram Patel and Paul Farmer published an important essay titled "The Moral Case for Global Mental Health Delivery"[64] in 2020. It is an impassioned plea for mental healthcare decisions to be driven by moral values, not just economic values. They highlight the fact that individuals with severe mental illnesses suffer multiple social and economic hardships, such as high rates of homelessness and incarceration, and die at younger ages compared to others. Poignantly they argue, "Our collective failure to respond to the needs of one of the most vulnerable groups of people in society is a catastrophic failure of humanity" (p. 109).

So what can you do? This is a very complex problem. If you want to learn more so that you can be an informed advocate, please check out any of these organizations that address global mental health. You may even find opportunities to participate in global projects.

- Grand Challenges Canada: Global Mental Health: https://www.grandchallenges.ca/programs/global-mental-health/
- Mental Health Innovation Network: https://www.mhinnovation.net/
- National Institute of Mental Health's Center for Global Mental Health Research: https://www.nimh.nih.gov/about/organization/cgmhr/index.shtml
- Child Family Health International: https://www.cfhi.org/
- United for Global Mental Health: https://unitedgmh.org/
- World Health Organization, Mental Health: www.who.int/health-topics/mental-health#tab=tab_1

If you are inspired to devote your career to global mental health, make sure to search for graduate programs that include this emphasis. It is not common in graduate programs, but if you search, you can find graduate programs that offer this training or at least offer global education opportunities. You may also find faculty members who do research globally, and there may be opportunities to work on their projects. When I went to graduate school, I had never heard of global mental health and didn't know anyone working abroad. There have been exciting developments since then, but there is so much more to be done. This is a wide open area with great opportunities for the adventurous.

In Conclusion

This chapter is packed with lots of information. The truth is that it could easily have been double or triple the length because there are just so many interesting and creative innovations in mental healthcare. There are exciting intersections across the four major categories I've reviewed. For example, think about how technological innovations might help to expand access to care in global contexts or in integrated care settings. The possibilities are virtually limitless; I had to rein in my own desire to include more and more examples.

I hope you have felt inspired or at least curious about all these emerging shifts in mental healthcare. Remember that there is a place for everyone. Maybe you identify as a bit of a techy, and you love the idea of working on therapeutic video games or mobile apps. Alternatively, perhaps you shudder at the use of tech in mental health and imagine yourself working with community health partners in the United States or around the world, offering culturally sensitive support in underserved communities. Maybe you want to bridge these different areas to bring neuroscientific discoveries on emotional regulation into healthcare settings around the globe. Whatever inspires you, I urge you to be open to innovation, while also holding on to the core value of human connection that defines and brings meaning to our work.

14

Shared Wisdom and
Suggested Inspiration

I urge you to commit and take the leap. You won't be sorry. This career is incredibly meaningful and rewarding. But recognize the challenges, take responsibility, have humility, and accept that you are not infallible. (Saul, therapist in private practice and retired professor)

As you reach this final chapter, I hope that you are feeling the enthusiastic encouragement expressed in this opening quote. You've learned a lot about the awesome opportunities this career path offers as well as how to prepare for some of the weighty challenges. In this chapter, I'll reinforce and expand on some of the most important themes in this book, and I'll share more wisdom from experts, sending you off with a deeper understanding of the decisions you'll face moving forward, as well as how to maximize your training opportunities. Finally, I will offer recommendations of resources where you can learn more about the topics addressed in these pages. My goal is to inspire your further explorations as you chart your career path.

Balancing Dualities: The Yin and Yang of Mental Health

Throughout this book I've identified competing priorities in mental healthcare and discussed the need for balance numerous times. The most prominent example is the need to respect both the healing art and the science of mental healthcare, as discussed in Chapters 11 and 12. But our field is full of many examples of these types of dualities. The ancient yin/yang figure from Daoism (also referred to as Taoism) is a helpful symbolic illustration of how potentially opposing forces can actually be complementary or interdependent (Figure 14.1). Consider how this graphic represents a fluid balance of some of the dualities in our field as described in this section.

Nature Versus Nurture

If you've taken any psychology classes, you've likely learned about the tension between theories of human behavior based on nature versus nurture. This duality

Figure 14.1 Yin Yang Symbol

has been at the core of much of the history of psychology for more than 100 years. Are mental health problems the result of nature, such as genetic, anatomical, biochemical, or other innate characteristics? Or are they a result of experiences and environmental influences, such as family upbringing, exposure to trauma, toxins, community, or societal factors? Many are fascinated by these big questions about the extent to which our personalities and behavior are predetermined versus shaped by our experiences.

Answers to these questions point toward what kind of treatment is likely to be most effective. For example, if we conclude that mental illnesses are caused by biochemical imbalances, then the most effective interventions may be pharmaceutical agents to change biochemistry. Alternatively, if we believe that mental illnesses are caused by experiences, then we need to intervene to address those experiential factors. In the history of mental healthcare, there have been dramatic pendulum swings from dominant explanations that emphasize nature (e.g., genetics, brain anatomy, biochemistry) to those emphasizing nurture (e.g., social learning, trauma).[1] Attempts to crown the victor in the nature versus nurture debate have repeatedly failed, leaving us with a more complex understanding of how these potentially opposing forces interact with each other.

This is admittedly an oversimplification of a complicated debate, but it nevertheless serves to highlight a basic duality at the core of this field. If you are looking for absolute right or wrong answers to these types of big questions, you will be sorely disappointed. Our field is full of ambiguities and answers that start with "It depends." I hope I've reignited your interest in grappling with these types of dualities; I'll offer a few more to contemplate as you embark on this career.

Feeling Versus Thinking

One of the main draws of this career is that it fully engages our hearts as well as our brains. We are often balancing strong feelings versus intellectual analysis, and at times, these forces point us in opposite directions. I've encouraged you to trust your intuition (i.e., gut feelings), but I've also argued that everyone's intuition can be flawed; therefore, we need to employ critical analysis and objective measurement for sound decision-making. This presents another good reminder to envision the yin/yang example of complementarity and integration. We don't want either side to over-power the other but rather for our "feeling self" and our "thinking self" to work in concert. This is also something that we model for our clients who may be struggling to integrate their own feelings and cognitions.

Integrating our feelings and our intellect is easier said than done. I imagine that we all can think of times when our feelings have overwhelmed or paralyzed our intellect. Likewise, sometimes we may try to make rational decisions based entirely on intellectual analysis, ignoring pesky feelings. That's when we often learn that ignoring our feelings can backfire. Think about how you use both your feelings and your intellect for decision-making. Remember that balance is an aspiration to strive for; it's not necessarily something we can always expect to achieve.

Flexibility Versus Structure

Here's another potentially frustrating but absolutely critical duality. Being a mental health professional requires a great deal of flexibility, like the ability to adapt to unpredictable events and capitalize on unforeseen opportunities. However, it also requires strong organizational skills and the ability to prepare plans in advance, persevering in the pursuit of goals in the face of obstacles. Too much flexibility can result in a lack of progress, but holding too tight to structure in the face of unforeseen developments can also derail progress and potentially interfere with the therapeutic relationship.

When I talk to students about this duality I often see frustration on their faces, and some are brave enough to verbalize it: "So you want me to be very flexible to meet my clients' shifting needs at any given time AND you want me to have an agenda, provide structured skill-building activities, and persist in the pursuit of identified goals. How can I do both?" I don't blame them for being frustrated; this is not an easy balance to achieve. I tell them that the way I address this challenge is that I always have a semi-structured plan in mind, driven by the goals, but I give myself permission to put that plan on hold temporarily if needed. Being intentional about this decision-making is what is essential so that you don't feel unmoored. With experience, you'll gain skills in knowing when to hold tight to your structured plan and when to pause it for unforeseen crises or opportunities.

Empathy Versus Confrontation

Expressing empathy for our clients through active listening and reflection as well as providing warm, compassionate support are absolutely essential. These are core elements of the healing art of therapy (often referred to as the "common factors" as described in Chapter 11). However, at times we need to confront our clients with hard truths and we need to push them to face anxiety-provoking situations or try out new behaviors and ways of interacting with others. This is another challenging duality. Therapists are usually very good at expressing empathy, yet many, especially trainees, feel uncomfortable confronting their clients. Just remember that one of the most compassionate ways you can help someone is by supportively and constructively coaching them on necessary but difficult behavioral changes. Empathy is essential in therapy, but it is not sufficient.

Authenticity Versus Maintaining Boundaries

This is yet another tricky duality for therapists to juggle. We know that being genuine and authentic helps to build a strong therapeutic alliance with our clients. When clinicians are inauthentic, when they try to pretend to share experiences with clients in a superficial way, this often backfires. So it's clear to me that inauthenticity is unwise. However, how authentic and transparent should we be with our clients? We are taught about the critical need to maintain appropriate boundaries and limits to the therapeutic relationship. Everyone I know struggles a bit with this tension. Authenticity is healing, unless it's not. How are we to know the difference?

This plays out in many different ways. To what extent is it therapeutic for the therapist to authentically self-disclose aspects of their own background, personal life, or experiences to the client? And as therapists, we know we shouldn't share all of our authentic responses or thoughts about the client, but when might sharing an authentic response be therapeutic? For example, if we are particularly bored or frustrated by a client, we should use that feeling to better understand what's going on; but we shouldn't share our authentic reaction. What about the boundaries around accepting a gift from a client? A natural response would be to accept, but would that authentic response violate boundaries?

Oftentimes there will be clear answers to these questions but not always. You'll learn more about how to navigate this duality in graduate school, but it will likely be a persistent tension throughout your career. My advice is to imagine an inner critic who asks pointed questions about your intent: Is your self-disclosure something that you think will be beneficial to the client? Or are you simply sharing something you feel like sharing for your own benefit? This type of inner critic helps us to use authenticity in a disciplined way, which is the goal.

Humility Versus Confidence

At different points in this book I've discussed the need for mental health professionals to be both humble and confident. How can we be both? Humility often comes easily for beginning therapists who may feel uncertain about their skills starting out. They need to be strongly encouraged to convey confidence for the sake of their clients, given the importance of boosting positive expectations. But we also need to retain some humility, especially regarding potential biases in our judgment. As discussed in Chapter 8, we need to practice cultural humility, with curiosity to learn more about others' experiences.

So here is another tricky balance: demonstrating confidence to boost our clients' expectations for success while also expressing humble curiosity about their unique experiences and needs. No wonder trainees often look befuddled and frustrated when instructed to embody seemingly contradictory characteristics like this. How can you be all these things at the same time? Once again, I believe the yin/yang symbol can help to serve as a reminder of fluid complementarity and balance.

Work–Family Life Balance

On top of the unique dualities that mental health professionals need to balance, there is the more universal work–life balance that everyone confronts regardless of career path. When I surveyed practicing clinicians for their advice to you, several responded with comments about the challenges of balancing a career with family life. It is notable that all those who contributed such comments identify as mothers. I'm not suggesting that fathers don't experience some of the same challenges; I know they do. However, it didn't surprise me that it was mothers who raised these points unsolicited by any specific question about family life. I find their comments very poignant and am sharing some here in their entirety. They speak for themselves and provide wisdom for you to contemplate.

> For better or for worse, I grew up with lots of mental health provider family members so I felt I had a decent idea of what this career choice would entail. But I didn't anticipate how much I would struggle with work/life balance and boundaries. It might be the life stage I'm in currently, but I wish I would have been more aware of how starting a family would impact my career trajectory. Although I wouldn't change anything about when we started our family or how many children we have, I would have been a bit more intentional about my child-free years and checked off a few more professional "to-do's" before adding child/family commitments into the mix. Other than that I doubt I would change anything—all my experiences (even the mis-steps) have been valuable learning opportunities and I doubt I'd be where I am now without them. Sometimes though, I do wonder if a different career would have been a better fit and facilitated a healthier balance. But then again, I'm

not sure I would be as fulfilled if I would have become a professional paddle board instructor. (Florencia, professor and therapist)

The only thing I would do differently would be to delay some professional milestones and work part-time while my children were young. I think I could have had a satisfying career without having to follow the standard academic trajectory. One can always find ways that they could have accomplished more "If only . . ." So I think I would have been as happy with a lesser career if I chose to delay some career advances while I started my family. (Carolyn, professor and therapist)

I now have two young beautiful children. Nothing would have prepared me for the change that occurred in me, and my desire to be with them, when they were born. I did not do a good job setting up my life to have young children before they were born and I think it's hard to start developing these skills later in life. So, my advice is, to the extent that it's possible, set up your life so that you have the flexibility to incorporate and balance all of the things that are important to you. It may require changing old goals and habits, and it's OK. (Angela, therapist in a hospital and instructor)

I very much appreciate the honesty reflected in these comments. While the focus is on balancing career and parenting, these same tensions can apply to all aspects of work–life balance. I can certainly relate to the tensions these mothers experienced. Parenting young children while building a career is extraordinarily challenging. The same is true for other caregiving responsibilities such as caring for ill family members. Even when one shares responsibilities with a partner and has sufficient resources, it is difficult; and it is all the more so without such supports.

The most stressful part of my life (so far) has been when my child was a toddler, my mother was terminally ill, and I was building my professional career. I can easily summon up memories of the deep exhaustion I experienced and my disappointment when I felt I couldn't fulfill every expectation as well as I'd hoped. But I can also summon powerful feelings of pride for what I was able to do. Some of my most meaningful memories of that stressful time are actually humorous: I distinctly remember leading a serious professional phone meeting while accompanying my daughter on amusement rides at the county fair. Other memories are more poignant, such as writing a research paper in a cancer center while seated next to my mother as she drifted in and out of sleep while receiving chemotherapy. I know these are not unique experiences. Every working parent, caregiver, or partner has many such examples of trying to juggle responsibilities.

The pandemic has exponentially increased work–life challenges for parents and caregivers. I marvel at parents who are facilitating homeschooling while also fulfilling their work responsibilities. The toll of these demands will become clear over time. I sincerely hope that wider recognition of these pressures on parents and caregivers will drive policy initiatives for greater support for child and family care and education.

A comprehensive discussion of strategies to manage tensions in work–life balance is beyond the scope of this book, but I will share some advice. First of all, try to be as intentional as you can be about your career decisions. As noted by the three mothers quoted, think carefully about your values and priorities, and let those guide your decisions, recognizing that those values and priorities may shift.

This book is designed to help you make well-informed, intentional career decisions. Too often, students may fall into a particular career path without full knowledge of its implications or of other options. Also problematic are career choices made solely on the basis of what others think is best for us. See Jill's response below regarding what she learned in retrospect about her own career decisions.

> I would prioritize my own values earlier rather than choosing what I thought my mentors would approve of. (Jill, therapist in private practice)

Secondly, no matter how intentional you are in your decision-making, your goals or circumstances are likely to change over time. Give yourself the freedom to shift course as needed. Emphasizing different personal or professional priorities at different stages in one's life makes developmental sense. I've learned this lesson when faced with unexpected life events.

I always prided myself on being very goal-directed, following a planned linear trajectory from step A to the desired outcome of step Z. Yet through the years I've learned that unexpected events or opportunities will sometimes jumble the plan, leaving my intended A-to-Z trajectory resulting in something resembling alphabet soup. Frankly, the most meaningful developments in my life have been those that were unexpected and totally unpredictable. So here I go again, urging you to be intentional in your decision-making yet, at the same time, to give yourself freedom to redirect and change course. I believe if you use your values as your compass, you can balance this seeming contradiction.

Jill (who definitely should be a career counselor) sums this up beautifully. She also highlights an important point: You will have opportunities to shift directions. Very few career decisions are irreversible.

> The path to a rich and satisfying career is not, nor need not be, linear. There is no "right" or "best" way forward—we make choices that have consequences, some we like, some we don't, and we learn from those consequences and either choose to stay the course or pivot. (Jill, therapist in private practice)

Additional Career Advice

The mental health professionals quoted throughout this book have shared valuable wisdom with you already. In this section, I offer additional advice for you to consider moving forward.

Find Good Mentors

> I was never good at networking or at building mentorship relationships. I always worried that I was a nuisance. If I could go back in time, I would have been more proactive at fostering relationships with mentors, and maintaining these relationships over time. (Angela, therapist in a hospital and instructor)

> I was blessed to have strong mentors and I would highly recommend that new clinicians start off careers with a strong mentor and truly be "under their wing" for a period of time to allow for skill development and confidence. It is really important to practice with confidence. (Mary, professor and therapist in private practice)

Finding good mentors is valuable in any career, but it's not always easy. Perhaps, like Angela, you are reluctant to "bother" potential mentors. If so, look for opportunities to help out on specific projects or events. Getting involved in clubs or extracurricular activities is another great way to connect with potential mentors. Those of us who are lucky enough to be in mentorship roles enjoy supporting highly motivated students and colleagues, so you are not a nuisance. And besides, if you reach out to a potential mentor and are rebuffed, it's time to find a different mentor.

It can be challenging to find the time and the nerve to reach out to potential mentors in an academic or a work setting, but it will be worth your effort. Mentors don't have to be senior leaders in your field; they just need to be a few years ahead of you in your chosen trajectory. One of my mentors early on was just a couple years ahead of me, but she taught me a great deal about applied research. Also, remember that you may choose to emulate some aspects of a mentor's career but not others. That's fine. In fact, it's preferable. The goal isn't to try to imitate a mentor. You are forging your own path, and I hope you will find wise guides to support you on your journey.

Focus on a Specialization, but Don't Rush

> Find your niche—figure out what populations, presenting problems, or modalities you enjoy or are good at and become a relative master/expert in that. It's unrealistic to think you'll be able to do or know it all. (Florencia, professor and therapist)

> Vision for yourself what you want to do; the therapeutic work that you might enjoy the most. Do you want to specialize in a certain population or issue? It will not hurt your practice to limit your practice. (Marcia, therapist in schools and private practice)

Here is yet another nuanced balance to achieve. As our experts note, finding your niche or specialization is valuable. No one can be an expert in everything. But I urge you to take some time before honing in on your desired specialization. Graduate school, especially the early part, is the time to explore many different topics and types of work. Seek out opportunities to expand your experience with different populations and mental health service contexts. There will be plenty of time to specialize later on.

Some students are laser-focused on one narrow specialization before they even begin graduate study. I respect that a determined focus can be motivating, but if it restricts your interest in a broad range of training experiences, it can also be limiting. Perhaps you have a specific long-term career goal in mind, such as working with military veterans struggling with addiction or adolescent males with eating disorders or same-sex couples contemplating marriage. Use your specific goal as motivation, but don't put blinders on to limit your training. And, alternatively, don't worry if you do not have a specific focus yet (with a caveat here that it is wise to be able to speak about some general interests in a graduate school interview or essay). Graduate school is the time to build a broad foundation of knowledge and skills. You can add more specialized skills on top of this strong foundation later.

Treat Clients Respectfully

> Sometimes when I'm writing reports, I re-read what I've written specifically to check that I have not become lazy and judgmental. Recently I read a colleague's description of a parent, which included the words "be ready to deal with mom as she has her own mental issues." It was necessary to change that wording immediately to reflect the integrity of that parent, who is doing her best. Respect for every client in our thoughts, our behavior and our words is difficult when we are exhausted, but it is one of the most important parts of our work. If we are judgmental when we work with our clients, why should they want to be honest and vulnerable with us? (Marcia, therapist in schools and private practice)

This may seem like unnecessary advice, but it's an important reminder. Sometimes when clinicians are stressed or just having a bad day, they may lapse into disrespectful ways of communicating to and about clients. For example, I've been in meetings where clinicians speak about their clients in pejorative ways, labeling them as "horrible parents," "liars," "fakers," "a train wreck," or "total psychopaths." As noted throughout this book, you will meet people who behave in ways that are harmful, deceitful, and sometimes shocking. I'm not suggesting that you ignore or sugarcoat these behaviors but rather that you remember to describe behaviors as opposed to applying pejorative labels to human beings.

I confess that there have been times I've not followed this advice when I've been particularly outraged or frustrated by a client's behavior (or even a colleague's behavior, to be honest). This is human. However, I have seen how this type of labeling can sabotage therapy and bias my judgment. It is much more constructive to describe specific behaviors than to label a person's identity. So, for example, instead of labeling someone as a "horrible parent," I should describe how the parent employs discipline strategies that are counterproductive. Likewise, instead of saying someone is a "liar," I should say their reports or perceptions of events are often inconsistent with others' reports or with available facts. These may seem like superficial semantic shifts, but they are essential for focusing on behaviors that can be changed versus reinforcing destructive core identities.

While most mental health professionals avoid speaking disrespectfully to clients directly, they may lapse into less constructive habits when writing notes about the client (as reflected in Marcia's quote). I've seen this pattern fairly often. Busy professionals rush to write a required session note and resort to pejorative labels about a client instead of describing behavior. Even labeling a client with a common term such as "resistant" can be problematic. This label is often applied to clients who seem unmotivated to fully engage in therapy or who avoid the topics or tasks therapists suggest. I'm not a fan of this label because it is too easy to pin on a client who may be struggling to engage in therapy for any number of reasons. It is more constructive to work with the client to figure out what would be motivating.

On the practical side, it's also important to remember that clients have a legal right to access all their records. If pejorative labels are found in those records, especially with an absence of objective descriptions of behaviors, it reflects poorly on the provider and can be harmful to the client. In addition, these records are often reviewed by other providers to guide concurrent or future treatment, so descriptive accounts are more useful. You have a ways to go before you'll be writing notes about clients, but I recommend training yourself to recognize when you lapse into pejorative labeling of individuals and work to shift that to describing specific behaviors. This shift will serve you well as a future clinician.

Foster Collaborative Professional Relationships

> Help others, not just clients/patients, but your colleagues, peers, friends. Be collaborative, not competitive. Don't hold the view that life/work is a zero-sum game. Network, network, network. Get to know people. Present at conferences and participate in professional organizations. (Kathy, professor and therapist)

This advice is not specific to this career path, but I believe it is particularly salient for this career. To thrive as a mental health professional, one needs a strong professional and personal mutual support system. This is not a career to pursue as a "lone wolf." Collaboration and consultation are essential. And, given that there is plenty of work to go around, a competitive approach is unnecessary.

If you have trouble finding a professional network, try looking for special interest groups within the discipline-specific professional organizations. Chapter 4 listed many of these discipline-specific professional organizations and their contact information. Each of these organizations has multiple subgroups for specific interests.

Most states also have a professional organization for each discipline. In addition, there are many cross-disciplinary professional organizations focused on different types of therapy (e.g., the Association for Behavioral and Cognitive Therapies and the American Group Psychotherapy Association). There are also groups for mental health professionals from specific racial or ethnic communities and other identities such as LGBTQ+. Keep a lookout for conferences that address topics of interest to you; these can also be good opportunities to meet like-minded professionals. Most organizations encourage student membership with discounted rates, so joining as a graduate student is feasible and a great way to start building a professional network.

Recommendations for Additional Resources

In this final section I will offer a variety of recommended resources for learning more about the topics raised in this book. Some resources offer career advice for becoming a therapist, while others are more for general interest. The general interest recommendations include stories and perspectives that have expanded my empathy and understanding of diverse human experiences. I've found inspiration through these resources and hope that some will inspire you too.

Books About Being a Therapist

The six books listed under this heading address what it's like to be a psychotherapist. The first three (by Gottlieb, Pipher, and Yalom) offer general descriptions and insights and would be appropriate to read at any stage of your career journey. The last three (by Cozolino, Kottler, and Willer) offer more detailed advice about beginning a practice and would be most relevant for when you begin practicing.

I've selected brief quotes from each of the books to give you a sample of their authors' wisdom; think of these as teasers to tempt you to read more. Each author has a slightly different approach to describing how psychotherapy works, some of which will be consistent with what you've read in this book and some of which will diverge a bit. Even though this can be confusing to reconcile, I think it's valuable to sample a variety of sources to build your own approach.

Please note that all the resources I recommend are listed in alphabetical order by authors' last names, not in any preferential order.

Maybe You Should Talk to Someone: A Therapist, Her Therapist, and Our Lives Revealed[2] by Lori Gottlieb

> Therapists use three sources of information when working with patients: What the patients say, what they do, and how we feel when we're sitting with them.... As a supervisor drilled into us during training, "What you feel on the receiving end of an encounter with a patient is real—use it!" (p. 121)

Therapy is about understanding the self that you are. But part of getting to know yourself is to unknow yourself—to let go of the limiting stories you've told yourself about who you are so that you aren't trapped by them, so you can live your life and not the story you've been telling yourself about your life. (p. 151)

Letters to a Young Therapist: Stories of Hope and Healing[3] by Mary Pipher

I love the work. Sometimes people ask if it is depressing to spend all day listening to problems. I tell them, "I am not listening to problems. I am listening for solutions." (p. xxv)

Even as doing therapy has helped me see all of the cruelties and stupidities that we humans commit, it has also reinforced my belief, developed in my childhood, that most people are basically decent. (p. 178)

The Gift of Therapy: An Open Letter to a New Generation of Therapists and Their Patients[4] by Irvin Yalom

Keep in mind the therapist's great power—power that, in part, stems from our having been privy to our patients' most intimate life events, thoughts, and fantasies. Acceptance and support from one who knows you so intimately is enormously affirming. (p. 14)

In general, the field of therapy focuses far too much on the past—on parental figures, long-ago events, and trauma—and too often neglects the future—our mortality, the fact that we, like all living creatures, wish to persist in our own being and yet are aware of inevitable death. (p. 4 of New Thoughts, New Developments addendum section)

The Making of a Therapist: A Practical Guide for the Inner Journey[5] by Louis Cozolino

When we begin training, we embark on two simultaneous journeys: one outward into the professional world and the other inward, through the labyrinth of our own psyches. (p. xv)

Our own failures help us to remain open to the struggles of others; our personal victories give us the optimism and courage to inspire those struggling with their lives. (p. 7)

On Being a Therapist[6] by Jeffrey Kottler

Our profession attracts the psychologically maimed and wounded for the best of reasons. Some of us were abused, neglected, or damaged as children. Others among us suffer from depression, anxiety, addictions, and other emotional struggles that led us to seek help and, perhaps ultimately, led us to seek training as a way to make the most from our experiences.... Rather than disqualifying us, having been wounded can provide us with special understanding and compassion for others—if we are aware of these issues and work on them in supervision and in our own therapy. (p. 176)

The Beginning Psychotherapist's Companion[7] by Jan Willer

As a beginning psychotherapist, you will be anxious, and you need to be able to talk about these feelings with your supervisor.... Your relationship with your supervisor must be solid and supportive for you to be able to develop confidence in difficult clinical situations. (p. 22)

Psychotherapists of all theoretical stripes recognize that it is normal to have emotional reactions to clients. One of the most challenging tasks before you is learning to understand your feelings about the client. Sometimes these feelings will be helpful in therapy, and at other times they will confuse you: this is normal. (p. 370)

General Resources

In this section I will recommend books, podcasts, and other content that may be of interest to you. It's intended as a kick-off to inspire you to keep exploring.

Books: Memoirs and Case Histories

I recommend reading (or listening to audio book) memoirs of all kinds. These first-hand accounts can give us insights into life experiences very different from our own. Seek out all kinds of memoirs, not just those focused on mental health or addiction challenges. Anything that opens and expands your perspectives on diverse human experiences will prepare you for a career in mental health.

Without a doubt, fiction also expands our horizons, builds our empathy skills, and enriches our lives in many ways. There are few things I enjoy more than losing myself in a wonderful work of fiction. However, I'm going to focus on nonfiction recommendations because people's taste in fiction can vary so much that I don't want to presume my favorites would resonate with you. Just know that I heartily recommend reading all types of fiction too.

I selected 20 nonfiction memoirs or case studies that directly address mental health and addiction or other topics that are highly relevant in therapy, such as grief, aging, work, family conflict, gender identity, academic challenges, body image, immigration, racial or ethnic identity, and sexual orientation. This eclectic set of books was selected without any specific criteria other than to represent diversity in experience and expression. I apologize in advance if your favorite was neglected; many worthy books were not included, and I urge you to find others that speak to you.

Each of these books gives you the opportunity to imagine inhabiting a different life, thus expanding your empathy skills. They provide important insights into diverse and often dramatic experiences. These insights are sometimes raw and painful, but just as often, they inspire us with resilience and hope.

> *Fun Home: A Family Tragicomic* by Alison Bechdel (Houghton Mifflin, 2006).
>
> *She's Not There: A Life in Two Genders* by Jennifer Finney Boylan (Crown, 2003).
>
> *Dry* by Augusten Burroughs (Picador, 2003).
>
> *Boy Erased: A Memoir* by Garrard Conley (Riverhead Books, 2016).
>
> *A Year of Magical Thinking* by Joan Didion (Alfred A. Knopf, 2005).
>
> *A Mind Spread Out on the Ground* by Alicia Elliot (Doubleday, 2019).
>
> *Hunger: A Memoir of (My) Body* by Roxanne Gay (HarperCollins, 2017).
>
> *Thinking in Pictures, Expanded Edition: My Life with Autism* by Temple Grandin (Doubleday, 1995).
>
> *Lab Girl* by Hope Jahren (Alred A. Knopf, 2016).
>
> *An Unquiet Mind: A Memoir of Moods and Madness* by Kay Redfield Jamison (Alfred A. Knopf, 1995).
>
> *Hidden Valley Road: Inside the Mind of an American Family* by Robert Kolker (a case study) (Doubleday, 2020).
>
> *Heavy: An American Memoir* by Kiese Laymon (Scribner, 2018).
>
> *Gaining: The Truth About Life After Eating Disorders* by Aimee Liu (Grand Central Publishing, 2008).
>
> *On the Move: A Life* by Oliver Sacks (Alfred A. Knopf, 2015).
>
> *The Center Cannot Hold: My Journey Through Madness* by Elyn Saks (Hachette Books, 2007).
>
> *My Age of Anxiety: Fear, Hope, Dread and the Search for Peace of Mind* by Scott Stossel (Alfred A. Knopf, 2014).
>
> *Darkness Visible: A Memoir of Madness* by William Styron (Penguin Random House, 1989).
>
> *The Noonday Demon: An Atlas of Depression* by Andrew Sullivan (Scribner, 2011).
>
> *Burro Genius* by Victor Villasenor (Rayo, 2004).
>
> *The Collected Schizophrenias* by Esme Weijun Wang (Greywolf Press, 2019).

I also want to recommend the book *Caste: The Origins of Our Discontents*, by Isabel Wilkerson (Penguin Random House, 2020). While it is neither a memoir nor a case study, this is the best book I have read addressing diversity, equity, and inclusion issues. It is extraordinarily well written and well researched; I believe it should be required reading for everyone entering this career, or any other for that matter.

Additional Recommendations

I've discovered an additional resource that offers some of the same benefits as memoirs in a very accessible format. *The Moth Podcast* and *The Moth Radio Hour* broadcast firsthand true stories from ordinary people (i.e., non-celebrities). Many are taped in live story slams throughout the world. I am hooked on these broadcasts that showcase how extraordinary "ordinary" people can be. I love the variety; some center around dramatic traumas, while others highlight more subtle drama in family or romantic relationships, career transitions and mentorship, cross-cultural experiences, or identity transformations. Listening to these personal narratives is compelling, educational, and entertaining. Sometimes they are full of clever humor, and other times they are emotionally raw. I listen while out walking, and I find myself laughing out loud or shedding a tear more frequently than I'd like to admit. The stories are often very moving, and I admire the storytellers' courage.

There are a variety of other podcasts that offer content relevant to becoming a mental health professional. These include Brene Brown's *Unlocking Us*; NPR's *Hidden Brain*; CBC's *Other People's Problems*, *The Happiness Lab*, and *Therapy for Black Girls*; and Wendy Mogel's *Nurture vs. Nurture*, just to name a few. There are also many podcasts that can expand our knowledge of different cultural contexts such as *Throwing Shade* and *Code Switch*. And there are documentaries such as the brilliant *Crip Camp* that educate and enlighten about how societal attitudes and opportunities have evolved and where we still have much work to be done.

YouTube provides additional content to learn more about being a mental health professional. *The Psych Show*, hosted by Ali Mattu, offers advice about this career. In addition, Judy Ho has many videos on YouTube with insights into different types of diagnoses and treatment. Esther Perel offers unique perspectives on couples counseling in videos and a blog. Many academic experts have lectures posted on YouTube, and some post sample therapy sessions. When you read something about a therapeutic approach that intrigues you, like cognitive behavior therapy, acceptance and commitment therapy, interpersonal psychotherapy, family systems therapy approaches, or dialectical behavior therapy, search for a video example to see what it looks like in action. In addition, there are many TED Talks about issues related to mental health and addictions.

A variety of websites also offer useful resources to learn more about mental health problems and treatments. PsychHub (psychhub.com) is a relatively new and fast-growing site with a wealth of resources, including brief videos about different treatment approaches. Advocacy organizations such as Mental Health America (www.mhanational.org) and the National Alliance on Mental Illness (www.nami.org) also provide a variety of education resources and potential opportunities to get involved. There are also organizations for specific mental health topics such as the Anxiety and Depression Association of America (adaa.org), the National Child Traumatic Stress Network (www.nctsn.org), the National Eating Disorders Association (www.nationaleatingdisorders.org), and Autism Speaks (www.autismspeaks.org). The Center for Deployment Psychology (deploymentpsych.org) offers training and resources for military mental health, and PsychArmor (psycharmor.org) offers terrific additional resources for those who support military members.

Please consider all these recommendations as potential starting points for your continuing explorations into this career. There are so many additional resources I could suggest, but I've tried to limit this to a manageable list. The truth is, any book, movie, podcast, or blog that intrigues you and expands your perspectives on the range of human experience will be valuable. Likewise, experiences that help you gain self-awareness will also be extraordinarily valuable. The possibilities are endless; maybe it is travel, volunteer work, personal therapy, journaling, reading or writing poetry or music, producing visual art, practicing yoga or meditation, or another spiritual ritual. These are just some of the ways people may gain self-awareness. Think what new activity you could add to expand your horizons, looking both outwardly and inwardly.

In Conclusion

I wrote this book to help people who are interested in a career as a mental health professional make well-informed, intentional decisions. But I had a selfish interest as well. There is a tremendous need for more mental health professionals across the world, and I want to ensure that those professionals are well prepared, personally and professionally. It's not enough just to have more mental health professionals. We need to have more effective, ethical, and culturally sensitive professionals. My goal was to give you the information and resources you need to become one of them.

This last chapter is intended as a send-off for you to begin your unique journey as a mental health professional. I've suggested a packing list for your journey, confident that the advice from experts and the suggested resources will help you reach your desired destination. In keeping with this metaphor, remember that your path may wind or even circle back or stall at times, and that's alright. The unexpected detours will offer new insights and opportunities or at least the chance to build perseverance and, ultimately, resilience. Use your core values as your compass, and have clarity about your ultimate goal. Each experience will be a stepping stone in your journey. Some may be ragged or slippery, whereas others will be smooth. That's what makes for an interesting path.

I wish you the best as you embark on this meaningful and rewarding journey!

Notes

Introduction

1. Swartz, H. A. (2020). The role of psychotherapy during the COVID-19 pandemic. *American Journal of Psychotherapy, 73*(2), 41–42. https://doi.org/10.1176/appi. psychotherapy.20200015
2. Yohanna, D. (2013). Deinstitutionalization of people with mental illness: Causes and consequences. *AMA Journal of Ethics: Virtual Mentor, 15*(10), 886–891. https://doi.org/ 10.1001/virtualmentor.2013.15.10.mhst1-1310
3. Weir, K. (2013, November). Feel like a fraud? *gradPSYCH Magazine, 11*(4). www.apa.org/ gradpsych/2013/11/fraud
4. Tracey, M.D. (2006, March). Older and wiser: Students weigh in on their decision to take up psychology as a second career. *gradPSYCH Magazine, 4*(2). www.apa.org/gradpsych/ 2006/03/wiser

Chapter 1

1. Allan, B. A., Autin, K. L., & Duffy, R. D. (2014). Examining social class and work meaning within the psychology of working framework. *Journal of Career Assessment, 22*(4), 543–561. https://doi.org/10.1177/1069072713514811
2. Allan, B. A., Duffy, R. D., & Collisson, B. (2018). Helping others increases meaningful work: Evidence from three experiments. *Journal of Counseling Psychology, 65*(2), 155–165. https://doi.org/10.1037/cou0000228
3. Wrzesniewski, A., McCauley, C., Rozin, P., & Schwartz, B. (1997). Jobs, careers, and callings: People's relations to their work. *Journal of Research in Personality, 31*(1), 21–33. https://doi.org/10.1006/jrpe.1997.2162
4. Baird, K., & Kracen, A. C. (2006). Vicarious traumatization and secondary traumatic stress: A research synthesis. *Counselling Psychology Quarterly, 19*(2), 181–188. https://doi. org/10.1080/09515070600811899
5. Gottman, J. M. (1994). *Why marriages succeed or fail.* Fireside.
6. Azuri, J., Ackshota, N., & Vinker, S. (2010). Reassuring the medical students' disease— Health related anxiety among medical students. *Medical Teacher, 32,* e270–e275. https:// doi.org/10.3109/0142159X.2010.490282
7. Hardy, M. S., & Calhoun, L. G. (1997). Psychological distress and the "medical student syndrome" in abnormal psychology students. *Teaching of Psychology, 24*(3), 192–193. https://doi.org/10.1207/s15328023top2403_10
8. Seligman, M. E. (1995). The effectiveness of psychotherapy. The *Consumer Reports* study. *American Psychologist, 50*(12), 965–974. https://doi.org/10.1037/0003-066X.50.12.965
9. Adler, A. (n.d.). *Quotable quote.* Goodreads. Retrieved August 9, 2020, from https://www. goodreads.com/quotes/623973-follow-your-heart-but-take-your-brain-with-you
10. Einstein, A. (1931). *Living philosophies.* Simon and Schuster.

11. Garland, A. F., Haine-Schlagel, R., Brookman-Frazee, L., Baker-Ericzen, M. J., Trask, E. V., & Fawley-King, K. (2013). Improving community-based mental health care for children: Translating knowledge into action. *Administration and Policy in Mental Health and Mental Health Services, 40*(1), 6–22. https://doi.org/10.1007/s10488-012-0450-8

12. Chorpita, B. F., Daleiden, E. L., Ebesutani, C., Young, J., Becker, K. D., Nakamura, B. J., Phillips, L., Ward, A., Lynch, R., Trent, L., Smith, R. L., Okamura, K., & Starace, N. (2011). Evidence-based treatments for children and adolescents: An updated review of indicators of efficacy and effectiveness. *Clinical Psychology: Science and Practice, 18*(2), 154–172. https://doi.org/10.1111/j.1468-2850.2011.01247.x; Spring, B. (2007). Evidence-based practice in clinical psychology: What it is, why it matters; what you need to know. *Journal of Clinical Psychology, 63*(7), 611–631. https://doi.org/10.1002/jclp.20373

13. Linden, D. (2006). How psychotherapy changes the brain—The contribution of functional neuroimaging. *Molecular Psychiatry, 11*(6), 528–538. https://doi.org/10.1038/sj.mp.4001 816; Weingarten, C. P., & Strauman, T. J. (2015). Neuroimaging for psychotherapy research: Current trends. *Psychotherapy Research: Journal of the Society for Psychotherapy Research, 25*(2), 185–213. https://doi.org/10.1080/10503307.2014.883088

14. Kandel, E. R. (2013, September 6). The new science of mind. *New York Times.* https://www.nytimes.com/2013/09/08/opinion/sunday/the-new-science-of-mind.html?searchResult-Position=10

Chapter 2

1. Adapted loosely from Wampold, B. E. (2011). *Qualities and actions of effective therapists.* American Psychological Association.

2. Goleman, D. (1995). *Emotional intelligence: Why it can matter more than IQ.* Bantam Books.

3. Burford, B., Carter, M., Morrow, G., Rothwell, C., Illing, J., & McLachlan, J. (2011). *Professionalism and conscientiousness in healthcare professionals.* Durham University School of Medicine and Health.

4. Hardy, M. S., & Calhoun, L. G. (1997). Psychological distress and the "medical student syndrome" in abnormal psychology students. *Teaching of Psychology, 24*(3), 192–193. https://doi.org/10.1207/s15328023top2403_10

Chapter 4

1. Bureau of Labor Statistics, US Department of Labor (2021). *Occupational Outlook Handbook. Substance Abuse, Behavioral Disorder, and Mental Health Counselors.* Retrieved December 13, 2021, from https://www.bls.gov/ooh/community-and-social-service/substance-abuse-behavioral-disorder-and-mental-health-counselors.htm

2. Swartz, H. A. (2020). The role of the psychotherapy during the COVID-19 pandemic. *American Journal of Psychotherapy, 73*(2), 41–42. https://doi.org/10.1176/appi.psychotherapy.20200015

3. Data in this table were compiled from multiple sources, including the Substance Abuse and Mental Health Services Administration's Workforce Report to Congress (2013); Bureau of Labor Statistics, Statistics by Occupation; *US News & World Report*; Payscale.com; https://www.apa.org/workforce/; https://www.humanservicesedu.org/occupation-career-outlook.html; https://www.bls.gov/ooh/community-and-social-service/substance-abuse-behavioral-disorder-and-mental-health-counselors.htm#tab-8

4. Harris, G. (2011, March 5). Talk therapy doesn't pay, so psychiatry turns instead to drug therapy. *New York Times*.

Chapter 5

1. National Academies of Sciences, Engineering, and Medicine. (2018). *Evaluation of the Department of Veterans Affairs Mental Health Services*. National Academies Press. https://doi.org/10.17226/24915. Retrieved from https://www.nap.edu/read/24915/chapter/10

2. Scott, K., & Lewis, C. C. (2015). Using measurement-based care to enhance any treatment. *Cognitive Behavioral Practice, 22*(1), 49–59. https://doi.org/10.1016/j.cbpra.2014.01.010

3. Lilienfeld, S. O., & Arkowitz, H. (2014, January). Just say no? *Scientific American Mind, 25*(1), 70–71. https://doi.org/10.1038/scientificamericanmind0114-70; Shaffer, D., Garland, A. F., Vieland, V., Underwood, M., & Busner, C. (1991). The impact of curriculum-based suicide prevention programs. *Journal of the American Academy of Child and Adolescent Psychiatry, 30*(4), 588–596. https://doi.org/10.1097/00004583-199107000-00010

4. Cuellar, A. (2015). Preventing and treating child mental health problems. *The Future of Children, 25*, 111–134; Wang, P. S., Berglund, P., Olfson, M., Pincus, H. A., Wells, K. B., & Kessler, R. C. (2005). Failure and delay in initial treatment contact after first onset of mental disorders in the National Comorbidity Survey Replication. *Archives of General Psychiatry, 62*(6), 603–613. https://doi.org/10.1001/archpsyc.62.6.603

5. Haine-Schlagel, R., Brookman-Frazee, L., Fettes, D. L., Baker-Ericzen, M., & Garland, A. F. (2012). Therapist focus on parent involvement in community-based youth psychotherapy. *Journal of Child and Family Studies, 21*(4), 646–656. https://doi.org/10.1007/s10826-011-9517-5

6. Garland, A. F., Saltzman, M., & Aarons, G. (2000). Adolescent satisfaction with mental health services: Development of a multidimensional scale. *Evaluation and Program Planning, 23*(2), 165–175. https://doi.org/10.1016/S0149-7189(00)00009-4

7. Constantino, M. J., & DeGeorge, J. (2007). *Believing is seeing: Clinical implications of research on patient expectations*. Society for the Advancement of Psychotherapy. http://www.societyforpsychotherapy.org/patient-expectations-research

8. Christidis, P., Lin, L., & Stamm, K. (2018, April). An unmet need for mental health services. *Monitor on Psychology, 49*(4), 19. http://www.apa.org/monitor/2018/04/datapoint

9. Leong, F. T., & Kalibatseva, Z. (2011). Cross-cultural barriers to mental health services in the United States. *Cerebrum: The Dana Forum on Brain Science, 2011*, 5.

10. Vespa, J. (2018, March 13). *The U.S. joins other countries with large aging populations*. US Census Bureau. https://www.census.gov/library/stories/2018/03/graying-america.html

11. Sewell, D. D. (2916, November 15). *Older adults are being overlooked when it comes to mental health care*. Care for Your Mind. https://careforyourmind.org/older-adults-are-being-overlooked-when-it-comes-to-mental-health-care/

12. Ong, A. D., Uchino, B. N., & Wethington, E. (2016). Loneliness and health in older adults: A mini-review and synthesis. *Gerontology, 62*(4), 443–449. https://doi.org/10.1159/000441651

Chapter 6

1. Kottler, J. A. (2017). *On being a therapist* (5th ed.). Oxford University Press.

2. Krueger, D. W. (1986). *The last taboo: Money as a symbol and reality in psychotherapy and psychoanalysis*. Brunner/Mazel.
3. Kottler, J. A. (2017). *On being a therapist* (5th ed.). Oxford University Press.
4. Christidis, P., Lin, L., & Stamm, K. (2018, April). *An unmet need for mental health services*. American Psychological Association. https://www.apa.org/monitor/2018/04/datapoint
5. Cohen Veterans Network. (2018, October 10). *America's mental health 2018* [PowerPoint slides]. https://www.cohenveteransnetwork.org/wp-content/uploads/2018/10/Research-Summary-10-10-2018.pdf
6. Centers for Medicare & Medicaid Services. (2020, April 15). *The mental health parity and addiction equity act (MHPAEA)*. https://www.cms.gov/CCIIO/Programs-and-Initiatives/Other-Insurance-Protections/mhpaea_factsheet
7. Career Tool Kit. (n.d.). *Free career test*. https://www.careertoolkit.com/

Chapter 7

1. Ethics codes for each discipline: ACA Ethics Code: https://www.counseling.org/knowle dge-center/ethics; AAMFT ethics code: https://www.aamft.org/Legal_Ethics/Code_of _Ethics.aspx; APA ethics code: https://www.apa.org/ethics/code; National Association of Social Workers Ethics Code: https://www.socialworkers.org/About/Ethics/Code-of-Ethics/Code-of-Ethics-English; Ethical Principles of Nursing: https://pmhealthnp.com/ pmhnp-topics/nursing-ethics/; American Psychiatric Association ethics code: https:// www.psychiatry.org/psychiatrists/practice/ethics
2. Koocher, G. P., & Keith-Spiegel, P. (2016). *Ethics in psychology and the mental health professions* (4th ed.). Oxford University Press.
3. Durrant, J., & Ensom, R. (2012). Physical punishment of children: Lessons from 20 years of research. *CMAJ: Canadian Medical Association Journal, 184*(12), 1373–1377. https:// doi.org/10.1503/cmaj.101314
4. Fontes, L. A. (2005). *Child abuse and culture: Working with diverse families*. Guilford Press.
5. DeAngelis, T. (2008). *Coping with a client's suicide*. American Psychological Association.https://www.apa.org/gradpsych/2008/11/suicide
6. Roth, A. (2018). *Insane: America's criminal treatment of mental illness*. Basic Books.; Ford, M. (June 8, 2015). America's largest mental hospital is a jail. *The Atlantic*. https://www. theatlantic.com/politics/archive/2015/06/americas-largest-mental-hospital-is-a-jail/ 395012/?utm_source=share&utm_campaign=share
7. US Department of Education. (n.d.). *What is FERPA?* Protecting Student Privacy.https:// studentprivacy.ed.gov/faq/what-ferpa
8. Hartocollis, A. (2018, May 12). His college knew of his despair. His parents didn't, until it was too late. *New York Times*. https://www.nytimes.com/2018/05/12/us/college-student-suicide-hamilton.html
9. Anderson, S. K., & Handelsman, M. M. (2010). *Ethics for psychotherapists and counselors: A proactive approach*. John Wiley & Sons.
10. Barnett, J. E. (2019). The ethical practice of psychotherapy: Clearly within our reach. *Psychotherapy, 56*(4), 431–440. http://dx.doi.org/10.1037/pst0000272
11. Novotney, A. (2017, February). *A growing wave of online therapy*. American Psychological Association. https://www.apa.org/monitor/2017/02/online-therapy
12. Barnett, J. E. (2019). The ethical practice of psychotherapy: Clearly within our reach. *Psychotherapy, 56*(4), 431–440. http://dx.doi.org/10.1037/pst0000272

13. Beauchamp, T. L., & Childress, J. F. (2012). *Principles of biomedical ethics* (7th ed.). Oxford University Press.

Chapter 8

1. Cross, T., Bazron, B., Dennis, K., & Isaacs, M. (1989). *Towards a culturally competent system of care* (Vol. 1). Georgetown University Child Development Center, CASSP Technical Assistance Center.
2. U.S. Department of Health and Human Services. (2001). *Mental Health: Culture, Race, and Ethnicity A Supplement to Mental Health: A Report of the Surgeon General.* Rockville, MD: U.S. Department of Health and Human Services, Substance Abuse and Mental Health Services Administration, Center for Mental Health Services. HHS Publication No. (SMA) 01-3613.
3. Chao, P. J., Steffen, J. J., & Heiby, E. M. (2012). The effects of working alliance and client–clinician ethnic match on recovery status. *Community Mental Health Journal, 48*(1), 91–97. https://doi.org/10.1007/s10597-011-9423-8
4. Shin, S., Chow, C., Camacho-Gonsalves, T., Levy, R. J., Allen, I. E., & Leff, H. S. (2005). A meta-analytic review of racial–ethnic matching of African American and Caucasian American clients and clinicians. *Journal of Counseling Psychology, 52*(1), 45–63. https://doi.org/10.1037/0022-0167.52.1.45; Flaskerud, J. H. (2009). Matching client and therapist ethnicity, language, and gender: A review of research. *Issues in Mental Health Nursing, 11*(1), 321–336. https://doi.org/10.3109/01612849009006520
5. Meyer, O. L., & Zane, N. (2013). The influence of race and ethnicity in clients' experiences of mental health treatment. *Journal of Community Psychology, 41*(7), 884–901. https://doi.org/10.1002/jcop.21580
6. Tervalon, M., & Murray-García, J. (1998). Cultural humility versus cultural competence: A critical distinction in defining physician training outcomes in multicultural education. *Journal of Health Care Poor Underserved, 9*(2), 117–125. https://doi.org/10.1353/hpu.2010.0233
7. Anderson, H., & Goolishian, H. (1992). The client is the expert: A not-knowing approach to therapy. In S. McNamee & K. Gergen (Eds.), *Social construction and the therapeutic process* (pp. 25–39). Sage Publications.
8. Dovidio, J. F., & Fiske, S. T. (2012). Under the radar: How unexamined biases in decision-making processes in clinical interactions can contribute to health care disparities. *American Journal of Public Health, 102*(5), 945–952. https://doi.org/10.2105/AJPH.2011.300601
9. Olbert, C. M., Nagendra, A., & Buck, B. (2018). Meta-analysis of Black vs. White racial disparity in schizophrenia diagnosis in the United States: Do structured assessments attenuate racial disparities? *Journal of Abnormal Psychology, 127*(1), 104–115. https://doi.org/10.1037/abn0000309
10. Gara, M. A., Minsky, S., Silverstein, S. M., Miskimen, T., & Strakowski, S. M. (2019). A naturalistic study of racial disparities in diagnoses at an outpatient behavioral health clinic. *Psychiatric Services (Washington, D.C.), 70*(2), 130–134. https://doi.org/10.1176/appi.ps.201800223
11. Fadus, M. C., Ginsburg, K. R., Sobowale, K., Halliday-Boykins, C. A., Bryant, B. E., Gray, K. M., & Squeglia, L. M. (2020). Unconscious bias and the diagnosis of disruptive behavior disorders and ADHD in African American and Hispanic youth. *Academic Psychiatry: The Journal of the American Association of Directors of Psychiatric Residency*

Training and the Association for Academic Psychiatry, 44(1), 95–102. https://doi.org/10.1007/s40596-019-01127-6

12. World Health Organization. (2021). *Gender and women's mental health.* https://www.who.int/teams/mental-health-and-substance-use/gender-and-women-s-mental-health#:~:-text=Gender%20bias%20occurs%20in%20the,or%20present%20with%20identical%20symptoms

13. Jacobson, R. (2014, July 1). Psychotropic drugs affect men and women differently. *Scientific American Mind.* https://www.scientificamerican.com/article/psychotropic-drugs-affect-men-and-women-differently/#:~:text=Yet%20women%20are%20now%20almost,likely%20to%20experience%20side%20effects

14. Rodriguez-Seijas, C., Morgan, T. A., & Zimmerman, M. (2020). Is there a bias in the diagnosis of borderline personality disorder among lesbian, gay, and bisexual patients? *Assessment, 28*(3), 724–738. https://doi.org/10.1177/1073191120961833

15. Bodner, E., Palgi, Y., & Wyman, M. F. (2018). Ageism in mental health assessment and treatment of older adults. In L. Ayalon & C. Tesch-Römer (Eds.), *Contemporary perspectives on ageism* (pp. 241–262). Springer. https://doi.org/10.1007/978-3-319-73820-8_15

16. Dovidio, J. F., & Fiske, S. T. (2012). Under the radar: How unexamined biases in decision-making processes in clinical interactions can contribute to health care disparities. *American Journal of Public Health, 102*(5), 945–952. https://doi.org/10.2105/AJPH.2011.300601

17. Project Implicit. (n.d.). *Preliminary information.* Harvard University. https://implicit.harvard.edu/implicit/takeatest.html

18. Alegria, M., Atkins, M., Farmer, E., Slaton, E., & Stelk, W. (2010). One size does not fit all: Taking diversity, culture and context seriously. *Administration and Policy in Mental Health, 37*(1–2), 48–60. https://doi.org/10.1007/s10488-010-0283-2

19. Centers for Disease Control and Prevention. (2020, April 3). *Adverse childhood experiences (ACEs).* https://www.cdc.gov/violenceprevention/aces/index.html

20. Khullar, D. (2017, June 8). *How prejudice can harm your health. The New York Times.* https://www.nytimes.com/2017/06/08/upshot/how-prejudice-can-harm-your-health.html

21. Williams, D. R. (2018). Stress and the mental health of populations of color: Advancing our understanding of race-related stressors. *Journal of Health and Social Behavior, 59*(4), 466–485. https://doi.org/10.1177/0022146518814251

22. Substance Abuse and Mental Health Services Administration. (2008–2015). *National Survey on Drug Use and Health.*

23. Substance Abuse and Mental Health Services Administration. (2015, April 15). *Racial/ethnic differences in mental health service use among adults.* https://www.samhsa.gov/data/report/racialethnic-differences-mental-health-service-use-among-adults

24. Griffin, M., Krause, K. D., Kapadia, F., & Halkitis, P. N. (2018). A qualitative investigation of healthcare engagement among young adult gay men in New York City: A P18 cohort substudy. *LGBT Health, 5*(6), 368–374. https://doi.org/10.1089/lgbt.2017.0015

25. Garland, A. F., Lau, A. S., Yeh, M., McCabe, K. M., Hough, R. L., & Landsverk, J. A. (2005). Racial and ethnic differences in utilization of mental health services among high-risk youths. *The American Journal of Psychiatry, 162*(7), 1336–1343. https://doi.org/10.1176/appi.ajp.162.7.1336

26. American Psychiatric Association. (2017, December 19). *Mental health disparities: Diverse populations.* https://www.psychiatry.org/psychiatrists/cultural-competency/education/mental-health-facts

27. Treatment Advocacy Center. (n.d.). *Criminalization of mental illness*.https://www.treatmentadvocacycenter.org/key-issues/criminalization-of-mental-illness/

28. Reingle Gonzalez, J. M., & Connell, N. M. (2014). Mental health of prisoners: Identifying barriers to mental health treatment and medication continuity. *American Journal of Public Health, 104*(12), 2328–2333. https://doi.org/10.2105/AJPH.2014.302043

29. Buche, J., Gaiser, M., Rittman, D., & Beck, A. J. (2018, June). *Characteristics of the behavioral health workforce in correctional facilities*. University of Michigan Workforce Research Center. Retrieved December 30, 2020, from http://www.behavioralhealthworkforce.org/wp-content/uploads/2016/09/Y2FA2P1_BHWRC_Corrections-Full-Report.pdf

30. Reingle Gonzalez, J. M., & Connell, N. M. (2014). Mental health of prisoners: Identifying barriers to mental health treatment and medication continuity. *American Journal of Public Health, 104*(12), 2328–2333. https://doi.org/10.2105/AJPH.2014.302043

31. Prison Policy Initiative. (2016). *Racial and ethnic disparities in prisons and jails.* https://www.prisonpolicy.org/graphs/pie2016_race.html

32. Child Welfare Information Gateway. (2021). Child welfare practice to address racial disproportionality and disparity. U.S. Department of Health and Human Services, Administration for Children and Families, Children's Bureau. https://www.childwelfare.gov/pubs/issue-briefs/racial-disproportionality/

33. Child Welfare Information Gateway & Children's Bureau. (2016). *Racial disproportionality and disparity in child welfare*. US Department of Health and Human Services. https://www.childwelfare.gov/pubPDFs/racial_disproportionality.pdf

34. Baams, L., Wilson, B. D. M., & Russell, S .T. (2019). LGBTQ youth in unstable housing and foster care. *Pediatrics, 143*(3), Article e2017421.

35. Garland, A. F., Landsverk, J. A., & Lau, A. S. (2003). Racial/ethnic disparities in mental health service use among children in foster care. *Children and Youth Services Review, 25*(5–6), 491–507. https://doi.org/10.1016/S0190-7409(03)00032-X

36. Garland, A. F., Landsverk, J. L., Hough, R. L., & Ellis-MacLeod, E. (1996). Type of maltreatment as a predictor of mental health service use for children in foster care. *Child Abuse & Neglect, 20*(8), 675–688. https://doi.org/10.1016/0145-2134(96)00056-7

37. Weir, K. (2016, November). Inequality at school: What's behind the racial disparity in our education system? *Monitor on Psychology, 47*(10), 42. https://www.apa.org/monitor/2016/11/cover-inequality-school

38. Gershenson, S., Holt, S. B., & Papageorge, N. W. (2016). Who believes in me? The effect of student–teacher demographic match on teacher expectations. *Economics of Education Review, 52*, 209–224. https://doi.org/10.17848/wp15-231

39. Gregory, A., Hafen, C. A., Ruzek, E., Mikami, A. Y., Allen, J. P., & Pianta, R. C. (2016). Closing the racial discipline gap in classrooms by changing teacher practice. *School Psychology Review, 45*(2), 171–191. https://doi.org/10.17105/SPR45-2.171-191

40. Bradshaw, C. P., Mitchell, M. M., O'Brennan, L. M., & Leaf, P. J. (2010). Multilevel explorations of factors contributing to the overrepresentation of Black students in office discipline referrals. *Journal of Educational Psychology, 102*(2), 508–520. https://doi.org/10.1037/a0018450

41. Nelson, L., & Lind, D. (2015, February, 24). *The school to prison pipeline, explained.* Justice Policy Institute. http://www.justicepolicy.org/news/8775

42. Gregory, A., Hafen, C. A., Ruzek, E., Mikami, A. Y., Allen, J. P., & Pianta, R. C. (2016). Closing the racial discipline gap in classrooms by changing teacher practice. *School Psychology Review, 45*(2), 171–191. https://doi.org/10.17105/SPR45-2.171-191

43. Centers for Disease Control and Prevention. (2015). *Understanding bullying* [Fact Sheet]. https://www.cdc.gov/violenceprevention/pdf/bullying-factsheet508.pdf

44. Hatzenbuehler, M. L., Birkett, M., Van Wagenen, A., & Meyer, I. H. (2014). Protective school climates and reduced risk for suicide ideation in sexual minority youths. *American Journal of Public Health, 104*(2), 279–286. https://doi.org/10.2105/AJPH.2013.301508

45. Wallace, J. B. (2019, September, 26). Students in high achieving schools are now named an at-risk group, study says. *The Washington Post.*https://www.washingtonpost.com/lifestyle/2019/09/26/students-high-achieving-schools-are-now-named-an-at-risk-group/

46. US Department of Health and Human Services, Health Resources and Services Administration, & National Center for Health Workforce Analysis. (2017, August). *Sex, race, and ethnic diversity of U.S. health occupations (2011–2015).* https://bhw.hrsa.gov/sites/default/files/bureau-health-workforce/data-research/diversity-us-health-occupations.pdf

47. Data USA. (n.d.). *Explore, map, compare, and download U.S. data.* https://datausa.io/

48. Wilson, C. (2017, April 5). The 50 jobs where people work the longest. *Time.* https://time.com/4726657/retirement-age-jobs/

Chapter 9

1. American Psychiatric Association. (2013). *Diagnostic and statistical manual of mental disorders* (5th ed.).

2. Kessler, R. C., Amminger, G. P., Aguilar-Gaxiola, S., Alonso, J., Lee, S., & Ustün, T. B. (2007). Age of onset of mental disorders: A review of recent literature. *Current Opinion in Psychiatry, 20*(4), 359–364. https://doi.org/10.1097/YCO.0b013e32816ebc8c

3. Scott, K., & Lewis, C. C. (2015). Using measurement-based care to enhance any treatment. *Cognitive and Behavioral Practice, 22*(1), 49–59. https://doi.org/10.1016/j.cbpra.2014.01.010; Bickman, L., Kelley, S. D., Breda, C., de Andrade, A. R., & Riemer, M. (2011). Effects of routine feedback to clinicians on mental health outcomes of youths: Results of a randomized trial. *Psychiatric Services, 62*(12), 1423–1429. http://dx.doi.org/10.1176/appi.ps.002052011

Chapter 10

1. Kottler, J. A. (2017). *On being a therapist* (5th ed.). Oxford University Press.

2. Ibid.

3. Ibid.

4. Maslach, C. (2001). What have we learned about burnout and health? *Psychology and Health, 16*(5), 607–611. https://doi.org/10.1080/08870440108405530

5. Morse, G., Salyers, M. P., Rollins, A. L., Monroe-DeVita, M., & Pfahler, C. (2012). Burnout in mental health services: A review of the problem and its remediation. *Administration and Policy in Mental Health, 39*(5), 341–352. https://doi.org/10.1007/s10488-011-0352-1

6. Kottler, J. A. (2017). *On being a therapist* (5th ed.). Oxford University Press.

7. Occupational Health and Safety. (2020, May 19). *Healthcare workers suffer from PTSD and burnout during COVID 19.* https://ohsonline.com/articles/2020/05/19/healthcare-workers-suffer-from-ptsd-and-burnout-during-covid19.aspx

8. Figley, C. R. (Ed.). (1995). *Compassion fatigue: Coping with secondary traumatic stress disorder.* Brunner/Mazel.

9. Bride, B. E., Radney, M., & Figley, C. R. (2007). Measuring compassion fatigue. *Clinical Social Work Journal, 35,* 155–163. https://doi.org/10.1007/s10615-007-0091-7

10. Newell, J. M., & MacNeil, G. A. (2010). Professional burnout, vicarious trauma, secondary traumatic stress, and compassion fatigue: A review of theoretical terms, risk factors, and preventive methods for clinicians and researchers. *Best Practices in Mental Health, 6*(2), 57–68.

11. Ibid.

12. Aarons, G. A., Sommerfeld, D. H., Hecht, D. B., Silovsky, J. F., & Chaffin, M. J. (2009). The impact of evidence-based practice implementation and fidelity monitoring on staff turnover: Evidence for a protective effect. *Journal of Consulting and Clinical Psychology, 77*(2), 270–280. https://doi.org/10.1037/a0013223

13. Neff, K. D. (2003b). The development and validation of a scale to measure self-compassion. *Self and Identity, 2*(3), 223–250. https://doi.org/10.1080/15298860309027

14. Ibid.

15. Schomaker, S. A., & Ricard, R. J. (2015). Effect of a mindfulness-based intervention on counselor–client attunement. *Journal of Counseling & Development, 93*(4), 491–498. https://doi.org/10.1002/jcad.12047; Shapiro, S. L., Brown, K. W., & Biegel, G. M. (2007). Teaching self-care to caregivers: Effects of mindfulness-based stress reduction on the mental health of therapists in training. *Training and Education in Professional Psychology, 1,* 105–115. https://doi.org/10.1037/1931-3918.1.2.105

16. Kottler, J. A. (2017). *On being a therapist* (5th ed.). Oxford University Press.

17. Oxford English Dictionary. (n.d.). Navel-gazing. In *Oxford English dictionary online.* https://www.lexico.com/en/definition/navel-gazing

18. Hernandez-Wolfe, P., Killian, K., Engstrom, D., & Gangsei, D. (2014). Vicarious resilience, vicarious trauma, and awareness of equity in trauma work. *Journal of Humanistic Psychology, 55*(2), 153–172. https://doi.org/10.1177/0022167814534322

19. Kottler, J. A. (2017). *On being a therapist* (5th ed.). Oxford University Press.

Chapter 11

1. Frank, J. D. (1974). *Persuasion and healing: A comparative study of psychotherapy* (2nd ed.). Schocken Books, p. 76.

2. Laska, K. M., Gurman, A. S., & Wampold, B. E. (2014). Expanding the lens of evidence-based practice in psychotherapy: A common factors perspective. *Psychotherapy, 51*(4), 467–481. http://dx.doi.org/10.1037/a0034332

3. Frank, J. D. (1974). *Persuasion and healing: A comparative study of psychotherapy* (2nd ed.). Schocken Books, p. 136.

4. Pipher, M. (2016). *Letters to a young therapist* (rev. ed.). Basic Books.

5. Greenberg, R. P., Constantino, M. J., & Bruce, N. (2006). Are patient expectations still relevant for psychotherapy process and outcome? *Clinical Psychology Review, 26*(6), 657–678. https://doi.org/10.1016/j.cpr.2005.03.002

6. Finniss, D. G., Kaptchuk, T. J., Miller, F., & Benedetti, F. (2010). Biological, clinical, and ethical advances of placebo effects. *Lancet, 375*(9715), 686–695. https://doi.org/10.1016/S0140-6736(09)61706-2

7. Young, C. (2006). What happens when people wait for therapy? Assessing the clinical significance of the changes observed over the waiting period for clients referred to a primary care psychology service. *Primary Care Mental Health, 4.* http://www.mhfmjournal.com/

old/open-access/what-happens-when-people-wait-for-therapy-assessing-the-clinical-significance-of-the-changes-observed-over-the-waiting-periodfor-c.pdf

8. Greenberg, R. P., Constantino, M. J., & Bruce, N. (2006). Are patient expectations still relevant for psychotherapy process and outcome? *Clinical Psychology Review*, *26*(6), 657–678. https://doi.org/10.1016/j.cpr.2005.03.002

9. Ibid.

10. Greenberg, G. (2018, November 7). What if the placebo effect isn't a trick? *New York Times*. https://www.nytimes.com/2018/11/07/magazine/placebo-effect-medicine.html?-searchResultPosition=2

11. US Food and Drug Administration. (2021, April). *Fraudulent coronavirus 2019 (COVID-19) products*. https://www.fda.gov/consumers/health-fraud-scams/fraudulent-coronavirus-disease-2019-covid-19-products

12. Pipher, M. (2016). *Letters to a young therapist* (rev. ed.). Basic Books.

13. Flückiger, C., Del Re, A. C., Wampold, B. E., Symonds, D., & Horvath, A. O. (2012). How central is the alliance in psychotherapy? A multilevel longitudinal meta-analysis. *Journal of Counseling Psychology*, *59*(1), 10–17. https://doi.org/10.1037/a0025749

14. Laska, K. M., Gurman, A. S., & Wampold, B. E. (2014). Expanding the lens of evidence-based practice in psychotherapy: A common factors perspective. *Psychotherapy*, *51*(4), 467–481. http://dx.doi.org/10.1037/a0034332; Martin, D. J., Garske, J. P., & Davis, M. K. (2000). Relation of the therapeutic alliance with outcome and other variables: A meta-analytic review. *Journal of Consulting and Clinical Psychology*, *68*(3), 438–450. https://doi.org/10.1037/0022-006X.68.3.438

15. Bordin, E. S. (1979). The generalizability of the psychoanalytic concept of the working alliance. *Psychotherapy: Theory, Research & Practice*, *16*(3), 252–260. https://doi.org/10.1037/h0085885

16. Meyer, O. L., & Zane, N. (2013). The influence of race and ethnicity in clients' experiences of mental health treatment. *Journal of Community Psychology*, *41*(7), 884–901. https://doi.org/10.1002/jcop.21580

17. Rogers, C. R. (1951). *Client-centered therapy: Its current practice, implications and theory*. Houghton Mifflin.

18. Rogers, C. R. (1980). *A way of being*. Houghton Mifflin.

19. Cameron, S. K., Rodgers, J., & Dagnan, D. (2018). The relationship between the therapeutic alliance and clinical outcomes in cognitive behaviour therapy for adults with depression: A meta-analytic review. *Clinical Psychology and Psychotherapy*, *25*(3), 446–456. https://doi.org/10.1002/cpp.2180

20. Saunders, R., Buckman, J. E. J., Cape, J., Fearon, P., Leibowitz, J., & Pilling, S. (2019). Trajectories of depression and anxiety symptom change during psychological therapy, *Journal of Affective Disorders*, *249*, 327–335. https://doi.org/10.1016/j.jad.2019.02.043

21. Gottlieb, L. (2019). *Maybe you should talk to someone: A therapist, her therapist, and our lives revealed*. Houghton Mifflin Harcourt, p. 154.

Chapter 12

1. Feyman, R. P. (1999). *The pleasure of finding things out*. Perseus Publishing.

2. Einstein, A. (1931) *Living philosophies*. Simon and Schuster.

3. Sackett, D. L., Straus, S. E., Richardson, W. S., Rosenberg, W. M. C., & Haynes, R. B. (2000). *Evidence-based medicine: How to practice and teach EBM* (2nd ed.). Churchill Livingstone.

4. Stewart, R. E., Marcus, S. C., Hadley, T. R., Hepburn, B. M., & Mandell, D. S. (2018). State adoption of incentives to promote evidence-based practices in behavioral health systems. *Psychiatric Services*, *69*(6), 685–688. https://doi.org/10.1176/appi.ps.201700508

5. Tavris, C. (2003, February 8). Mind games: Psychological warfare between therapists and scientists. *The Chronicle of Higher Education*, *49*, B7. https://www.chronicle.com/article/mind-games-psychological-warfare-between-therapists-and-scientists/

6. Lilienfeld, S. O., Ritschel, L. A., Lynn, S. J., Cautin, R. L., & Latzman, R. D. (2015). Science–practice gap. In R. L. Cautin & S. O. Lilienfeld (Eds.), *The encyclopedia of clinical psychology*. https://doi.org/10.1002/9781118625392.wbecp566

7. Weisz, J. R., Donenberg, G. R., Han, S. S., & Weiss, B. (1995). Bridging the gap between laboratory and clinic in child and adolescent psychotherapy. *Journal of Consulting and Clinical Psychology*, *63*(5), 688–701. https://doi.org/10.1037//0022-006x.63.5.688

8. For examples, see dedicated journals: *Implementation Research and Practice*, https://journals.sagepub.com/home/irp and *Implementation Science*, https://implementationscience.biomedcentral.com/

9. Hoagwood, K., Burns, B. J., Kiser, L., Ringeisen, H., & Schoenwald, S. K. (2001). Evidence-based practice in child and adolescent mental health services. *Psychiatric Services*, *52*(9), 1179–1189. https://doi.org/10.1176/appi.ps.52.9.1179

10. Aarons, G. A., Fettes, D. L., Flores, L. E., & Sommerfeld, D. H. (2009). Evidence-based practice implementation and staff emotional exhaustion in children's services. *Behavior Research and Therapy*, *47*(11), 954–960. https://doi.org/10.1016/j.brat.2009.07.006

11. Chorpita, B. F., & Weisz, J. R. (2009). *MATCH-ADTC: Modular approach to therapy for children with anxiety, depression, trauma, or conduct problems*. PracticeWise.

12. Garland, A. F., Hawley, K. M. Brookman-Frazee, L., & Hurlburt, M. (2008). Identifying common elements of evidence-based psychosocial treatments for children's disruptive behavior problems. *Journal of the American Academy of Child and Adolescent Psychiatry*, *47*(5), 505–514. https://doi.org/10.1097/CHI.0b013e31816765c2; Garland, A. F., Accurso, E. C., Haine-Schlagel, R., Brookman-Frazee, L., Roesch, S., & Zhang, J. J. (2014). Searching for elements of evidence-based practices in children's usual care and examining their impact. *Journal of Clinical Child and Adolescent Psychology*, *43*(2), 201–215. https://doi.org/10.1080/15374416.2013.869750; Chorpita, B. F., Becker, K. D., & Daleiden, E. L. (2007). Understanding the common elements of evidence-based practice: Misconceptions and clinical examples. *Journal of the American Academy of Child and Adolescent Psychiatry*, *46*(5), 647–652. https://doi.org/10.1097/chi0b013e318033ff71

13. Bickman, L., Kelley, S. D., Breda, C., deAndrade, A. R., & Riemer, M. (2011). Effects of routine feedback to clinicians on mental health outcomes of youths: Results of a randomized trial. *Psychiatric Services*, *62*(12), 1423–1429. https://doi.org/10.1176/appi.ps.002052011; Lambert, M. J., Whipple, J. L., & Kleinstäuber, M. (2018). Collecting and delivering progress feedback: A meta-analysis of routine outcome monitoring. *Psychotherapy*, *55*(4), 520–537. https://doi.org/10.1037/pst0000167

14. Garland, A. F., Kruse, M., & Aarons, G. A. (2003). Clinicians and outcome measurement: What's the use? *The Journal of Behavioral Health Services & Research*, *30*(4), 393–405. https://doi.org/10.1007/BF02287427

15. Jensen-Doss, A., Becker Haimes, E. M., Smith, A. M., Lyon, A. R., Lewis, C. C., Stanick, C. F., & Hawley, K. M. (2018). Monitoring treatment progress and providing feedback is viewed favorably but rarely used in practice. *Administration and Policy in Mental Health*, *45*(1), 48–61. https://doi.org/10.1007/s10488-016-0763-0

16. Garb, H. N. (1998). *Studying the clinician: Judgment research and psychological assessment.* American Psychological Association; Garb, H. N. (2005). Clinical judgment and decision making. *Annual Review of Clinical Psychology, 1*(1), 67–89. https://doi.org/10.1146/annurev.clinpsy.1.102803.143810

17. Garland, A. F., Aarons, G. A., Hawley, K., & Hough, R. L. (2003). Relationship of youth satisfaction with services and changes in symptoms and functioning. *Psychiatric Services, 54*(11), 1544–1546. https://doi.org/10.1176/appi.ps.54.11.1544

18. Bickman, L. (2008). A measurement feedback system (MFS) is necessary to improve mental health outcomes. *Journal of the American Academy of Child and Adolescent Psychiatry, 47*(10), 1114–1119. https://doi.org/10.1097/CHI.0b013e3181825af8

19. Ibid.

20. Chorpita, B. F., Bernstein, A., Daleiden, E. L., & The Research Network on Youth Mental Health. (2008). Driving with roadmaps and dashboards: Using information resources to structure the decision models in service organizations. *Administration and Policy in Mental Health, 35*(1–2), 114–123. https://doi.org/10.1007/s10488-007-0151-x; Lambert, M. J., & Burlingame, G. M. (2007, October 1). *Uniting practice-based evidence with evidence-based practice.* Behavioral Healthcare Executive. https://www.psychcongress.com/article/uniting-practice-based-evidence-evidence-based-practice

Chapter 13

1. Bickman, L. (2020). Improving mental health services: A 50-year journey from randomized experiments to artificial intelligence and precision mental health. *Administration and Policy in Mental Health, 47*(5), 795–843. https://doi.org/10.1007/s10488-020-01065-8

2. Gonzalez, R. (2017, October, 17). Virtual therapists help veterans open up about PTSD. *Wired.* https://www.wired.com/story/virtual-therapists-help-veterans-open-up-about-ptsd/ Fiske, A., Henningsen, P., & Buyx, A. (2019). Your robot therapist will see you now: Ethical implications of embodied artificial intelligence in psychiatry, psychology, and psychotherapy. *Journal of Medical Internet Research, 21*(5), Article e13216. https://doi.org/10.2196/13216

3. https://willrobotstakemyjob.com/clinical-and-counseling-psychologists.

4. Blum, D. (2021, January 12). Therapists are on TikTok. And how does that make you feel? *New York Times.*

5. Swartz, H. A. (2020). The role of psychotherapy during the COVID-19 Pandemic. *American Journal of Psychotherapy, 73*(2), 41–42. https://doi.org/10.1176/appi.psychotherapy.20200015

6. Hilty, D. M., Ferrer, D. C., Parish, M. B., Johnston, B., Callahan, E. J., & Yellowlees, P. M. (2013). The effectiveness of telemental health: A 2013 review. *Telemedicine Journal and e-health: The Official Journal of the American Telemedicine Association, 19*(6), 444–454. https://doi.org/10.1089/tmj.2013.0075

7. Kluger, J. (2020, August 27). Online therapy, booming during the coronavirus pandemic, may be here to stay. *Time.* https://time.com/5883704/teletherapy-coronavirus/

8. Andersson, G., & Titov, N. (2014). Advantages and limitations of internet-based interventions for common mental disorders. *World Psychiatry: Official Journal of the World Psychiatric Association (WPA), 13*(1), 4–11. https://doi.org/10.1002/wps.20083

9. Vigerland, S., Lenhard, F., Bonnert, M., Lalouni, M., Hedman, E., Ahlen, J., Olén, O., Serlachius, E., & Ljótsson, B. (2016). Internet-delivered cognitive behavior therapy for children and adolescents: A systematic review and meta-analysis. *Clinical Psychology Review, 50*, 1–10. https://doi.org/10.1016/j.cpr.2016.09.005

10. Pohl, M. (2020). 325,000 mobile health apps available in 2017—Android now the leading mHealth platform. *Research 2 Guidance Newsletter.* Retrieved April 17, 2021, from https://research2guidance.com/325000-mobile-health-apps-available-in-2017/

11. Krebs, P., & Duncan, D. T. (2015). Health app use among US mobile phone owners: A national survey. *JMIR mHealth and uHealth, 3*(4), Article e101. https://doi.org/10.2196/mhealth.4924

12. Wasil, A. R., Venturo-Conerly, K. E., Shingleton, R. M., & Weisz, J. R. (2019). A review of popular smartphone apps for depression and anxiety: Assessing the inclusion of evidence-based content. *Behaviour Research and Therapy, 123*, Article 103498. https://doi.org/10.1016/j.brat.2019.103498.

13. Ibid.

14. Wykes, T. (2019). Racing towards a digital paradise or a digital hell? *Journal of Mental Health, 28*(1), 1–3. https://doi.org/10.1080/09638237.2019.1581360

15. WoeBot Health. Retrieved September 5, 2020, from https://woebothealth.com/

16. Rosenfeld, A., Benrimoh, D., Armstrong, C., Mirchi, N., Langlois-Therrien, T., Rollins, C., Tanguay-Sela, M., Mehltretter, J., Fratila, R., Israel, S., Snook, E., Perlman, K., Kleinerman, A., Saab, B., Thoburn, M., Gabbay, C., & Yaniv-Rosenfeld. (2019). *Big data analytics and AI in mental healthcare.* https://arxiv.org/abs/1903.12071

17. Schueller, S. M., Tomasino, K. N., & Mohr, D. C. (2017). Integrating human support into behavioral intervention technologies: The efficiency model of support. *Clinical Psychology: Science and Practice, 24*(1), 27–45. https://doi.org/10.1111/cpsp.12173

18. Bickman, L. (2020). Improving mental health services: A 50-year journey from randomized experiments to artificial intelligence and precision mental health. *Administration and Policy in Mental Health, 47*(5), 795–843. https://doi.org/10.1007/s10488-020-01065-8

19. Quiroz, J. C., Geangu, E., & Yong, M. H. (2018). Emotion recognition using smart watch sensor data: Mixed-design study. *JMIR Mental Health, 5*(3), Article e10153. https://doi.org/10.2196/10153

20. Boukhechba, M., Chow, P., Fua, K., Teachman, B. A., & Barnes, L. E. (2018). Predicting social anxiety from global positioning system traces of college students: Feasibility study. *Journal of Medical Internet Research, 5*(3), Article e10101. https://doi.org/10.2196/10101

21. Gharani, P., Suffoletto, B., Chung, T., & Karimi, H. A. (2017). An artificial neural network for movement pattern analysis to estimate blood alcohol content level. *Sensors, 17*(12), Article 2897. https://doi.org/10.3390/s17122897

22. Schueller, S. M., Aguilera, A., & Mohr, D. C. (2017). Ecological momentary interventions for depression and anxiety. *Depression and Anxiety, 34*(6), 540–545. https://doi.org/10.1002/da.22649

23. Colombo, D., Fernández-Álvarez, J., Patané, A., Semonella, M., Kwiatkowska, M., Garcia-Palacios, A., et al. (2019). Current state and future directions of technology-based, ecological momentary assessment and intervention for major depressive disorder: A systematic review. *Journal of Clinical Medicine, 8*(4), Article 465. https://doi.org/10.3390/jcm8040465

24. Bickman, L. (2020). Improving mental health services: A 50-year journey from randomized experiments to artificial intelligence and precision mental health. *Administration and Policy in Mental Health, 47*(5), 795–843. https://doi.org/10.1007/s10488-020-01065-8

25. von der Heiden, J. M., Braun, B., Müller, K. W., & Egloff, B. (2019). The association between video gaming and psychological functioning. *Frontiers in Psychology, 10,* Article 1731. https://doi.org/10.3389/fpsyg.2019.01731

26. EndeavorRx. https://www.endeavorrx.com/

27. Merry, S. N., Stasiak, K., Shepherd, M., Frampton, C., Fleming, T., & Lucassen, M. F. G. (2012). The effectiveness of SPARX, a computerised self help intervention for adolescents seeking help for depression: Randomised controlled non-inferiority trial. *BMJ, 344,* Article e2598. https://doi.org/10.1136/bmj.e2598

28. Ibid.

29. Dennis, T. A., & O'Toole, L. J. (2014). Mental health on the go: Effects of a gamified attention-bias modification mobile application in trait-anxious adults. *Clinical Psychological Science, 2*(5), 576–590. https://doi.org/10.1177/2167702614522228

30. Granic, I., Lobel, A., & Engels, R. C. M. E. (2014). The benefits of playing video games. *American Psychologist, 69*(1), 66–78. https://doi.org/10.1037/a0034857

31. Weir, K. (2018, February). Virtual reality expands its reach. *Monitor on Psychology, 49*(2). https://www.apa.org/monitor/2018/02/virtual-reality

32. Gerardi, M., Cukor, J., Difede, J., Rizzo, A., & Rothbaum, B. O. (2010).Virtual reality exposure therapy for post-traumatic stress disorder and other anxiety disorders. *Current Psychiatry Reports, 12*(4), 298–305. https://doi.org/10.1007/s11920-010-0128-4

33. Weir, K. (2018, February). Virtual reality expands its reach. *Monitor on Psychology, 49*(2).https://www.apa.org/monitor/2018/02/virtual-reality

34. Boeldt, D., McMahon, E., McFaul, M., & Greenleaf, W. (2019). Using virtual reality exposure therapy to enhance treatment of anxiety disorders: Identifying areas of clinical adoption and potential obstacles. *Frontiers in Psychiatry, 10,* Article 773. https://doi.org/10.3389/fpsyt.2019.00773

35. Segovia, K. Y., & Bailenson, J. N. (2009). Virtually true: Children's acquisition of false memories in virtual reality. *Media Psychology, 12*(4), 371–393. https://doi.org/10.1080/15213260903287267

36. Topol, E. J. (2019). High-performance medicine: The convergence of human and artificial intelligence. *Nature Medicine, 25*(1), 44–56. https://doi.org/10.1038/s41591-018-0300-7

37. Bickman, L. (2020). Improving mental health services: A 50-year journey from randomized experiments to artificial intelligence and precision mental health. *Administration and Policy in Mental Health, 47*(5), 795–843. https://doi.org/10.1007/s10488-020-01065-8

38. Guntuku, S. C., Yaden, D. B., Kern, M. L., Ungar, L. H., & Eichstaedt, J. C. (2017). Detecting depression and mental illness on social media: An integrative review. *Current Opinion in Behavioral Sciences, 18,* 43–49. https://doi.org/10.1016/j.cobeha.2017.07.005

39. Rezaii, N., Walker, E., & Wolff, P. (2019). A machine learning approach to predicting psychosis using semantic density and latent content analysis. *npj Schizophrenia, 5,* Article 9. https://doi.org/10.1038/s41537-019-0077-9

40. Saxe, G. N., Ma, S., Ren, J., & Aliferis, C. (2017). Machine learning methods to predict child posttraumatic stress: A proof of concept study. *BMC Psychiatry, 17*(1), Article 223. https://doi.org/10.1186/s12888-017-1384-1

41. Love-Koh, J., Peel, A., Rejon-Parrilla, J. C., Ennis, K., Lovett, R., Manca, A., Chalkidou, A., Wood, H., & Taylor, M. (2018). The future of precision medicine: Potential impacts for health technology assessment. *PharmacoEconomics, 36*(12), 1439–1451. https://doi.org/10.1007/s40273-018-0686-6

42. Javanbakht, A., & Alberini, C. M. (2019). Editorial: Neurobiological models of psycho-therapy. *Frontiers in Behavioral Neuroscience, 13*, Article 144. https://doi.org/10.3389/fnbeh.2019.00144

43. Courchesne, E., Gazestani, V. H., & Lewis, N. E. (2020). Prenatal origins of ASD: The when, what, and how of ASD development. *Trends in Neurosciences, 43*(5), 326–342. https://doi.org/10.1016/j.tins.2020.03.005

44. Javanbakht, A., & Alberini, C. M. (2019). Editorial: Neurobiological models of psycho-therapy. *Frontiers in Behavioral Neuroscience, 13*, Article 144. https://doi.org/10.3389/fnbeh.2019.00144

45. Perry, B. D. (2009). Examining child maltreatment through a neurodevelopment lens: Clinical applications of the neurosequential model of therapeutics. *Journal of Loss and Trauma, 14*(4), 240–255. https://doi.org/10.1080/15325020903004350

46. Fisher, P. A., Stoolmiller, M., Gunnar, M. R., & Burraston, B. O. (2007). Effects of a therapeutic intervention for foster preschoolers on diurnal cortisol activity. *Psychoneuroendocrinology, 32*(8–10), 892–905. https://doi.org/10.1016/j.psyneuen.2007.06.008

47. Felitti, V. J. (2002). The relation between adverse childhood experiences and adult health: Turning gold into lead. *The Permanente Journal, 6*(1), 44–47.

48. Beauchaine, T. P., Gatzke-Kopp, L., & Mead, H. K. (2007). Polyvagal theory and devel-opmental psychopathology: Emotion dysregulation and conduct problems from pre-school to adolescence. *Biological Psychology, 74*(2), 174–184. https://doi.org/10.1016/j.biopsycho.2005.08.008

49. Ibid.

50. Scult, M. A., Fresco, D. M., Gunning, F. M, Liston, C., Seeley, S. H., García, E., & Mennin, D. S. (2019). Changes in functional connectivity following treatment with emotion regu-lation therapy. *Frontiers in Behavioral Neuroscience, 13*, Article 10.https://doi.org/10.3389/fnbeh.2019.00010

51. Shields, G. S., Spahr, C. M., & Slavich, G. M. (2020). Psychosocial interventions and im-mune system function: A systematic review and meta-analysis of randomized clinical trials. *JAMA Psychiatry, 77*(10), 1031–1043. https://doi.org/10.1001/jamapsychiatry.2020.0431

52. Roman, M., & Irwin, M. R. (2020). Novel neuroimmunologic therapeutics in depres-sion: A clinical perspective on what we know so far. *Brain Behavior Immunology, 83*, 7–21. https://doi.org/10.1016/j.bbi.2019.09.016

53. Velasquez-Manoff, M. (2020, August 28). The brain implants that could change humanity. *The New York Times*.https://www.nytimes.com/2020/08/28/opinion/sunday/brain-machine-artificial-intelligence.html

54. Ibid.

55. Harrington, A. (2019). *Mind Fixers: Psychiatry's Troubled Search for the Biology of Mental Illness.* (New York, N.Y: W.W. Norton & Company, Inc.).

56. Agency for Healthcare Research and Quality. (n.d.). *What is integrated behavioral health?* https://integrationacademy.ahrq.gov/about/what-integrated-behavioral-health

57. Asarnow, J. R., Rozenman, M., Wiblin, J., & Zeltzer, L. (2015). Integrated medical–behavioral care compared with usual primary care for child and adolescent behavioral health: A meta-analysis. *JAMA Pediatrics, 169*(10), 929–937. https://doi.org/10.1001/jamapediatrics.2015.1141

58. World Health Organization. (n.d.). *Depression.* Retrieved September 26, 2020, from https://www.who.int/health-topics/depression#tab=tab_1

59. Wang, P. S., Aguilar-Gaxiola, S., Alonso, J., Angermeyer, M. C., Borges, G., Bromet, E. J., Bruffaerts, R., de Girolamo, G., de Graaf, R., Gureje, O., Haro, J. M., Karam, E. G., Kessler, R. C., Kovess, V., Lane, M. C., Lee, S., Levinson, D., Ono, Y., Petukhova, M., ... Wells, J. E. (2007). Use of mental health services for anxiety, mood, and substance disorders in 17 countries in the WHO world mental health surveys. *Lancet, 370*(9590), 841–850. https://doi.org/10.1016/S0140-6736(07)61414-7

60. Wainberg, M. L., Scorza, P., Shultz, J. M., Helpman, L., Mootz, J. J., Johnson, K. A., Neria, Y., Bradford, J. E., Oquendo, M. A., & Arbuckle, M. R. (2017). Challenges and opportunities in global mental health: A research-to-practice perspective. *Current Psychiatry Reports, 19*(5), Article 28.https://doi.org/10.1007/s11920-017-0780-z

61. Eaton, J., McCay, L., Semrau, M., Chatterjee, S., Baingana, F., Araya, R., Ntulo, C., Thornicroft, G., & Saxena, S. (2011). Scale up of services for mental health in low-income and middle-income countries. *Lancet, 378*(9802), 1592–1603. https://doi.org/10.1016/S0140-6736(11)60891-X

62. Ibid.

63. Garland, A. F. (2019, February 19). *Improving school readiness in Ethiopia: The data and the lived experience.* Global Ed Leadership. https://globaledleadership.org/2019/02/19/improving-school-readiness-in-ethiopia-the-data-and-the-lived-experience/?fbclid=IwAR0LEKYaA19fH6gCn1i-ha76O-74XInF6GE79ecx-QjtxMvH0RmSQu3Swno

64. Patel, V., & Farmer, P. E. (2020). The moral case for global mental health delivery. *Lancet, 395*(10218), 108–109. https://doi.org/10.1016/S0140-6736(19)33149-6

Chapter 14

1. Harrington, A. (2019). *Mind fixers: Psychiatry's troubled search for the biology of mental illness.* W. W. Norton & Company.

2. Gottlieb, L. (2019). *Maybe you should talk to someone: A therapist, her therapist, and our lives revealed.* Houghton Mifflin Harcourt.

3. Pipher, M. (2016). *Letters to a young therapist: Stories of hope and healing.* Basic Books.

4. Yalom, I. D. (2017). *The gift of therapy: An open letter to a new generation of therapists and their patients.* HarperCollins Publishers.

5. Cozolino, L. (2004). *The making of a therapist: A practical guide for the inner journey.* W. W. Norton & Company.

6. Kottler, J. A. (2017). *On being a therapist* (5th ed.). Oxford University Press.

7. Willer, J. (2014). *The beginning psychotherapist's companion* (2nd ed.). Oxford University Press.

Index

For the benefit of digital users, indexed terms that span two pages (e.g., 52–53) may, on occasion, appear on only one of those pages.

Tables and figures are indicated by *t* and *f* following the page number.

abuse, reporting, 100–1
academic career path, 7–8, 71
academic ethics, 103, 106
acceptance, 19, 25
accomplishment, decreased sense of, 143
accreditation agencies, 39, 48, 49, 53, 55, 66
Accreditation Commission for Education in
    Nursing, 64
active listening, 159
addiction counseling, 50, 51
addictions, 131
ADHD (attention deficit hyperactivity disorder),
    113, 116, 179–80
adjunct faculty, 71
Adler, Alfred, 15
administrative demands, 93–94
adolescents
    career opportunities with, 75–76
    confidentiality and, 99
    courses on, 125
    inequities in schools, 116
    LGBTQ+ youth, 115
    suicide risk, 116
    video games for, 179–80
    working with, 51, 74–76, 101–2
adoption, 53–54, 82
adult populations, 76–78
    career opportunities with, 77–78
    geriatric, 78–80
advanced patient-centered medical home
    model, 185–86
advanced practice resident nurses
    (APRNs), 63–64
advocacy
    coursework on, 132
    organizations, 119, 204–5
    work in, 74, 85–86
affiliated organization coverage, 86
Affordable Care Act, 185–86
age, representation in workforce, 118
age groups, 68*f*, 68
ageism, 113
AI. *See* artificial intelligence
Alzheimer's disease, 101

American Association of Marital and Family
    Therapy (AAMFT), 97, 119
American Counseling Association (ACA), 97
American Psychological Association (APA), 59,
    97, 119
Anderson, S.K., 104
anxiety disorders, 10, 181
APA. *See* American Psychological Association
art, of psychotherapy, 15–16, 162, 163*f*
artificial intelligence, 178, 181–82
aspirational ethics, 106–7, 188
assessment. *See* psychological testing
attention-bias modification training, 180
attention deficit hyperactivity disorder (ADHD),
    113, 116, 179–80
attitude, 19
audits, 94
authenticity, 5, 6, 159, 193
autism, 183
automation risk, 175

balance. *See also* dualities
    art *versus* science of psychotherapy, 15–16,
        162, 163*f*
    of work–family life, 194–96
bandit algorithm, 179
Barnett, Jeffrey, 105
The Beginning Psychotherapist's Companion
    (Willer), 202
behavioral health, term, 185–86
belief systems, 19, 25
bereavement, 79
biases, 84, 112–13, 116, 125, 147, 171
Bickman, Leonard, 181
billing, 94
biopsychosocial approach, 126–27
board certification, 63, 64
books, as resources
    on being a therapist, 200–2
    memoirs and case histories, 202–3
borderline personality disorder, 113
boundaries, 97–98, 105, 139, 193
brain function. *See* neuroscience
BrainGate, 184

brain injuries, 60–61, 70, 76, 132, 184
brain-reading/-writing technologies, 184–85
brainstorming, 104
budgeting, 83
bureaucracy, 42, 85, 91–92, 93, 94
burnout
  detrimental effects of, 143, 144
  prevalence, 143
  protecting against, 144–46
  related concepts, 143
  self-awareness and, 144
  self-monitoring for, 145
  warning signs of, 142–43
business, of mental healthcare, 83–84
business planning, 83
business sector opportunities, 68–69, 78, 80

career as therapist
  advice on, 196–200
  balance in, 15–16, 26, 190–94
  books on, 200–2
  as calling, 10, 84
  challenges in, 4, 13–14, 142
  disappointments, 14–15
  inspiration through, 10
  journey of, 205
  meaningfulness, 9–12
  motivations for choosing, 1–2, 26–29, 38
  opportunities (*see* career opportunities)
  possibilities in, 14, 67–68, 82
  potential fit of (*see* career fit)
  rewarding aspects, 9, 13, 70–71, 148, 161
  specializations, 67–68, 68*f*, 197–98
  steps to, 31*f*, 31, 35, 45
  success in, 14–15
  types of work for, 67–68, 68*f*, 69–71
career counseling, 76, 133
career fit
  for counseling, 50–51, 133
  graduate coursework and, 136–37
  for marital and family therapy, 53–54
  overview, 2–3, 18, 29–30
  personal strengths and, 18–23
  for psychiatric nursing, 65
  for psychiatry, 63
  for psychology, 60–61
  of social work, 56
  testing out, 29
  weaknesses and, 23–26
career goals, 37, 55, 196, 198
career opportunities, 2, 46
  with adolescents, 75–76
  with adult populations, 77–78
  with children, 73–74
  with couples, 80–81
  with families, 82

  with older adults, 79–80
  throughout career, 13–14
career paths, 2
caring attitude, 21
case histories, 202–3
case management, 56, 70, 73
Caste (Wilkerson), 203
challenges, 4, 13–14
change, inspiring, 150
children
  adverse events, experience of, 115–16, 183
  career opportunities with, 73–74
  caregivers involvement in therapy, 72–73
  confidentiality and, 99
  corporal punishment of, 100
  courses on child development, 124, 125
  emotional dysregulation in, 183
  parent–child conflicts, 53–54, 82
  reporting abuse of, 100–1
  with special needs, 82
  video games for, 179–80
  working with, 72–74
child welfare system, 56, 100, 115
client-associated stress, 139
clients. *See also* therapeutic relationship;
      specific population
  biases, 171
  canceling services for, 84–85
  coping skills, 77
  dependency on therapy, 23
  diversity of, 4, 111–12, 158
  environmental factors, 54
  expectations about therapy, 76–77, 151–56
  exploitation of, 23, 97–98, 105–6, 156
  financial resources, 84–85, 86, 91
  harm, risk of, 101
  hospitalization of, 101
  insurance coverage, 85–87
  labeling, 198–99
  motivations to seek therapy, 72, 74, 77
  outcomes, 14–15, 142, 159, 169
  versus patients, 61
  respect for, 198–99
  satisfaction with therapy, 171–72
  stories revealed in therapy, 10–12
  term, xi
clinical counselors, 49
clinical decision-making, 172
clinical faculty, 71
clinical judgment, 170–71
clinical outcomes, 14–15, 142, 159, 169
clinical psychology, 57–58
clinical supervision, 22, 41–42, 71, 135–36. *See also*
      practicum
clinicians. *See* therapists
cognitive-behavioral theory, 126, 152, 177

cognitive dissonance, 171
cognitive flexibility, 20
collaboration, 22–23, 199–200
collaborative care, 185–86
college majors, 31–32
Commission on Accreditation for Marriage and
    Family Therapy Education (COAMFTE), 53
Commission on Collegiate Nursing Education, 64
common factors, 150
communication skills, 20–21
community-based nonprofits, 79, 91
community mental health counselors, 49
community placements, 134
community psychology, 59
comorbidities, 131
compartmentalizing, ability for, 25, 79, 144
compassion, 4–5, 158
compassion fatigue, 11, 143, 144
compassion satisfaction, 148–49
computer courses, 133–34
confidence, 19, 41, 151–52, 194
confidentiality, 98–99, 101, 103, 105
conflict, comfort with, 21–22
confrontation, empathy *versus*, 193
congruence, 159
conscientiousness, 21
conscious bias, 112–13
consultation-liaison nursing, 64
consultations, 104, 199–200
consulting, 70
continuing education, 44
continuous learning, 145
coping skills, 77, 144
coronavirus pandemic. *See* COVID-19 pandemic
Council for Accreditation of Counseling and
    Related Educational Programs (CACREP), 48
Council on Social Work Education (CSWE),
    55, 119
counseling
    graduate school admissions, 48–49
    informational resources, 52
    licensing/credentialing, 49–50
    minority student opportunities in, 118
    overview, 47, 47*t*, 48
    potential fit for interests, 50–51
    skills course, 129
    subspecialties, 48
    theories of, 125–26
counseling psychology, 49, 57–58
counselors, 48, 49. *See also* therapists
couples work, 11, 80–81. *See also* marital and
    family therapy
court testimony, 102–3
cover letters, 43–44
COVID-19 pandemic, 2, 25, 79, 143, 156, 176, 177
Cozolino, Louis, 201

credentialing. *See* licensing/credentialing
criminal justice system, 78, 102, 115
criminal profiling, 102
criminal psychology. *See* forensic psychology
crisis assessment, 131
crisis intervention, 131
critical thinking skills, 22
criticism, sensitivity to, 24
Cross, T., 111
cross-disciplinary opportunities, 71
cultural competent care, 111–12
cultural diversity, 109–10
cultural humility, 112
cultural issues, 125
cultural sensitivity, 106, 111
culture, of mental health, 32
curiosity, 22
curriculum vitae (CV), 33

Daoism, 190
data-mining, 181–82
debt, 87, 89
decision-making, 99, 104–5, 172
degree paths, 2, 7
    choosing, 46
    combined degree programs, 65
    by discipline, 47*t*
    salaries and, 89
    tuition costs and, 87–88
"deinstitutionalization" movement, 3–4
Department of Veterans Affairs (VA), 69
depersonalization, 142–43
depression, 113, 179, 187
Desta, Menelik, 187
developmental psychopathology, 127
Diagnostic and Statistical Manual 1 (DSM), 126
diagnostic bias, 112–13, 116
diagnostic criteria, 102, 126, 171
disabilities, therapists with, 117–18
disability, leading cause of, 187
disappointments, 14–15
disciplines. *See* mental health disciplines
discrimination, 27, 109, 110, 114, 117
disparities, in mental healthcare, 108, 110, 114–16
dissertations, 58
diversity issues, 108, 111
    courses on, 125
    resources on, 118–19
    workforce representation, 116–19
divorce work, 81
doctoral programs
    applying to, 37–38
    disciplines requiring degree in, 47, 57, 58
    master's degree prerequisite, 59
    salaries with degree, 89
    types of degrees, 58

doctor of nursing practice (DNP), 64
doctor of osteopathy (DO), 62–63
doctor of psychology (PsyD), 58
domestic violence, 78, 80, 81, 130
dualities, 190
    authenticity *versus* maintaining boundaries, 193
    empathy *versus* confrontation, 193
    feeling *versus* thinking, 192
    flexibility *versus* structure, 192
    humility *versus* confidence, 194
    nature *versus* nurture, 190–91
duty, 96

eating disorders, 76, 204–5
ecological approach, 54
ecological momentary assessment devices, 178–79
educational degrees. *See specific degree*
effectiveness, 142–43
Einstein, Albert, 16, 164
elder abuse reporting, 100, 101
elderly populations. *See* geriatric adults
electronic record systems, 94
emergencies, 105, 131, 139
emotional arousal, 139
emotional exhaustion, 142–43
emotional intelligence, 18–19
emotion regulation therapy, 184
empathy, 4–5, 18–19, 138–39, 159, 167
    versus confrontation, 193
empirically supported treatments, 168
employee wellness, 68–69
employment. *See* job search
EndeavorRx, 179–80
entrepreneurship, 83, 91–92
equity, 108, 118–19
ethics
    accountability and, 96
    aspirational, 106–7
    codes, 21, 96, 97
    consequences for violating, 105–6
    courses in, 128
    in decision-making, 99, 104–5
    versus laws, 97
    new challenges with innovations, 105
    in research and teaching, 103, 106
    in technology use, 181
Ethics for Psychotherapists and Counselors
    (Anderson), 104
Ethiopian School Readiness Initiative, 187
ethnic disparities, 114–16
ethnic identity, 109
event-related stress, 140
evidence-based medicine, term, 165–66
evidence-based practice, 5, 16, 165–69
    benefits of, 167
    courses on, 130

directive *versus* non-directive support, 167
    identifying, 167–68
    implementation, 168
    promotion of, 166
    science–practice gap and, 166–67
    tension over use of, 166
    term, xi, 165
    website resources on, 168–69
expectations
    addressing, 152–53
    boosting positivity, 151–52, 155
    counterproductive, 155–56
    importance of, 151–56
    placebo effect and, 154–55
    power of, 150, 151, 152, 154
    unrealistic, 155–56
exposure therapy, 180–81

Facebook's Reality Labs, 184
faculty mentors, 59–60, 88
faculty positions, 71
faith-based counseling, 50, 69, 76, 78
false memories, 181
Family Educational Rights and Privacy Act
    (FERPA), 103
family legal issues, 102
family life balance, 194–96
family systems theories, 126
family therapy. *See* marital and family therapy
Farmer, Paul, 188
feedback
    giving to clients, 21, 24
    in graduate courses, 129
    as measurement system, 169, 171–72, 179
    from supervisors, 22, 135
feeling *versus* thinking, 192
fees, setting, 84, 86, 91
Feyman, Richard, 163
field placement, 40
fieldwork. *See* practicum
financial aid, 88
financial considerations, 83–84. *See also* salaries
    ambivalence about, 84–85
    costs of graduate school, 40, 87–88
    debt, 87, 89
    of private practice, 91–93
flexibility, 5, 20, 192
Food and Drug Administration (FDA),
    156, 179–80
forensic mental health practice, 102–3
forensic psychology, 58
foster care, 53–54, 73, 115–16
Frank, Jerome, 150, 151, 160

gender
    bias, 113

expectations, 109–10
representation in mental health
  professions, 116–17
genetic testing support, 80
geographic location, 40, 90
geriatric adults, working with, 78–80
geriatric counseling field, 50
The Gift of Therapy (Yalom), 201
global mental health, 187–89
global projects, 188
goals
  career-related, 37, 55, 196, 198
  for graduate school, 34, 35
  of therapy, 20, 72, 75, 153, 156, 157, 159,
    171, 192
Goleman, Daniel, 18–19
Gottlieb, Lori, 160, 200
government agencies, employment in, 69
government insurance, 86
grade point average (GPA), 38, 48–49, 53, 55,
    64, 121–22
graduate assistantships, 58, 59–60, 88, 118
graduate coursework. *See also specific topics*
  advanced, 129–34
  delivery of, 122–34
  foundational, 124–29
  overview of, 123–34
Graduate Record Examination (GRE) scores, 35,
    38, 48–49
graduate school
  accreditation of programs, 39, 48, 49, 53, 55, 64
  application process (*see* graduate school
    admissions)
  clinical supervision and, 22, 41–42, 71, 135–36
  combined degree programs, 65
  cost of, 40, 87–88
  course topics overview, 41, 123–34
  differences from undergraduate
    experience, 121–23
  employment during, 88–89
  faculty mentors in, 59–60, 88
  grade point average in, 121–22
  practice training (*see* practicum)
  preparation for, 121
  program duration, 40
  return on investment, 87–89
  selecting, 39–40
  social life in, 123
graduate school admissions
  application process, 34–36
  in counseling, 48–49
  for doctoral programs, 37–38
  interviews for, 36–37
  in marital and family therapy, 53
  personal essay for, 34–35
  potential pitfalls, 38–39

program fit and, 35, 38–39
program selection, 39–40
in psychiatric nursing, 64
in psychiatry, 62–63
in psychology, 59–60
recommenders, choosing, 34
in social work, 55
undergraduate experiences and, 33
grants, 87
Greenberg, Gary, 154
grief, 79
group dynamics, 133
group homes, 3–4
group therapy, 133

Handelsman, M.M., 104
Harrington, Anne, 185
Head Start, 107
healing arts, 15–16, 150, 162, 163*f*
healing role, 156
healthcare disparities, 114
health insurance, 85–87, 91
health psychology, 133
Health Resources and Services Administration
    (HRSA), 119
help, therapist asking for, 22–23
helper role, 26, 149, 163
homicide risk, 105
hope, inspiring, 19–20, 150, 154
hospice care settings, 79
hospital work settings, 74, 76, 77, 80, 90
human connection, 15–16, 157, 162, 174–75, 189
human development, 124–25
humanistic approach, 160
human sexuality. *See* sexuality
human suffering, 10–11
humility, 23–24, 112, 194

identity issues, 79, 109, 124
immigrant families, 74
immunology, 184
impaneled providers, 91–92
Implicit Association Test, 113
implicit bias. *See* biases
imposter syndrome, 6, 141
improvement, motivation for, 22
inclusion
  courses on, 125
  personal reflections on, 108–10
  resources on, 118–19
income. *See* salaries
industrial/ organizational psychology, 61
infertility support, 81
innovations, 105
institutional review boards (IRBs), 103, 106
insurance, 85–87, 91

integrated behavioral healthcare, 78, 133, 185–87
intellectual curiosity, 22
internal personal stress, 140–41
international organizations, 29, 65, 69, 187, 188
international work, 48, 69, 77, 82, 187
internet gaming disorder, 179
internet therapy, 177–82
internships. *See* practicum
interpersonal skills, 39
interviews, for graduate school, 36–37
intuition, 23–24, 192

job growth, 46, 47*t*
job opportunities. *See* career opportunities
job satisfaction, 148–49
job search, 42–44
    casting a wide net, 44
    networking and, 43
    postgraduate practice for licensure and, 42–43
    preparing materials for, 43–44
job shadowing, 18
Juste, Robert, 184
juvenile justice system, 82, 115

Kandel, Eric, 16
Kaptchuk, Ted, 154
kindness, 21
Kottler, Jeffrey, 84, 139, 148, 201

labels, 198–99
laboratory–clinic gap, 166–67
language skills, 20–21
laws, 78, 97, 128
lawsuits, 96
learning
    curiosity for, 22
    willingness toward, 24–25
legal issues
    confidentiality, 98–99, 103
    liabilities, 96
    overview, 96, 97–102
    reporting requirements, 100–2
legal privilege, 98–99
legislation, development, 78
Letters to a Young Therapist (Pipher), 151, 201
LGBTQ+ community, 75, 81, 110, 115, 117
Licensed Clinical Social Worker (LCSW), 55
Licensed Independent Clinical Social Worker, 56
Licensed Professional Clinical Counselors
    (LPCCs), 49
licensing/credentialing
    in counseling, 49–50
    exams for, 44
    loss of licensure, 97, 105–6
    maintaining, 44

in marital and family therapy, 53
practice requirements for, 42–43
in psychiatric nursing, 64
in psychiatry, 63
in psychology, 60
salaries and, 89–90
in social work, 55
summary by discipline, 47*t*
life balance, 194–96
life stages, 124–25
listening skills, 12–13, 20, 159
loneliness, problem of, 78–79

machine learning, 181–82
The Making of a Therapist (Cozolino), 201
malpractice, 96
mandatory reporting, 100–1
marginalized communities, 108, 110, 114–15
marital and family therapy (MFT)
    couples work, 11, 52–54
    family therapy, 52–53
    graduate school admissions, 53
    informational resources, 54
    licensing/credentialing, 53
    minority student opportunities in, 119
    overview, 47, 47*t*, 52–53
    parenting issues, 11, 12–13, 73
    potential fit for interests, 53–54
marketing, 91–92, 175
Maslach, Christina, 142
master's degree, 47, 59, 89
master's in public health (MPH), 65
master's thesis, 128
Mattu, Ali, 204
Maybe You Should Talk to Someone (Gottlieb),
    160, 200–1
meaningfulness, career, 9–12
measurement-based care, 169–72
media, opportunities in, 69, 73, 76, 77, 79, 82
Medicaid, 86
Medical College Admissions Test, 62–63
medical doctors (MDs), 62, 63
medical school, 62–63
medical student syndrome, 13
Medicare, 86
medications
    management, 62
    pharmacology courses, 131–32
    prescribing, 113
memoirs, as resources, 202–3
memory loss issues, 67–68, 79
mental health
    culture of, 32
    global contexts, 187–89
    mobile apps for, 177–78

parity in, 85–86
  stigma and, 4, 77, 78, 86, 114, 186, 187
Mental Health America, 85–86
mental healthcare
  access to, 77, 85–86, 114
  barriers to treatment, 77, 85–86, 115, 142
  business of, 83–84
  delivery of services, 132, 166–67, 185–87, 188
  demand for, 2, 46
  disciplines in (*see* mental health disciplines)
  disparities in, 108, 110, 114–16
  effectiveness of, 16, 115, 127, 152
  funding for, 85–87
  future developments in, 2–3
  undervaluing of, 84
  unmet needs for, 85, 186–87
mental health counselors, 48, 49. *See also*
    counseling
mental health disciplines. *See also specific discipline*
  choosing between, 46
  descriptions, 47
  job growth in, 46
  overview of, 46, 47*t*
  term, xi, 2
  types of work, 67–68, 68*f*, 69–71
Mental Health Parity and Addiction Equity Act, 86
mental health professionals. *See* therapists
mental health services. *See* mental healthcare
mental illnesses, 50–51, 57, 61, 62, 126
  among incarcerated population, 115
  criminalization of, 102
  diagnosing, 102, 112–13, 116, 126, 171
  personal experience as career motivator, 27–28
  social determinants of, 114, 188
  of therapists, 27
mentors, 59–60, 88, 197
MFT. *See* marital and family therapy
Mind Fixers (Harrington), 185
mindfulness, 80, 146
minority student opportunities, 118–19
mobile apps, 105, 177–78
modular approaches, 168
"The Moral Case for Global Mental Health
    Delivery" (Patel), 188
Moth Podcast, 204
Moth Radio Hour, 204
motivation
  of children and adolescents in therapy, 72, 74
  reasons for career choice, 1–2, 26–29, 38
  of therapist for self-improvement, 22
multicultural issues, 125
Musk, Elon, 184

National Alliance on Mental Illness, 85–86
National Board for Certified Counselors, 118

National Health Service Corps, 119
national organizations, 66, 204–5
nature *versus* nurture, 190–91
navel-gazing, 148
negative outcomes, 14–15, 142
networking, 43, 93, 123, 136
neuralinks, 184
neurograins, 184
neuropsychology, 60–61, 76, 79
neuroscience, 127, 132, 182–85
niche, finding, 197–98
nonprofit organizations, 69, 73, 87
nursing. *See* psychiatric nursing
nurture, nature *versus*, 190–91

Obamacare, 185–86
occupational hazards, 11, 138, 144
occupations. *See* mental health disciplines
On Being a Therapist (Kottler), 84, 139, 148, 201–2
openness, 19, 25, 159
opportunities. *See* career opportunities
optimism, 19–20, 152, 154
organizational culture, 68–69
organizational skills, 20, 21, 192
organizational systems, as course topic, 132
outcomes. *See* clinical outcomes
out-of-pocket costs, 86
outreach methods, 175
overconfidence, 23–24

paperwork requirements, 93–94, 140
paraprofessionals, 187
parenting skills, 11, 12–13, 73
parents, in child therapy, 72–73, 75
Parkinson's disease, 184
part-time jobs, 89, 92
pastoral (faith-based) counseling, 50, 69, 76, 78
Patel, Vikram, 188
patients, *versus* clients, 61
peer support, 92, 104, 145
personal experiences of therapists
  as career motivator, 27–28
  with psychotherapy, 27–28, 147–48
  specialized skills through, 90
personal growth, as therapist, 12–13
personal life, stress and, 140
personal strengths, 18–23
Persuasion and Healing (Frank), 150
PhD degree, 58. *See also* doctoral programs
philanthropy, 87
phobias, 180
Pipher, Mary, 151, 201
placebo effect, 154
podcasts, 204
policy issues, as course topic, 132

populations, 72–82. *See also specific population*
  overview of possibilities, 67–68, 68f, 71
  during practicum, 135–36
  specializing in, 197–98
  vulnerable communities, 54
positive expectations, 151–52, 155
positive psychology, 132
post-traumatic stress disorder, 99, 143–44, 181
practicum, 6, 40, 41, 134–36
  balancing with coursework, 41
  finding placements on your own, 134–35
  importance of supervision, 135–36
  licensure requirements for, 42–43
  networking opportunities, 136
  on-site *versus* community placements, 134
  program-facilitated placements, 134–35
  time requirements, 89
precision medicine, 182
premarital counseling, 80, 81
prevention programs, 132
primary care behavioral health, 78, 185–86
prisoners, mental illness, 115
private health insurance, 86
private practice
  business expenses, 91
  income, 91
  marketing for, 91–92
  pros and cons of, 91–93
problem-solving, 4–5
productivity demands, 140
professional boundaries, 97–98, 105, 139, 193
professional identity, 41, 136
professional networking, 136
professional organizations, 118–19
professional reputation, 43, 90
program development, 70–71, 74, 77
program evaluation, 70–71, 127, 128
PsyberGuide (OneMindPsyberGuide.org), 177–78
PsychHub, 204–5
psychiatric disorders. *See* mental illnesses
psychiatric hospitals, 3
psychiatric nursing
  graduate school admissions, 64
  informational resources, 65
  licensing/credentialing, 64
  minority student opportunities in, 119
  overview, 47, 47t, 63–64
  potential fit interests, 65
  subspecialities, 64
psychiatry
  graduate school admissions, 62–63
  informational resources, 63
  licensing/credentialing, 63
  minority student opportunities in, 119
  overview, 47, 47t, 62

potential fit for interests, 63
  subspecialties, 62
psychoeducation providers, 76
psychological first-aid, 131
psychological testing
  courses in, 57, 130
  employment in, 70
  in forensic mental health practice, 102
  measurement-based care and, 169–72
  of older adults, 79
  of school children, 73
psychologists, 118
psychology
  defined, 56–57
  graduate school admissions, 59–60
  informational resources, 61
  licensing/credentialing, 60
  mental health of students of, 13
  minority student opportunities in, 119
  overview, 47, 47t, 56–57
  potential fit for interests, 60–61
  subspecialities, 57–59
psychometric testing. *See* psychological testing
psychoneuroimmunology, 184
psychopathology, 126–27
psychopharmacology, 131–32
psychotherapy, 62. *See also* therapeutic
    relationship
  approaches, 130, 167
  balancing art and science of, 15–16, 162, 163f
  client motivations for seeking, 72, 74, 77
  client stories revealed in, 10–12
  common factors of, 150
  effectiveness, 16, 19, 150
  expectations and, 151–56
  founding father of, 15
  goals of, 20, 72, 75, 153, 156, 157, 159,
    171, 192
  modalities in, 70, 176
  placebo effect and, 154–55
  promoting value of, 16
  rationale, discussing with client, 152
  remote communications, 13–14, 25, 105,
    175–82
  skepticism about, 16
  term, xi
  theories of, 125–26
  therapists' personal experience of, 147–48
  timing stress in, 141–42
The Psych Show, 204
public insurance, 86
public services, 86

racial bias, 112–13
racial disparities, 114–16, 117

reasonable suspicion, 100
record keeping, 94
records, access, 199
referrals, making, 22–23, 101
reflective listening, 159
refugees, working with, 74
registered nurse (RN) license, 64
rehabilitation counseling, 50
rejection, sensitivity to, 24
religious beliefs, 25
remote learning, 88
remote therapy, 13–14, 25, 105, 175–82
reporting
    of child or elder abuse, 100–1
    of suicide risk, 101–2
research
    career in, 71
    ethics in, 103, 106
    experience in, 5–6, 33, 37–38
    lag time in application of, 166–67
    methods course, 127–28
residencies, 40, 63, 134. *See also* practicum
residential facilities, 79, 90
resilience, 148–49
resolution, need for, 25–26
resources
    books, memoirs and case histories, 202–3
    books on being a therapist, 200–2
    on diversity, equity, and inclusion in
        training, 118–19
    on evidence-based practice, 168–69
    podcasts, 204
    recommendations, 200–5
    video, 204–5
    websites, 66, 168–69, 204–5
respect, for clients, 198–99
résumés, 43–44
retirement age, 118
risk assessment, 101–2
robots, 175, 178
Rogers, Carl, 158–59
role-playing exercises, 122–23, 129, 167

Sackett, David, 165–66
safety issues, 80, 139
salaries, 46, 89–90
    by degree level, 89
    by discipline, 47t
    experience and, 90
    geographic location and, 90
    licensure and, 89–90
    in private practice, 91
    reputation and, 90
    specialized skills and, 90
    workplace setting and, 90

schizophrenia, 112
scholarships, 39, 58, 88, 117, 118, 119
school counselors, 49, 51. *See also* counseling
school-to-prison pipeline, 116
school work settings, 73, 75, 82
science
    advances in, 13–14
    versus art of psychotherapy, 15–16,
        162, 163f
    attitudes about, 163, 166, 172–73
    embracing, 16, 162, 163
science–practice gap, 166–67
scientific thinking, 163–65
scope of practice, 50
secondary traumatic stress, 143–44
self-absorption, 148
self-awareness, 13, 22, 144, 146–48
self-care, 144–45
self-compassion, 145–46
self-doubt, 140–41
sensitivity, 24
services. *See* mental healthcare
sex therapy, 81
sexuality, 113, 131. *See also* LGBTQ+ community
silence, sitting in, 20
skepticism, 16, 115, 170, 172
skill-building courses, 129
skills, 18–23
social anxiety, 77
social desirability bias, 171
social justice issues, 106–7, 108, 188
social media
    boundaries and, 97–98, 105
    for older adults, 80
social networking, 123
social support, 145
social work
    graduate school admissions, 55
    informational resources, 56
    licensing/credentialing, 55
    minority student opportunities in, 119
    overview, 47, 47t, 54
    potential fit for interests, 56
    subspecialities, 55
    values of, 56
societal biases, 84
societal pressures, 74
SPARX (Smart, Positive, Active, Realistic, X-
        Factor Thoughts), 179–80
specialization, 67–68, 68f, 197–98
specialized skills, 90
standardized measures, 165, 169, 170–71
standardized testing, for graduate school,
        35, 48–49
stigma, 4, 77, 78, 86, 114, 186, 187

stress
    burnout and, 142–44
    client-associated, 139
    due to inability to help, 142
    event-related, 140
    internal personal, 140–41
    sources, overview of, 138–42
    timing issues, 141–42
    of work environment, 140
structure, flexibility *versus*, 20, 192
student loans, 88
substance abuse, 27, 76, 77, 131, 169, 178–79, 181
Substance Abuse and Mental Health Services
    Administration (SAMHSA), 119
success, 14–15, 142, 149
suicide risk, 76, 101–2, 103, 105, 116, 139
supervision, 22, 41–42
support groups, 75, 77, 78, 80

Taoism, 190
task shifting, 187
teaching
    bias in education, 116
    careers in, 71
    ethics in, 103, 106
technology
    courses in, 133–34
    employment in, 69
    ethical challenges with, 105
    innovations, 174–82
    for internet-based therapy, 177–82
    learning how to use, 22
    for remote therapy, 13–14, 25, 105, 175–82
    trade-offs with, 174–75
    wearable, 178–79
TED talks, 204
teletherapy, 25, 175–76. *See also* remote therapy
theoretical courses, 125–26
therapeutic relationship, 15, 156–60
    beginnings and endings, 141–42
    boundaries, 97–98, 105, 139, 193
    building, 158–60
    conflict in, 21–22
    contributing elements to, 157–58
    cultural competence and, 111
    emotional bond in, 157
    resolution to, 25–26
    term, xi, 155
    trust in, 21, 158
    values, differing, 19, 25
therapist–client relationship. *See* therapeutic
    relationship
therapists. *See also* career as therapist
    attitude, 19, 159
    biases, 84, 112–13, 116, 125, 147, 171
    biases of, 13

books on being, 200–2
as clinical scientists, 163–65
collaboration between, 22–23, 199–200
confidence, 19, 41, 151–52, 194
judgmental behavior of, 159, 198
learning new things, 22, 24–25
life events of, 140
mental image of, 9
personal experience of psychotherapy,
    27–28, 147–48
personal growth, 12–13
respecting clients, 198–99
self-disclosure, 193
steps to becoming, overview, 31*f*, 31, 35, 45
strengths of, 18–23
term, xi, 1
trigger issues of, 18, 27–28, 147
weaknesses, 23–26
therapy, term, xi. *See also* counseling;
    psychotherapy
thesis projects, 37–38, 128
thinking, feeling *versus*, 192
transdiagnostic treatment models, 168
trauma
    course on, 130–31
    secondary traumatic stress, 143–44
    vicarious traumatization, 143–44
treatment models
    empirically supported, 168
    modular systems, 168
    transdiagnostic, 168
treatment progress, 171
tribal nations, 76
triggers, 18, 27–28, 147
trustworthiness, as therapist, 21, 158
tuition costs, 87–88

unconditional positive regard, 159
unconscious bias, 112–13
undergraduate degree, 31–33
unsuccessful client outcomes, 142, 153

value systems, 19, 25
verbal skills, 20–21
veterans, working with, 69, 77, 102, 181
Veterans Administration, 86, 102
vicarious resilience, 148–49
vicarious traumatization, 11, 143–44
video games, 73, 179–80
video resources, 204–5
video therapy. *See* remote therapy
violence, 10, 16, 131
    domestic, 78, 80, 81, 130
    public media consulting on, 76
    school-related, 73
virtual reality, 105, 180–81

volunteer experience, 29, 32–33, 188

weaknesses, 23–26
wearable technology, 178–79
website resources, 66, 168–69, 204–5
wellness, promotion, 50–51, 57, 68–69
Wilkerson, Isabel, 203
Willer, Jan, 202
Woebot, 178
work
    environmental stress, 140
    experience as undergraduate, 32–33, 38
    types of, 67–68, 68f, 69–71
workforce in mental healthcare
    diversity, 116–19
    growth, 46, 47t

working alliance. *See* therapeutic relationship
work–life balance, 194–96
work settings
    descriptions of, 68–69
    overview of, 67–68, 68f
    salaries and, 90
work–study opportunities, 88
World Health Organization, 113, 187
wrap-around care, 73

Yalom, Irvin, 201
yin yang, 190, 191f
youth. *See* adolescents; children
YouTube videos, 204

Zigler, Edward, 107